CONTEMPORARY LATIN AMERICAN FICTION

THE
MAGILL
BIBLIOGRAPHIES

Other Magill Bibliographies:

The American Presidents—Norman S. Cohen
Black American Women Novelists—Craig Werner
Classical Greek and Roman Drama—Robert J. Forman
Masters of Mystery and Detective Fiction—J. Randolph Cox
Nineteenth Century American Poetry—Philip K. Jason
Restoration Drama—Thomas J. Taylor
Twentieth Century European Short Story—Charles E. May
The Victorian Novel—Laurence W. Mazzeno
Women's Issues—Laura Stempel Mumford

CONTEMPORARY LATIN AMERICAN FICTION

An Annotated Bibliography

KEITH H. BROWER

Associate Professor of Spanish and Portuguese
Dickinson College

SALEM PRESS

Pasadena, California   Englewood Cliffs, New Jersey

Library of Congress Cataloging-in-Publication Data

Brower, Keith H.
    Contemporary Latin American fiction / Keith H.
    Brower.
        p.   cm. — (Magill bibliographies)
    ISBN 0-89356-660-8
    1. Latin American fiction—20th century—His-
tory and criticism—Bibliography.   2. Latin American fiction— 20th   century—Bio-bibliography.
I. Title. II. Series.
Z1609.F4B76   1989
[PQ7082.N7]
863—dc20   89-10825
                                                CIP

This book is dedicated to my father.

CONTENTS

CONTENTS

CONTENTS

EDITORIAL STAFF

ACKNOWLEDGMENTS

One does not usually complete a task such as the present volume without the help and support of many people, and my case is no different. I wish to thank Ellen Reinig at Salem Press for her enduring support as well as for her meticulous editing of the manuscript. My gratitude goes as well to the Charles A. Dana Foundation Student Intern Program of Dickinson College for providing me with two excellent interns, Lori Adamcik and Bonnie Brubaker, whose help in the preparation of this work was immeasurable. Special thanks go to my family, friends, and colleagues who have lent me their patient support and encouragement throughout my work on the project.

CONTEMPORARY LATIN AMERICAN FICTION

INTRODUCTION

When labeling anything "contemporary," the most difficult aspect of doing so is determining just how far back "contemporary" goes. Where does one draw the line? In the case of "contemporary Latin American fiction," however, the task is actually a relatively simple one. Latin American fiction as it enters the 1990's, in the hands of Gabriel García Márquez, Mario Vargas Llosa, Carlos Fuentes, Isabel Allende, and others, can certainly claim kinship, or "contemporariness," to the Latin American fiction of the 1960's, a period during which, in fact, some of these same authors produced what many consider their masterworks. It can trace its roots, however, to the tradition-breaking writers of the 1940's, such as Miguel Ángel Asturias, Augustín Yáñez, Clarice Lispector, João Guimãraes Rosa, and, most notably, Jorge Luis Borges. It is there, then, in the 1940's, that "contemporary Latin American fiction" begins.

What makes the major Latin American writers and their works of this rather extended period contemporaries of one another is their identification (albeit at times a somewhat loose one) with what has been called Latin America's "new narrative." Latin American fiction of the first part of the twentieth century (particularly between 1920 and 1940) was chiefly concerned with painting a realistic and detailed picture of external Latin American reality. In the works of this period, description frequently ruled over action, environment over character, and types over the individual. Social message, also, was often more important to the writer than was narrative artistry. "New narrative," is "new" by comparison to the type of narrative just described in that it: (1) releases Latin American fiction from its documentary nature, (2) turns its focus toward the inner workings of its fully individualized human characters, (3) presents various interpretations of reality, (4) expresses universal as well as regional and national themes, (5) invites reader participation, and (6) emphasizes the importance of artistic presentation of the story, particularly with respect to narrative voice, language, structure (and the corresponding element of time), and characterization. It is this type of narrative which in its many manifestations and degrees has dominated Latin American fiction since the 1940's and which makes contemporaries of Borges and Allende and of every major Latin American narrativist in between.

This new type of narrative not only has produced an artistic and captivating literary voice, but also has brought Latin American fiction to the forefront of world literature during the second half of the twentieth century. Correspondingly, contemporary Latin American fiction holds a prominent place in the English-speaking world in general, and in the United States in particular. This is reflected in many ways. Numerous periodicals, for example, from *The New York Times Book Review* to *Time* magazine, regularly review the latest novels (in English translation) of such authors as García Márquez, Vargas Llosa, Allende, and Jorge Amado. At the same time, the works of these and other Latin American writers often make the North

American best-seller lists and grace the shelves of trade bookstores throughout the United States. The number of college and university courses in which works by contemporary Latin American narrativists are treated has increased dramatically since Latin America's "new narrative" burst into the English-speaking world in the 1960's.

It should not be surprising, then, that this fiction has attracted an impressive amount of critical attention. Both the volume of criticism on contemporary Latin American fiction and the increase in it since the mid-1960's is reflected in the *MLA International Bibliography*. The 1965 edition of this bibliography lists approximately thirty scholarly books and articles published on contemporary Latin American fiction during that year, while the 1970 edition lists some one hundred and fifty. These numbers grow to just over three hundred and fifty in 1975, to more than four hundred in 1980, and to a similar number in 1985. It is with this vast body of criticism that the present bibliography concerns itself.

This bibliography contains more than six hundred entries covering twenty-three contemporary Latin American narrativists and more than one hundred individual works. Its target audience is essentially the English-speaking undergraduate student. It is therefore the nature and the interests of this audience which have established the parameters of the present volume with respect to language, the type of criticism listed, and the authors and works covered.

Because the target audience is English speaking, the present bibliography is limited to English-language criticism. This is a significant limitation since fully half (or more) of the available criticism on contemporary Latin American fiction is not written in English but in Spanish or Portuguese. (The reason for this is two-fold. A significant portion of the criticism is written and published in Spanish- or Portuguese-speaking countries, chiefly, but not exclusively, in Latin America; and the majority of the criticism readily available to the North American undergraduate student is written by college and university professors in the United States, most of whom speak Spanish and/or Portuguese and write in the language in which the works they analyze are written, their anticipated audience frequently being other scholars or graduate students studying Latin American literature, all of whom speak the language or languages used.) The present bibliography does not limit itself, however, to critical works which cite the English version of the novel or short story under discussion, or which use only English-language sources of reference, or which provide only English-language bibliographies. In other words, although the texts of all works of criticism listed in this bibliography are written in English, many of the same works cite the novel or short story under discussion in the original Spanish or Portuguese, or refer to other sources in languages other than English, or provide bibliographies in various languages. The student is informed of this, however, at the end of virtually every annotation. "Bibliography in Spanish, English, and French," for example, indicates that some works cited in the bibliography at the end of the critical work are in Spanish, others in English, and still others in French. Similarly, "Quotations in Spanish and English" indicates that some passages cited in the work are in Spanish while others are in English. "Titles and quotations in Spanish with English translations" indicates that though titles and quotations do appear in Spanish, English translations follow. Every effort has been made to provide detailed and accurate information on this aspect of the critical works cited so that the student is forewarned concerning the language(s) employed within the text of the critical work in question.

Beyond the language in which it is written, the criticism included in this bibliography has been selected based upon its availability and accessibility for the undergraduate student. The majority of the entries represent books or chapters of books (published, with but rare exceptions, between 1965 and 1989) which should be available (or obtainable through interlibrary loan) at a good undergraduate library. A significant portion of the entries, however, are drawn from numerous scholarly journals devoted wholly or in part to Latin American literature. Considerable effort has been made to list only those articles which appear in journals which, again, should be available at or through a good undergraduate library. In consideration of the audience as well, critical works which require extensive knowledge of certain types of literary analysis and theory (such as structuralism), for the most part, have been excluded. Most of the criticism of this type (as well as that which may be particularly difficult for the student to obtain) which does appear in the present bibliography has been included because it may represent the only English-language criticism on the author or work in question, or because it is simply too important to exclude.

The following three criteria have been used to determine which authors and works are and are not covered in the present volume: (1) availability in English translation; (2) probability of being treated in an undergraduate, English-language literature course in the United States; and (3) availability of English-language criticism. Some authors and works have been included because they have met all three of the above criteria (García Márquez and his *One Hundred Years of Solitude*, for example). Others have been included because they have met at least the first and third criteria (such as Osman Lins and his *Avalovara*). On the other hand, some have been excluded because they have managed to meet the first two criteria, but not the third. (Some of Jorge Amado's novels, for example, fit into this category.)

Following an opening section featuring books and articles dealing with contemporary Latin American fiction in general, the present bibliography is arranged alphabetically by author and English-language title (with book-length works, such as novels and short-story collections, listed first, individual short stories second). Each author's bibliography begins with a list of works (if such are available) concerning his or her life, followed by a general bibliography (entitled "Commentary") featuring criticism which deals with the author's works in general or with certain aspects of his or her writing. This is followed by individual sections, each of which treats one of the author's works. The student is strongly urged to consult not only the bibliographical entries listed for a specific work, but also the more general criticism provided under the "Commentary" section as well, since the critical pieces listed here often contain information which may help the student better understand the specific work in question.

Considering the various criteria used to establish which authors, titles, and critical works are included in this volume, this bibliography obviously cannot (and does not) pretend to provide a complete listing of the criticism written on contemporary Latin American fiction, even within the confines of English-language criticism on the subject. It does, however, present most of the readily available and accessible English-language criticism on the contemporary Latin American narrativists covered and should therefore serve its target audience well. The student who wishes to seek out further criticism (particularly that written in a language other than English, that more heavily based in literary theory, or that intended more for critics and graduate students) on the authors and works covered in this bibliography (and on those not covered as well) may refer to the previously mentioned *MLA International Bibliography*, which is available in the reference section of most college and university libraries.

General Studies

Books Abroad 44 (Winter, 1970): 7-50.

An issue devoted to the topic of "The Latin American Novel Today." Provides a wide-ranging collection of articles both on the Latin American novel of the "Boom" and on individual authors and their works largely within the context of the "Boom." Articles include an introduction by Mario Vargas Llosa, "Gabriel García Márquez: The Boom and the Whimper" by Wolfgang A. Luchting, "João Guimarães Rosa: The Third Bank of the River" by Gregory Rabassa, and "The New Latin American Novel" by Emir Rodríguez Monegal. Most titles and quotations in English.

Brotherston, Gordon. *The Emergence of the Latin American Novel*. London: Cambridge University Press, 1977.

Intended by the author as an introduction to the contemporary Latin American novel. Focuses on the works of eight major Spanish American novelists (Asturias, Carpentier, Juan Carlos Onetti, Rulfo, Cortázar, Vargas Llosa, García Márquez and José María Arguedas) who the author believes capture the essence of contemporary Latin American fiction by concerning themselves with Latin American settings and, more important, Latin American reality. An enlightening and widely read study of each author and the contemporary Latin American novel. Contains an index and a selected bibliography in Spanish, Portuguese, and English. Titles in Spanish and English. Quotations in English.

Brushwood, John S. *Mexico in Its Novel: A Nation's Search for Identity*. Austin: University of Texas Press, 1966.

As the description on the cover of the paperbound edition states, this work is "a perceptive examination of Mexican reality as revealed through the nation's novel." Covers the Mexican novel from 1521 to 1963, though the first chapter is dedicated to the Mexican novel from 1947 to 1963. Provides a solid study of works by Yáñez, Rulfo, and Fuentes and their relationship to the culture and society in which they were produced. Includes extensive coverage of works by less prominent authors whose works do not appear in this bibliography. An excellent study of the topic. Provides a detailed index and a chronological list of novels (1832-1963). Some titles in Spanish with English translations. Others only in Spanish. Quotations in English.

_____ . *The Spanish American Novel: A Twentieth-Century Survey.* Austin: University of Texas Press, 1975.
Simply put, the most important and most widely read work of its kind in the English-language criticism of the Spanish American novel of the twentieth century. In just over three hundred pages of text, Brushwood manages to cover, in strict chronological order, the novels of every major Spanish American novelist of this century as well as (remarkably) the works of numerous minor and frequently otherwise ignored novelists of the same period, thus presenting an exhaustive survey of the Spanish American novel from 1900 through the early 1970's. Supplemented by a list of novels arranged by year and country. A superb survey. Includes an excellent index. Titles in Spanish. Quotations in English.

_____ . "Two Views of the Boom: North and South." *Latin American Literary Review* 15 (January-June, 1987): 13-32.
Brushwood discusses the major writers, major works, important precursors and influences, significant dates, and principal characteristics of the "Boom" in an article which not only describes the "Boom" but which also seeks to determine both its lasting significance and the perception of it as a literary period by readers and critics in the United States as well as in Spanish America. A very good introduction to the nature of the "Boom." Titles in English or in English with Spanish translations.

Cortázar, Julio. "The Present State of Fiction in Latin America." *Books Abroad* 50 (Summer, 1976): 522-532.
In spite of its title, this article (the text of a lecture by Cortázar at a conference at the University of Oklahoma) is actually a discussion of the fantastic and its role in his life and works as well as in the works of a number of Río Plate region narrativists (such as Borges). Valuable because of its discussion of such a prevalent element of contemporary Latin American fiction, but particularly insightful because of Cortázar's frank, personal opinions on the fantastic and how he views it as a normal element of everyday life. Titles in English.

Donoso, José. *The Boom in Spanish American Literature: A Personal History.* New York: Columbia University Press, 1977.

A fascinating first-person account of the "Boom" period by one of its major figures. Donoso speaks of the literary climate in which he and other "Boom" writers began their careers. He discusses significant events and personalities which allowed the "Boom" to occur. He also confronts, and to a large degree repudiates, several common assumptions about the "Boom" period and its writers. He laces all this with information concerning his own personal situation within the "Boom," creating both a literary autobiography and an admittedly nonscholarly, though intriguing, inside history of the period. Virtually required reading after the more academic histories of the "Boom." Provides a good index. Titles of translated works in English. Titles of other works in Spanish with English translations when first cited, subsequently cited in Spanish.

Ellison, Fred P. *Brazil's New Novel*. Westport, Conn.: Greenwood Press, 1954.
A study of Brazil's socially oriented Northeastern novel, which flourished in Brazilian literature during the 1930's and the early 1940's and set a precedent for the social protest novels of following decades (for example, the novel of the Brazilian dictatorship). Provides individual chapters on each of this subgenre's major writers: José Lins do Rego, Jorge Amado, Graciliano Ramos, and Rachel de Queiroz. Highlighted by an excellent introduction which details the social, historical, and literary background from which the Northeastern novel sprang. Though somewhat dated (particularly concerning Amado), the book provides a fine overview of the Northeastern novel and is considered a classic work on this area of Brazilian literature. Contains a bibliography in Portuguese and English. Titles in English or in English with Portuguese translations. Quotations in English.

Esquenazi-Mayo, Roberto. "Marginal Notes on the Twentieth-Century Spanish American Novel." *Prairie Schooner* 39 (1986): 126-131.
This short article is a collection of commentaries or observations on the twentieth century Spanish American novel. In spite of its lack of depth (due to its length), the article still conveys clearly the difference between the "old" narrative produced before the 1940's and the "new" narrative produced by Borges, Cortázar, Rulfo, and Fuentes. Not a critical piece nor a history, but very good for what it is and achieving its modest purpose well. Titles in Spanish. Reference quotations in Spanish, French, and English.

Foster, David William. *Currents in the Contemporary Argentine Novel: Arlt, Mallea, Sábato, and Cortázar*. Columbia: University of Missouri Press, 1975.
Intended by the author "as a panorama of Argentine fiction" with emphasis on the twentieth century in general and the works of Cortázar, Sábato, Roberto Arlt, and Eduardo Mallea in particular. Foster dedicates a chapter of analysis to each of these authors, focusing on one of their major works while touching

on others. Each chapter begins with a separate thumbnail sketch of the author to be discussed. A fine introduction presents background on the Argentine novel, while a final chapter quickly covers works by authors not included in previous analysis in the volume (such as those of Puig). A bibliography in Spanish and English on the Argentine novel and the four major writers discussed. Titles and quotations in English.

_____ . *Studies in the Contemporary Spanish-American Short Story*. Columbia: University of Missouri Press, 1979.
Far from being as simple as its title suggests, this work is truly atypical in the area of Latin American fiction criticism. Based upon the concept of narrative *écriture*, the book focuses on a handful of stories by Rulfo, Borges, Cortázar, García Márquez, and Cabrera Infante. Works "are examined as particular strategies in the production of verbal art." Heavily laced with literary theory. An entire introductory chapter is dedicated to the concept of *écriture*. All primary and secondary references listed in bibliography are works of literary theory. An interesting study but obviously intended for a limited and initiated audience. Includes an index. Titles and quotations in Spanish.

Gallagher, D. P. "Latin American Fiction from 1940." In his *Modern Latin American Literature*. New York: Oxford University Press, 1973.
This seven-page chapter presents a concise summary of the nature of Latin American fiction since 1940, emphasizing primarily, as Gallagher says, "what exactly is 'new' in the so-called Latin American 'new novel.'" His discussion of these "new" elements focuses on the absence of didacticism, the presence and significance of fantasy, the dissatisfaction of Latin American authors with their respective societies, the failure of characters to communicate with one another, the questions of structure, and the use of language. Informative and very readable. Titles in Spanish.

Guibert, Rita. *Seven Voices: Seven Latin American Writers Talk to Rita Guibert*. Translated by Frances Partridge. New York: Alfred A. Knopf, 1973.
In-depth interviews with seven renowned Spanish American writers, five of whom (Borges, Asturias, Cortázar, García Márquez, and Cabrera Infante) appear in this bibliography. Most of the interviews are lengthy (averaging just over sixty pages), informative, and revealing. Guibert speaks casually with each writer (except in the case of Cortázar, whose interview takes place in writing) about, as she puts it, "literature and life, current events and trivia." An insightful book which, if nothing else, shows these literary giants as human beings. Not as important critically as it is interesting.

Harss, Luis, and Barbara Dohmann. *Into the Mainstream: Conversations with Latin American Writers*. New York: Harper & Row, 1967.

This book contains interview-based essays on the lives, careers, works, and thoughts of Carpentier, Asturias, Borges, Guimarães Rosa, Juan Carlos Onetti, Cortázar, Rulfo, Fuentes, García Márquez, and Vargas Llosa. Also contains a solid introduction to contemporary Latin American fiction at a critical time in its evolution (1967). A bit dated, but even this works in the book's favor, catching García Márquez, for example, just months before the publication of *One Hundred Years of Solitude*, and Vargas Llosa at only thirty-one years of age. Considered at the time of its publication a classic in contemporary Latin American fiction studies, it remains a classic more than twenty years later. Most titles only in original language. Some in English as well. Quotations in English.

Klein, Leonard S., ed. *Latin American Literature in the Twentieth Century: A Guide*. New York: Frederick Ungar, 1986.
A collection of ninety-two short overview essays by multiple contributors on the major Latin American (including Brazilian) writers of the twentieth century. Arranged by country or region with an introductory essay on literature in the twentieth century in each country or region. Also includes an article on Magic Realism. Index to authors covered. A "Further Works" section and a short bibliography appear at the end of each essay. Titles in essays are in Spanish or Portuguese with English translations. Titles in "Further Works" section are in the original language only. Provides mixed-language bibliographies. A good work to introduce individual authors to uninitiated readers, and a handy reference book.

Langford, Walter M. *The Mexican Novel Comes of Age*. Notre Dame, Ind.: University of Notre Dame Press, 1971.
A chronicle of the evolution of the Mexican novel with heavy emphasis on the 1950's and 1960's. A solid overview of works by Yáñez, Rulfo, and Fuentes. Also includes chapters dedicated to lesser-known Mexican novelists of the same period and a fine preface and conclusion dealing not only with the "Boom" in the Mexican novel but, by extension, in the Latin American novel as well. A list of authors' works and a critical bibliography appear at the end of each chapter. More general bibliography included at the end of the book. Contains an index and a bibliography in Spanish and English. Titles and quotations in English.

Latin American Literary Review 15 (January-June, 1987): 7-206. A special issue entitled "The Boom in Retrospect: A Reconsideration."
This issue contains fifteen articles (many lengthy) on the "Boom" in general or on works by "Boom" writers in particular. Articles of the first category include "Two Views of the Boom: North and South" by John S. Brushwood, "The First Seven Pages of the Boom" by William H. Gass, "Translating the

Boom: The Apple Theory of Translation" by Margaret Sayers Peden, and "Literature and History in Contemporary Latin America" by Richard J. Walter. Titles and quotations in English.

Leal, Luis. "The New Mexican Short Story." *Studies in Short Fiction* 8 (Winter, 1971): 9-19.
Beginning with the colonial period, this article briefly traces the history of the Mexican short story before turning its attention to the writer of the "new" Mexican short story: Arreola, Rulfo, and Fuentes. Considerable discussion of the works of these three writers, followed by the mention of several other writers who the author believes carry on the "new" tradition. A solid article, particularly valuable for how it establishes Arreola, Rulfo, and Fuentes as writers of the "new" Mexican short story and then discusses the nature of their works which earn for them that label. Most titles in Spanish. Some in English as well.

Levy, Kurt L. "The Contemporary Hispanic American Novel: Its Relevance to Society." *Latin American Literary Review* 3 (Fall/Winter, 1974): 7-21.
Levy cites what he calls "the penchant towards social concern" present in Spanish American literature since the chroniclers of the sixteenth century and then traces social concern in the Spanish American novel from Romanticism to the early 1970's, concentrating on the period between Mariano Azuela's *Los de abajo* (*The Underdogs*) in 1916 and *One Hundred Years of Solitude* (1967), concluding, in part, that social concern has remained strong in the Spanish American novel, though "the overwhelming force of nature gave way to collective social problems which in turn yielded increasingly to the dilemma of the individual conscience whatever his milieu." Levy is less certain, however, concerning the concrete changes the Spanish American novel has made in society. An interesting, detailed, and very readable study. Titles in Spanish with English translations. Quotations in English.

Lipp, Solomon. "The Anti-Castro Novel." *Hispania* 58 (May, 1975): 284-296.
Solomon delineates the characteristics of the anti-Castro novel and then goes on to discuss (largely through plot summary and critical comments) nine novels of this subgenre. His conclusions as well as his comments are overwhelmingly negative, finding most of the anti-Castro novels to be "wanting from an artistic point of view." Conceding that their aim is extraliterary, that they are above all thesis novels, he concludes that these novels will soon (as of 1975) run their course, that "there is nothing more to say." Titles and quotations in Spanish.

Mac Adam, Alfred J. *Modern Latin American Narratives*. Chicago: University of Chicago Press, 1977.

Described by the author as an "attempt to determine the distinctive features of what may seem to be a literary chaos," chiefly by examining a series of diverse narratives from the perspective of genre. Includes chapters on the works of twelve Latin American writers, from Machado de Assis and Cortázar to Guimarães Rosa and Donoso. Not particularly useful as a historical overview and heavily oriented to the reader already quite well versed in Latin American literature and even more knowledgeable in literary theory. A fine study, particularly as it pertains to the individual authors treated, but for a limited audience. Contains an excellent index and a very good selected bibliography in Spanish, Portuguese, French, and English. Titles in original language. Quotations in English.

McMurray, George R. "Current Trends in the Mexican Novel." *Hispania* 51 (September, 1968): 532-537.
Briefly citing Yáñez' *The Edge of the Storm* as a "turning point in the Mexican novel," and then mentioning Rulfo and Fuentes as the dominant Mexican writers of the period between 1947 and 1964, McMurray focuses here on a survey of the works of what he calls the seven most promising of the lesser-known Mexican novelists writing during 1965, 1966, and the first half of 1967. The writers discussed are Vicente Leñero, Tomás Mojarro, Salvador Elizondo, Gustavo Sainz, José Agustín, Raúl Navarrete, and Fernando del Paso. Of interest for its somewhat nonmainstream view of the Mexican novel of the 1960's. Titles in Spanish.

_____ . *Spanish American Writing Since 1941: A Critical Survey*. New York: Frederick Ungar, 1987.
This work, according to its author, "aims to acquaint readers of English with some major figures and trends of a literature that in recent years has transcended national borders and attracted worldwide recognition and critical acclaim." Almost half the book is dedicated to Spanish American fiction writers. Brief overviews are presented for each of Spanish America's most important narrativists, beginning with writers of the 1940's and 1950's who sent Spanish American narrative, as the author puts it, in "new directions," followed by more lengthy essays on the major writers of the "Boom." Minor writers are covered by country. Contains a selected English-language bibliography and an index of names and movements. Includes a good introduction. Overall, a fine starting point for the English-speaking reader. Titles in Spanish with English translations.

Menton, Seymour. *Prose Fiction of the Cuban Revolution*. Austin: University of Texas Press, 1975.
A survey of the more than two hundred novels and volumes of short stories related to the Cuban revolution published between 1959 and 1974. Includes works by both major and minor writers as well as works written in Cuba and

in exile by both Cubans and foreign writers. Examines the intimate relationship between the various phases of the revolution and the fiction produced during each phase. Includes twelve succinct conclusions concerning the prose fiction of the Cuban revolution. Also contains a chronology of novels and short stories as well as a lengthy bibliography (some of which is annotated), and a detailed index. An exhaustive study. Titles in Spanish. Almost all quotations in English.

_____ . "The Short Story of the Cuban Revolution, 1959-1969." *Studies in Short Fiction* 8 (Winter, 1971): 32-43.
A general overview of the subject at hand. Menton discusses the first decade of the short story of the Cuban revolution in comparison with the first decade of the short story following revolutions in other Latin American countries. He also discusses the relationship between the novel and the short story in Latin American literature during the 1960's and then moves on to a generational listing of Cuban short-story writers, followed by a discussion of the various types of stories written about the revolution. Article ends with the annotated bibliography of twelve anthologies dedicated to the short story of the Cuban revolution. One anthology in English. Titles in Spanish.

Ortega, Julio. *Poetics of Change: The New Spanish American Narrative*. Translated by Galen D. Greaser. Austin: University of Texas Press, 1984.
Not a history but a critical study of a series of Spanish American narratives which have produced, as the author terms it, "a systematic deconstruction of traditional writing," creating a type of narrative, a poetics which "deconstructs the notion of the text within the literary tradition." The author offers in-depth critical analysis of works he believes not only fit into this type of narrative but, in the case of some, actually established the model for it (works by Borges, Rulfo, Cortázar, Lezama Lima, and García Márquez). A very good introduction to the "poetics of change" which characterized the reshaping of Spanish American fiction. Includes an index of names. Titles and quotations in English.

Peden, Margaret Sayers, ed. *The Latin American Short Story: A Critical Study*. Boston: Twayne, 1983.
This work serves as a superb introduction to the Spanish American and Brazilian short stories. It features a chronology of some of the important dates in the history of the Latin American short story, an introduction by Peden, and chapters on the Brazilian short story by David William Foster, the Spanish American short story from Esteban Echeverría to Horacio Quiroga by Naomi Lindstrom, from Quiroga to Borges by John S. Brushwood, and from Borges to the present by George R. McMurray. Also contains a bibliography of anthologies and critical works in English as well as a separate listing of the same

in Spanish and Portuguese, and an index. Chapters divided into sections. Titles
in original language with English translations. Quotations in English. An excellent introductory volume.

Pupo-Walker, Enrique. "The Contemporary Short Fiction of Spanish America: An
Introductory Note." *Studies in Short Fiction* 8 (Winter, 1971): 1-8.
Just as the title implies, this article is an introduction to contemporary Spanish
American short fiction. It is not, however, a miniature history or even a
detailed overview of the genre. It is, instead, an essay on the nature and vitality
of the genre, quite short on names and titles, but long on reasoning and
presentation of characteristics. Most titles (very few altogether) are in Spanish.
Some in English as well. Quotations in English.

Rodríguez Monegal, Emir. "The Contemporary Brazilian Novel." In *Fiction in
Several Languages*, edited by Henri Peyre. Boston: Houghton Mifflin, 1968.
A solid article by the foremost critic of contemporary Latin American fiction,
tracing the evolution of the twentieth century Brazilian novel. Emphasizes the
diversity of the Brazilian novel, the influence of Brazilian Modernism, the
importance of the Northeastern novel, and the subsequent end of regionalism.
Guimarães Rosa and Lispector are discussed as the masters of the post-
regionalist novel. Concluding section places the contemporary Brazilian novel
within the context of Latin American literature. Article bursting with authors'
names. As complete as an eighteen-page article on the subject can be. Titles in
Portuguese.

_____ . "The New Latin American Novel." *Books Abroad* 44 (Winter,
1970): 45-50.
A classic introduction to the new type of novel which characterized the
"Boom" period. Rodríguez Monegal discusses the changes in scope, focus,
and language which differentiate the "new" Latin American novel from the
"old" Latin American novel. Calling them "efficient builders of great narrative machines," the critic discusses several of the new novelists, concluding
that the "all-embracing and over-experimental" new Latin American novelists
as a group represent the strongest potential foreign influence in narrative
"since the introduction of the Russian novelists to nineteenth-century France
and England, or of the modern Americans into postwar Europe." An excellent
article, particularly when read in tandem with Vargas Llosa's introduction in
the same issue. Titles in Spanish.

_____ . "The New Latin American Novelists." *TriQuarterly* 13/14
(1968/1969): 13-32.
Discusses the factors behind the development of the "new novel" in Latin
American literature and then discusses the major writers and works of this

genre in a generational or group fashion, beginning with the first breakers of Latin American narrative tradition in the 1940's: Borges, Carpentier, Asturias, and Leopoldo Marechal. Other writers discussed include Cortázar, Fuentes, Vargas Llosa, García Márquez, Cabrera Infante, Lezama Lima, and Puig. Emphasis on the nature of the new genre in the hands of these writers as well as both Latin American and foreign influences which help shape the writers' styles and interests. A very important article. Titles in Spanish.

_____ . "A Revolutionary Writing." *Mundus Artium* 3, no. 3 (1969/1970): 6-11.

In just six pages, the author delineates the reasons for and the results of the "tremendous leap," as he calls it, made by Latin American narrative from the late 1920's to the early 1960's. Among other things, he discusses the change of focus in Latin American narrative, the change in setting, the change in language, as well as the enormous popularity of Latin American narrative in Europe and in the United States, and the importance of Borges sharing the International Prize of Publishers with Samuel Beckett in 1961, thus launching the Argentine writer and his Latin American colleagues more visibly into international literary circles. An excellent, amazingly concise article, very good for understanding the emergence of the new Latin American narrative. Titles in English.

Schwartz, Kessel. *A New History of Spanish American Fiction.* Coral Gables: University of Miami Press, 1972.

A two-volume set. Volume 2 is subtitled "Social Concern, Universalism, and the New Novel" and covers the Spanish American novel from the late 1920's through 1969 with a full two-thirds of the book dedicated to the "New Novel." Schwartz treats the "New Novel" in four lengthy chapters (entitled "New Novel I," "New Novel II," and so on). The author not only presents an exhaustive chronology of the New Novels" produced in Spanish America (including numerous works written by largely ignored writers), but, more important, he also methodically traces and discusses the literary and extraliterary factors that helped create and then develop the "New Novel" in Spanish America. A thorough study. Includes a lengthy bibliography in Spanish and English and an index of authors and titles covered. Titles and quotations in Spanish.

_____ . "Themes, Trends, and Textures: The 1960's and the Spanish American Novel." *Hispania* 55 (December, 1972): 817-831.

An informative fourteen-page article with the first two pages dedicated to the changing nature of the Spanish American novel of the 1960's, with emphasis on technique, scope, and, most important, theme. Remainder of article is devoted to an exhaustive list of novelists (arranged according to decade of birth) and novels of the 1960's. Each novel receives at least a one- or two-sentence mention, with more attention given to major writers and works. This section of the article is interesting (even remarkable) for its degree of completeness as novelists and novels virtually ignored by many critics receive mention. Both sections of article are informative and useful. Titles in Spanish. Most quotations in Spanish. Some in English.

Schwartz, Ronald. *Nomads, Exiles, and Émigrés: The Rebirth of the Latin American Narrative, 1960-80*. Metuchen, N.J.: Scarecrow Press, 1980.

This work is the author's "attempt to popularize the 'new' Latin American novel in the United States for readers of English." Features chapters on ten major Spanish American novelists (among them Carpentier, Cortázar, Lezama Lima, García Márquez, Vargas Llosa, Cabrera Infante, Fuentes, Puig, and Donoso). Each chapter presents a brief biographical sketch of the author in question, an overview of his works (those translated into English), and an analysis of one of his novels. Also contains an interesting introduction and an even more interesting conclusion concerning the "Boom." Contains a selected English-language bibliography, including lists of each author's works translated to English and a good index. All titles and quotations in English. Especially suited for the reader with little or no knowledge of Latin American fiction.

Siemens, William L. "Latin American Long Fiction." In *Critical Survey of Long Fiction* (Foreign Language Series), edited by Frank N. Magill, vol. 5. Pasadena, Calif.: Salem Press, 1984.

An excellent, very readable twenty-one page survey of the Latin American novel (both Spanish American and Brazilian) beginning in the late eighteenth century. The survey essentially follows the individual literary periods or dominant trends and alternatingly treats Brazilian and Spanish American works and writers. Good discussion of the contemporary Latin American novel and the influences (both literary and extraliterary) and trends which have shaped it. Limited discussion of some of the period's major writers (such as Fuentes, Donoso, Cortázar, and García Márquez) and their works. Most titles in Spanish with English translations. Some (very few) in Spanish.

Sommers, Joseph. *After the Storm: Landmarks of the Modern Mexican Novel*. Albuquerque: University of New Mexico Press, 1968.

This book first examines the novel of the Mexican Revolution and then moves on to in-depth, chapter-long analyses of authors and works Sommers contends are responsible for "the major contours" of the modern Mexican novel: Yáñez (*The Edge of the Storm*), Rulfo (*Pedro Páramo*), and Fuentes (*Where the Air Is Clear* and *The Death of Artemio Cruz*). A thought-provoking conclusion. One of the most widely read and critically acclaimed studies in the criticism of contemporary Latin American fiction. Bibliographies (in Spanish and English) on the twentieth century Mexican novel in general and the authors and works discussed. Index. Titles and quotations in English.

Souza, Raymond D. "Language vs. Structure in the Contemporary Spanish American Novel." *Hispania* 52 (December, 1969): 833-839.
Using Yáñez' *The Edge of the Storm*, Cortázar's *Hopscotch*, and Cabrera Infante's *Three Trapped Tigers* as examples, Souza traces the "decided movement toward language as the almost exclusive concern of the novelist" in Spanish America. His contention is that as language becomes freer, less ordered, so too does the novel's structure, for linguistic freedom resists the limitations of logic and order. An interesting study connecting two usually unconnected narrative elements. Titles in Spanish. Quotations from novels in Spanish. Quotations from other sources in English, Spanish, and French.

_____ . *Major Cuban Novelists*. Columbia: University of Missouri Press, 1976.
Intended by the author as a "general survey of the development of the Cuban novel in the nineteenth and twentieth centuries." Features an excellent introduction which provides an overview of Cuba's novelistic production through 1971, citing several authors and their works, ranging from Gertrudís Gómez de Avellaneda to Severo Sarduy and Reynaldo Arenas. Core of the book consists of three detailed, chapter-long studies of the works of Carpentier, Lezama Lima, and Cabrera Infante. Text includes a solid summary which ties in well with the introduction. Also includes a rather lengthy bibliography (in Spanish and English) of criticism on the Cuban novel. A solid study of the three authors featured and an excellent introduction to and overview of the Cuban novel through 1971, with emphasis on the contemporary period. Titles and quotations in Spanish.

Stern, Irwin, ed. *Dictionary of Brazilian Literature*. Westport, Conn.: Greenwood Press, 1988.
Contains entries on all the Brazilian authors listed in this bibliography as well as entries on events and trends frequently reflected in contemporary Brazilian fiction (for example, "Dictatorship and Literature" and "Feminism and Literature"). Entries average one thousand words in length, but those dedicated to major authors (such as Amado) and wider-ranging topics (such as "New Writers") run between three and five pages. An excellent reference and starting point for the reader interested in contemporary Brazilian fiction. Titles and quotations (very few of the latter) in Portuguese with English translations.

Titler, Jonathan. *Narrative Irony in the Contemporary Spanish-American Novel*. Ithaca, N.Y.: Cornell University Press, 1984.

Intended by the author as an attempt "to explore the ways in which irony, as a figure of speech, a paradoxical turn of events, and a state of mind, helps explain several outstanding works of current Spanish-American fiction." Divided into two sections, the book first offers a study of "Static Irony" in four novels (by Fuentes, Rulfo, Puig, and Cabrera Infante) and then a study of "Kinetic Irony" in three others (by Vargas Llosa, Cortázar, and Issac Goldemberg). An informative introduction helps define irony (and particularly narrative irony) for the reader, and an equally informative epilogue helps place the "intimate connection between irony and the novel" into the context of the Spanish American novel. Contains a good index and a bibliography of works consulted in Spanish and English. Titles and quotations in English.

Tolman, John. "The Brazilian Novel." In *The Brazilian Novel*, edited by Heitor Martins. Bloomington: Indiana University, 1976.
An excellent "broad picture of the Brazilian novel," as the author puts it, intended for an uninitiated English-speaking audience and punctuated by a brief discussion of the social and political conditions which have accompanied each turn in the evolution of this novel. Includes mention of numerous novelists and their works with more lengthy discussion of major writers such as Machado de Assis and, from the contemporary period, Guimarães Rosa, Lispector, and Antonio Callado. A solid, brief introduction to the Brazilian novel. Titles in Portuguese with English translations.

Vargas Llosa, Mario. Introduction to "The Latin American Novel Today." *Books Abroad* 44 (Winter, 1970): 7-16.
Vargas Llosa briefly traces the history of the Latin American novel and then discusses the emergence of the new Latin American novel, delineating the thematic and technical characteristics which differentiate it from its predecessors. He also discusses the changing status of the Latin American novelist as well as the social, historical, and philosophical factors which contributed to the changes discussed. A truly excellent introduction to the Latin American novel as it stood in 1970. Titles in original language.

Vázquez Amaral, José. *The Contemporary Latin American Narrative*. New York: Las Américas, 1970.
An in-depth discussion of eleven Spanish American novels of the twentieth century, eight of which were published between 1940 and 1970, including works by Fuentes, Vargas Llosa, Carpentier, Asturias, García Márquez, and Cortázar. An introduction and conclusion, as well as a chapter on Latin American fiction as a new genre, help place the works discussed in historical, cultural, and literary context. Includes a good index. Titles and quotations in English.

ISABEL ALLENDE
Chile

Commentary

Foster, Douglas. "Isabel Allende Unveiled." *Mother Jones* (December, 1988): 42-46.

In an interview with Foster, Allende provides often-lengthy and always personal and insightful answers to questions on topics as diverse as the political situation in Chile, her feelings as an exile, her novel *Eva Luna*, how her own upbringing was different from that of her female characters, her similarities to García Márquez, her new marriage and life as a writer and suburban housewife in California, and her plans for new writings. An interesting and informative piece. Titles in English.

The House of the Spirit (La Casa de los espíritus)

Antoni, Robert. "Parody or Piracy: The Relationship of *The House of Spirits* to *One Hundred Years of Solitude*." *Latin American Literary Review* 16 (July-December, 1988): 16-28.

In part through the juxtaposition of passages from each novel, Antoni shows how the beginning sections of Allende's novel present striking parallels (through "language, technique, characters, and events") to García Márquez' *One Hundred Years of Solitude*. The critic also shows, however, that as the story progresses (as it shifts from Clara to Alba), the work becomes less like García Márquez' novel, as Allende's work abandons magic realism and "becomes the tragic political history of Chile." Antoni even cites a book-burning scene (by General "García") in *The House of the Spirits* which he suggests may signify, or at least parallel, Allende's declaration of literary independence. Antoni concludes that Allende's novel is a work which "may begin as an attempt to rewrite *One Hundred Years of Solitude*, but which discovers itself as a unique statement," and at the same time, he implies, uncovers Allende's own voice. An insightful piece. Titles and quotations in English with Spanish translations.

Engelbert, Jo Anne, and Linda Levine. "The World Is Full of Stories." *Review 34* (January-June, 1985): 18-20.

In a short interview conducted during her stay as a writer-in-residence at Montclair State College, Allende responds to questions concerning the four female characters of *The House of the Spirits*, the issue of machismo (particularly as it relates to her novel), and the topic of writing. An informative piece. Titles in English.

Grove, James. "*The House of the Spirits*." In *Magill's Literary Annual,* 1986, edited by Frank N. Magill, vol. 1. Pasadena, Calif.: Salem Press, 1986.

Grove begins his article with a brief discussion of the concept of the "total novel" and contends that *The House of the Spirits* is Allende's attempt at just such a novel. He then considers the writer's use of "both magical and social realism" in her work and the novel's theme. The bulk of the article, however, is devoted to an analysis of the principal characters of the work. Provides an introduction to the novel in question. "Sources for Further Study" section lists review articles of the work (in English). Titles and quotations in English.

JORGE AMADO
Brazil

Commentary

Branam, Harold. "Jorge Amado." In *Critical Survey of Long Fiction* (Foreign Language Series), edited by Frank N. Magill, vol. 1. Pasadena, Calif.: Salem Press, 1984.
A six-and-a-half-page overview of Amado's novels. Contains a list of his major works (some only in Portuguese), a summary of his work in other literary forms, and an assessment of his achievements. This is followed by a biographical sketch and an overview and analysis of some of his major works. A good introduction to Amado for the reader unfamiliar with the Brazilian author. Includes a list of his other major works (most in Portuguese only) and a short critical bibliography in English. Titles of translated works in English.

Chamberlain, Bobby J. "Unlocking the Roman à Clef: A Look at the 'In-Group' Humor of Jorge Amado." *The American Hispanist* 4, no. 28 (September, 1978): 12-16.
Claiming that some 688 of the 3,060 characters which populate Amado's novels actually exist (most being friends of Amado), Chamberlain sets out to identify many of these characters in several of the Brazilian author's works (such as *Gabriela, Clove, and Cinnamon*; *Tent of Miracles*; *Dona Flor and Her Two Husbands*; and *Tereza Batista: Home from the Wars*). More important, the critic shows the various ways in which Amado presents such characters and the reasons for which he does it. An exhaustively researched and interesting piece. Titles and quotations in Portuguese.

Ellison, Fred P. "Jorge Amado." In his *Brazil's New Novel: Four Northeastern Masters*. Westport, Conn.: Greenwood Press, 1954.
Although dated, this chapter provides a good background for the student of the post-1958 (the date considered the beginning of the writer's second phase) Jorge Amado. Includes a brief biographical sketch, but most of the chapter is dedicated to a discussion of Amado's socially oriented novels of the 1930's and 1940's. Reveals just how much the Brazilian author has changed since his first phase and, at the same time, just how much he has not. A widely read study. Interesting not in spite of its publication date but to a large degree because of it. Titles in English with Portuguese translations. Quotations in English.

Fitz, Earl E. "Jorge Amado." In *Latin American Literature in the Twentieth Century: A Guide*, edited by Leonard S. Klein. New York: Frederick Ungar, 1986.
A brief (roughly three-page) introduction to Amado's life and works. Emphasis on his major works (particularly *The Two Deaths of Quincas Wateryell* and *Gabriela, Clove, and Cinnamon*) and the thematic concerns and character

types which dominate his narrative. A good starting point for the reader unfamiliar with Amado. Provides a list of some of the Brazilian author's works (mostly in Portuguese) and a short critical bibliography in English.

Hamilton, Russell G. "Afro-Brazilian Cults in the Novels of Jorge Amado." *Hispania* 50 (May, 1967): 242-252.

Stating that most critics make the mistake of writing off the presence of Afro-Brazilian cults in Amado's works as "so much folklore" and that many under-estimate Amado's involvement in these cults, Hamilton uses his article "to trace the development of the Afro-Brazilian cults in most of Jorge Amado's novels and show how he finds cultural and spiritual values as well as aesthetic expression in them." Concentrates on the presence of *candomblé* in Amado's early works, but still insightful and informative for the student of the Brazilian author's post-1958 works as well. Includes background on how Amado got involved in Afro-Brazilian cults and how African religious culture has been treated in Brazilian literature in general. A solid article. Titles and quotations in Portuguese.

Keating, L. Clark. "The Guys and Dolls of Jorge Amado." *Hispania* 66 (September, 1983): 340-344.

A general examination of the various types of characters which populate Amado's novels and the roles and personalities Amado assigns to them. Several novels are mentioned, though most attention is paid to works not listed in this bibliography (with the exception of *The Two Deaths of Quincas Wateryell*). Not intended as an in-depth analysis of Amado's characters, but it does provide a good introduction to them for the uninitiated reader. Most titles in Portuguese. Some in English as well.

Nunes, Maria Luísa. "Jorge Amado." In *Dictionary of Brazilian Literature*, edited by Irwin Stern. Westport, Conn.: Greenwood Press, 1988.

A brief (roughly three-page) introduction to Amado's life and works. Discusses the two distinct phases of the Brazilian writer's career and the type of works which characterize each one. Brief discussion of some of Amado's major works (such as *Gabriela, Clove, and Cinnamon* and *Tent of Miracles*) and far less detailed mention of others. A good starting point for the reader unfamiliar with Amado. Includes a list of his works (most in both Portuguese and English) and a critical bibliography in English.

Tent of Miracles (Tenda dos milagres)

Fitz, Earl E. "The Problem of the Unreliable Narrator in Jorge Amado's *Tenda dos Milagres.*" *Kentucky Romance Quarterly* 30 (1983): 311-312.

Fitz mentions that the technical aspects of Amado's novels have received "short shrift" and contends that while this may have been justifiable with regard to the Brazilian writer's early works, it is not so with respect to his later works, particularly where narrative voice is concerned. The critic then presents a meticulous analysis of the narrator of *Tent of Miracles*, Fausto Pena, who, Fitz contends, "weaves in and out of the text and leads us through the often labyrinthine but always delightful digressions that make up his earthy, affecting story." Fitz calls Pena at one point "a special type of unreliable narrator, one whose innate simplicity and ingenuousness endear him to us at the same time that they lead him astray in the novel." A solid study. Titles and quotations in Portuguese.

Tereza Batista: Home from the Wars (Tereza Batista cansada de guerre)

Patai, Daphne. "Jorge Amado: Morals and Marvels." In her *Myth and Ideology in Contemporary Brazilian Fiction*. Rutherford, N.J.: Fairleigh Dickinson University Press, 1983.

In sections entitled "Narrative Technique," "Character and Act," "Myth and the Marvelous," and "The Ideology of Machismo" (complemented by an introduction and conclusion), Patai analyzes Amado's *Tereza Batista: Home from the Wars* with emphasis on the novel's popular and picturesque nature, as well as "the magical or supernatural aspect of myth" developed by the author. A lengthy (thirty pages) and detailed study. Very readable. Titles in Portuguese with English translations. Quotations in English.

The Two Deaths of Quincas Wateryell (A morte e a morte de Quincas Berro D'Água)

Fitz, Earl E. "Structural Ambiguity in Jorge Amado's *A morte e a morte de Quincas Berro d'Água*." *Hispania* 67 (May, 1984): 221-228.

Calling *The Two Deaths of Quincas Wateryell* "arguably Amado's finest overall technical achievement," Fitz goes on to prove why he believes this to be the case, citing the Brazilian author's "skill in weaving a fundamental ambiguity concerning what 'really happens' in the story into the actual structuring of the story itself." Fitz states that the careful wording of the narrative and its structure work together throughout the story to present several occurrences which may be classified both as real and as fantastic, making it "difficult, if not impossible, to say with absolute certainty what is true and what is not." Fitz breaks down the work into three sections and then in a detailed manner analyzes each section and the masterful intentional ambiguity employed by Amado in each part. An excellent article on a fascinating topic. Quotations in Portuguese.

Silverman, Malcolm. "Duality in Jorge Amado's *The Two Deaths of Quincas Wateryell*." *Studies in Short Fiction* 15 (Spring, 1978): 196-199.

A brief and concise examination of the "work's parallel if ambiguous philosophical and plot lines," beginning with the redundancy present in the novel's title through the two names and two lives of the main character and his supposed behavior after death. Silverman discusses the presence of duality in all these aspects of the work and offers possible explanations for some of the unusual events. His explanations are necessarily indefinite, however, since, as he states, Amado's narrator "skillfully bends characters and events without breaking them," rendering all explanations only possible at best. Quotations in English.

JUAN JOSÉ ARREOLA
Mexico

Biography

Washburn, Yulan. "Life and Works." In his *Juan José Arreola*. Boston: Twayne, 1983.

A lengthy (thirty-seven-page), detailed account of Arreola's life and career (more emphasis on the latter) through 1982. The only unified account of its kind, according to Washburn. Divided into three sections ("The Early Years"; "First Fruits [1946-1960]"; and "Maturity"), this chapter not only provides simple background information on the Mexican writer's life and a list of his literary accomplishments, it also integrates the two parts of Arreola's life, combining the man and the writer, providing an insightful picture of both. Titles in Spanish with English translations. Quotations in English.

Commentary

McMurray, George R. "Juan José Arreola." In *Latin American Literature in the Twentieth Century: A Guide*, edited by Leonard S. Klein. New York: Frederick Ungar, 1986.

A brief (two-and-a-half-page) introduction to Arreola's life and works. Emphasis on the dominant characteristics of his narrative, his similarities to Borges, and very limited discussion of some of his short stories (chiefly "The Switchman"). A good starting point for the reader unfamiliar with Arreola. Provides a list of his works in Spanish and a short critical bibliography in Spanish and English.

_____ . "New Directions." In his *Spanish American Writing Since 1941: A Critical Survey*. New York: Frederick Ungar, 1987.

McMurray devotes roughly three pages of this section of his book to a brief overview of Arreola's fiction. Following two paragraphs of introduction, the critic offers concise commentary on a number of the Mexican writer's stories, with "The Switchman" receiving the most attention (two paragraphs). A good introduction for the reader unfamiliar with Arreola. Titles in Spanish with English translations.

Washburn, Yulan. *Juan José Arreola*. Boston: Twayne, 1983.

An excellent overview of Arreola's life and works. Features a chronology and opening chapter on the Mexican writer's life and career (chiefly the latter), followed by chapters containing treatment of Arreola's works according to the writer's principal thematic concerns, these being, according to Washburn, "the existential and artistic situation of humankind, the man-woman relationship, theological concerns, and Mexico the homeland." A final chapter presents an assessment of Arreola's achievement and places him in Mexican literature.

Includes a good index, a bibliography of Arreola's works (mostly in Spanish), and an annotated critical bibliography (in Spanish and English). Titles in Spanish with English translations. Quotations in English.

Confabulario and Other Inventions (Confabulario y varia invención)

Burt, John R. "This Is No Way to Run a Railroad: Arreola's Allegorical Railroad and a Possible Source." *Hispania* 71 (December, 1988): 806-811.

An examination of Arreola's "The Switchman" with emphasis on its allegorical nature and its similarity to Nathaniel Hawthorne's "The Celestial Railroad." The allegorical elements of "The Switchman" are clearly pointed out and the parallels between Arreola's story and Hawthorne's thoroughly examined. Burt's conclusion is that the Mexican writer likely read Hawthorne's story at some point and then later, perhaps unintentionally, used it as a basis for his own story. Titles and quotations in Spanish.

Heusinkveld, Paula R. "Juan José Arreola: Allegorist in an Age of Uncertainty." *Chasqui* 13 (February-May, 1984): 33-43.

Heusinkveld contends that Arreola's stories in *Confabulario and Other Inventions* are allegories, at least in the modern sense of the word. She then defines the function and nature of both the traditional allegory and its twentieth century counterpart, and places Arreola's works firmly within the context of the modern version. The critic then examines three stories from *Confabulario* ("The Switchman," "Autrui," and "The Map of Lost Objects") as examples of modern (and Arreola's version of) allegory, before concluding, in part, that the allegories in this collection share five characteristics: "(1) a skeptical, pessimistic view of the world; (2) an anti-hero who lacks control of his circumstances; (3) symbols that convey man's limitations rather than his potential; (4) a lack of overt didactic intent; and (5) an absence of explicitly stated correspondences between fictional and real meaning levels." Another element she finds common to Arreola's allegories (though uncommon in the modern allegory in general) is humor. An excellent article. Titles and quotations from Arreola's stories in Spanish.

McMurray, George R. "Albert Camus' Concept of the Absurd and Juan José Arreola's 'The Switchman.'" *Latin American Literary Review* 11 (Fall/Winter, 1977): 30-35.

An analysis of Arreola's famous short story based on the Absurdist ideas of Camus set forth in the French writer's *The Myth of Sisyphus*. McMurray explains Camus' concept of the absurd and then interprets the various elements of Arreola's story (such as the actions of the stranger, of the switchman himself, and of the other travelers about whom the switchman speaks) as a poetic expression of absurdist philosophy, concluding that the stranger in the story is "an absurd man with the potential of becoming a hero like the passengers who carried the train across the abyss." McMurray even suggests that the story could be "a metaphor of modern man's awakening to Camus' famous question, 'Why?' " An interesting and highly readable study. Titles and quotations in English.

Menton, Seymour. "Juan José Arreola and the Twentieth Century Short Story." *Hispania* 42 (September, 1959): 295-308.
Menton states that Spanish American short story writers "faced the dilemma of being called *passes* for continuing to treat timeworn *criollo* themes or xenophiles for attempting to search for more universal themes." The works contained in Arreola's *Confabulario and Other Inventions*, Menton contends, provide a "possible solution to this dilemma." The critic then presents and overview of Arreola's stories, which he believes "constitute to a certain extent a compendium of the modern short story." An excellent introduction to Arreola's stories within the context of the twentieth century short story. Titles and quotations in Spanish.

MIGUEL ÁNGEL ASTURIAS
Guatemala

Biography

Callan, Richard J. "Asturias, the Man." In his *Miguel Ángel Asturias*. New York: Twayne, 1970.

Divided into two sections, this short chapter first provides a thumbnail sketch of Asturias' life (through 1970) and then addresses the Guatemalan writer's personal views on the nature and purpose of Latin American literature. Both sections are concise and informative. The second section should help the reader understand why Asturias writes as he does. Titles and quotations (very few of either) provided in English or in Spanish with English translations.

Commentary

Brotherston, Gordon. "America's Magic Forest: Miguel Ángel Asturias." In his *The Emergence of the Latin American Novel*. London: Cambridge University Press, 1977.

A good introduction to Asturias' fictional world, largely through a discussion of his novels *Men of Maize* (treatment of which covers roughly fifteen pages of the twenty-page chapter) and *El Señor Presidente*, with particular emphasis on the aspects of Asturias' background which allow him to capture so vividly the Indian elements expressed in his work (focusing on *Men of Maize*). Titles in Spanish with English translations (or vice versa). Quotations (except in one case where both the Spanish and English versions are provided because of the passage's—from *El Senor Presidente*—"strong phonetic qualities which defy translation") in English.

——————— . "The Presence of Mayan Literature in *Hombres de maíz* and Other Works by Miguel Ángel Asturias." *Hispania* 58 (March, 1975): 68-74.

Brotherston traces the presence of Mayan literature in *Men of Maize* and several stories by Asturias, concluding that, contrary to general perception, the Guatemalan writer's creative involvement ("involvement" being the key word here) with Mayan literature is minimal, that though he uses Mayan myths and themes, he maintains a rather Western and twentieth century distance (as opposed to writers such as José María Arguedas and Augusto Roa Bastos, whose works are much more authentically Indian in content). An interesting article challenging, in effect, mainstream opinion concerning the nature of an Indian presence in Asturias' works. Titles and quotations in Spanish.

Callan, Richard J. *Miguel Ángel Asturias*. New York: Twayne, 1970.

A solid survey of Asturias' life and works. Includes a chronology of important dates in the Guatemalan writer's personal and professional life, a chapter entitled "Asturias, the Man," chapter-long discussions of each of his major works, a chapter dedicated to his plays, and another dedicated to his short stories. A final chapter briefly discusses three novels not analyzed previously in the volume, in addition to the thematic focus of Asturias' overall literary production. An excellent introduction for the uninitiated reader. Includes a detailed index and an annotated bibliography in Spanish and English. Titles in Spanish with English translations. Quotations in English.

_____ . "Miguel Ángel Asturias." In *Latin American Literature in the Twentieth Century: A Guide*, edited by Leonard S. Klein. New York: Frederick Ungar, 1986.
A brief (three-and-a-half pages) introduction to Asturias' life and works. Focuses on his background in Indian literature and very briefly discusses his major works (most notably *El Señor Presidente*). Some attention as well to his poetry. A good starting point for the uninitiated reader. Provides a list of Asturias' works (some titles in Spanish with English translations, others only in Spanish) and a critical bibliography almost entirely in English.

_____ . "Miguel Ángel Asturias: Spokesman of His People." *Studies in Short Fiction* 8 (Winter, 1971): 93-102.
Callan begins by briefly comparing Asturias to Nathaniel Hawthorne, stating that both writers are concerned with "invention and creation rather than reporting, with transmuting reality rather than transcribing it," and then moves on to how Asturias incorporates both the real and the mythical into his works. Most of the article is dedicated to several tales by Asturias and their relationship, chiefly, with fertility myths and themes. Considerable reference to Jungian psychology. Titles and quotations in English.

Guibert, Rita. "Miguel Ángel Asturias." In her *Seven Voices: Seven Latin American Writers Talk to Rita Guibert*. Translated by Frances Partridge. New York: Alfred A. Knopf, 1973.
In an interview with Guibert (compiled from a series of hour-long interviews conducted at Asturias' Paris apartment, November 6-10, 1970), the Guatemalan author provides lengthy answers to questions about his ancestors, his interest in Indians, how he came to write *El Señor Presidente*, his contact with Surrealism and its influence on his work, his style, how he writes, his reaction to winning the Nobel Prize, critics, translations of his works, books that have influenced him, and many other topics. Informative, interesting, and personal. A photograph is included in center of book. Titles in Spanish with English translations.

Harss, Luis, and Barbara Dohmann. "Miguel Ángel Asturias, or the Land Where the Flowers Bloom." In their *Into the Mainstream: Conversations with Latin American Writers*. New York: Harper & Row, 1967.

An interview-based discussion of Asturias and his works. Contains many more direct quotations from the writer than most chapters in this excellent volume. Provides inside information, so to speak, on the background and writing of the three novels by Asturias covered in this bibliography, as the writer discusses, for example, the real-life dictatorship on which *El Señor Presidente* is based, his opinions on Indian myth, the use of language in his novels, and the nature of Latin American literature. An insightful piece and a fine, up-close introduction to Asturias and his works. Titles in Spanish with English translations. Quotations in English.

Lyons, Thomas E. "Miguel Ángel Asturias: Timeless Fantasy. The 1967 Nobel Prize for Literature." *Books Abroad* 42 (Spring, 1968): 183-189.
This article seems to have two purposes: (1) to introduce Miguel Ángel Asturias to the American reading public; and (2) to defend his selection as winner of the 1967 Nobel Prize for Literature. It achieves both purposes admirably. It introduces the "famous unknown author" by providing a very brief sketch of his life and by presenting an overview of his works, concentrating on some of the key elements which characterize his writing (for example, the presence of Indian myth, a poetic style). Defense of Asturias' worthiness as a Nobel laureate is made in part by the very same overview of his works, punctuated with comments obviously meant to defend his selection. An excellent introduction to Asturias and his works for the uninitiated reader. Titles in Spanish with English translations. Most quotations in English. Some in Spanish.

McMurray, George R. "New Directions," In his *Spanish American Writing Since 1941: A Critical Survey*. New York: Frederick Ungar, 1987.
McMurray devotes approximately four pages of this section of his book to a brief overview of Asturias' fiction. Following an opening paragraph on the Guatemalan writer's personal and literary background, the critic follows Asturias' career in chronological fashion, with *El Señor Presidente* and *Men of Maize* receiving the most attention (three paragraphs and two paragraphs respectively). A final paragraph summarizes the nature of his fiction. A good starting point for the reader unfamiliar with Asturias. Titles in Spanish with English translations.

Mead, Robert G., Jr. "Miguel Ángel Asturias and the Nobel Prize." *Hispania* 51 (May, 1968): 326-331.
An article intended (1) to evaluate Asturias' standing as a result of winning the Nobel Prize; (2) to decry the university-teaching profession for not being able to spread knowledge of the Guatemalan author's works more effectively; and (3) to introduce the writer and his works to those who, as of the article's publication, are still unfamiliar with him. Contains a brief look at Asturias'

life and career and limited discussion of his three novels covered in this bibliography. Of particular interest are direct comments from Asturias himself on how he writes and his view of Magic Realism. Titles in Spanish.

Men of Maize (Hombres de maíz)

Brotherston, Gordon. "America's Magic Forest: Miguel Ángel Asturias." In his *The Emergence of the Latin American Novel*. London: Cambridge University Press, 1977.

Brotherston devotes roughly fifteen pages of this twenty-page introduction to Asturias' fictional world to an overview discussion of *Men of Maize*. While the critic treats various aspects of the narrative, most attention is paid to how Asturias presents the Indian world and to the aspects of the Guatemalan author's background which allow him to present it as he does. Titles in Spanish with English translations (or vice versa). Quotations in English or in Spanish with English translations.

Callan, Richard J. "*Hombres de maíz.*" In his *Miguel Ángel Asturias*. New York: Twayne, 1970.

The first third of this chapter presents a discussion of the difficulties of Asturias' novel, followed by a detailed plot summary. The final two thirds are devoted to a discussion of the parallels which exist between the story and characters of *Men of Maize* and several fertility myths (both Mediterranean and Aztec), and of death and rebirth. Among the myths discussed are those of Dionysus, Attis, Venus and Adonis, Huitzilopochtli, Quetzalcoatl, Toci, Demeter and Persephone, and Isis and Osiris. Includes considerable references to the text which support the critic's theories. An interesting piece. Quotations in English.

——————— . "The Quest for the Feminine." In his *Miguel Ángel Asturias*. New York: Twayne, 1970.

A discussion of the concepts of sacrifice, death and rebirth, the Great Mother, and the quest for the Eternal Feminine present in *Men of Maize*. Includes considerable reference to Carl Jung's analytical psychology and the development of consciousness and numerous references to the text which illustrate the critic's theories. Heavily based in psychological criticism. Interesting. Best read in tandem with the "*Hombres de maíz*" [*Men of Maize*] chapter of the same volume. Quotations in English.

Prieto, René. "Tall Tales Made to Order: The Making of Myth in *Men of Maize* by Miguel Ángel Asturias." *Modern Language Notes* 101 (March, 1980): 354-365.

Prieto examines the presence of mythmaking, particularly as it applies to the conversion of reality into (potential) fiction, in *Men of Maize*, a novel in which "the bones" of Asturias' "literary creation are laid bare not merely to moti-

vate the reader's response, but specifically, to nurture it." Prieto concentrates
on the frequent presence of two unlike versions of several events in the novel,
as well as the open and obvious fiction making of the tale-telling characters in
the work. Prieto's contention is that Asturias "opted to reveal the genetic
process of his literary discourse, to show, in other words, how a tale comes
into being and to demonstrate the role of each and all individuals in the
development of myth," all, according to the critic, with the underlying intention of inviting the Guatemalan public to participate in social revolution. Titles
and quotations in English.

Mulata (Mulata de tal)

Martin, Gerald. "*Mulata de tal*: The Novel as Animated Cartoon." *Hispanic Review* 41 (1973): 397-415.

Attempting to discern how Asturias animates the various elements of his
fragmented novel, Martin contends that the Guatemalan writer achieves said
animation through what the critic calls the author's "cartoon technique." Martin states that in *Mulata* "metaphor and other linguistic devices are used to
give dynamic motion to the action, to fuse the heterogeneous elements
. . . into a homogeneous literary whole." The critic discusses the nature of
cartoons, from Walt Disney's Mickey Mouse to *Popeye* and *Tom and Jerry*, and
shows how Asturias uses some basic concepts of cartoon animation to "inject
an extraordinary motion into his narrative by animating myths and legends into
a swiftly flowing fairy tale." A fascinating perspective on the novel. Titles and
quotations from Asturias' novel in Spanish. Most other references in English.
Some in Spanish.

El Señor Presidente

Brotherston, Gordon. "America's Magic Forest: Miguel Ángel Asturias." In his *The
Emergence of the Latin American Novel*. London: Cambridge University Press,
1977.

Although the bulk (roughly fifteen of the twenty pages) of the chapter is
devoted chiefly to a discussion of *Men of Maize*, the final five pages offer a
treatment of *El Señor Presidente*, with emphasis on some of its connections to
Guatemalan history, its Joycean qualities, and, most of all, its destruction of
myth. A brief but informative section. Titles in Spanish with English translations (or vice versa). Quotations (with the exception of one—from the beginning of *El Señor Presidente*, "because of its strongly phonetic qualities which
defy translation") provided in both Spanish and English.

Callan, Richard J. "Babylonian Mythology in *El Señor Presidente*." In his *Miguel
Ángel Asturias*. New York: Twayne, 1970.

A study of Asturias' novel as a veiled portrayal of the Babylonian fertility
myth of Tammuz and Ishtar. Callan sees Camila as Ishtar, Don Miguel as
Tammuz, and both the President and Fedina Rodas as the Great Mother.

Includes considerable background information on Babylonian mythology and the Tammuz/Ishtar myth, which helps the reader unfamiliar with the subject. Also includes subdivisions entitled "Additional Mythological Parallels," "The Tammuz Myth in Depth Psychology," and "The Archetype of Dictatorship." Provides considerable discussion of Carl Jung and the relationship between his school of psychology and Asturias' novel. An interesting piece. Quotations in English.

_____ . *"El Señor Presidente."* In his *Miguel Ángel Asturias*. New York: Twayne, 1970.
This brief chapter provides an excellent plot summary, though the bulk of the chapter is dedicated to a study of the novel's theme. Callan contends that *El Señor Presidente* "is not intrinsically a political novel," but is instead, a work of, as he puts it, "metaphysical conflict," based upon "the old pagan and medieval theme of fertility." He then provides considerable textual proof to support his claim. An interesting piece. Quotations in English.

Campion, Daniel. "Eye of Glass, Eye of Truth: Surrealism in *El Señor Presidente*." *Hispanic Journal* 3 (Fall, 1981): 123-135.
Calling *El Señor Presidente* "a thoroughly engaged political work whose central motif is based on surrealist doctrine," Campion seeks, in part at least, to "reconcile the novel's obvious aim of social protest with its almost unrelievedly bleak development and conclusion." He does this by pursuing the presence of surrealism in the novel, chiefly as it pertains to the motif of the eye of glass and the eye of truth. In the process he both praises and criticizes the interpretations of other critics and concludes that the novel is intended as a counter-myth, "one that inspires imagination and surrealist revolt in the reader if not the characters." The novel is negative, but its intention and hope for the future are positive. Quotations in Spanish, English, and French.

Franz, Thomas R. "Three Hispanic Echoes of Tolstoi at the Close of World War II." *Hispanic Journal* 6 (Fall, 1984): 37-51.
In this article on the presence of Leo Tolstoi's *War and Peace* in *El Señor Presidente*, Yáñez' *The Edge of the Storm* and Spaniard Camilo José Celas' *La colmena* (*The Hive*), Franz devotes most of his attention (roughly three pages) concerning Asturias' novel to "symbolic use of the comet" and "the abduction of the novel's heroine" in this work and *War and Peace*. The critic also cites numerous other traces of Tolstoi in Asturias' novel, such as "the achievement of objectivity by placing the narrative mind and voice within the minds and voices of all the novel's characters in all their little bifurcating monads of existence." An interesting piece. Titles and quotations of the Hispanic works in Spanish. All others in English.

Martin, Gerald. "*El Señor Presidente* and How to Read It." *Bulletin of Hispanic Studies* 47 (1970): 223-243.

Contending that most readers and critics have misunderstood *El Señor Presidente*, chiefly because they have not understood Asturias' fictional method, Martin sets out to show the true nature of the novel in the hope that others will use his findings as a starting point for their own interpretations of the work. He views the novel "as a poetic work in which plot and characters become simply motifs in the completed pattern," making the work self-referential and giving each element of this complex work an "intimate and organic relationship to the metaphorical substratum." Martin goes on to call the work "a systematic and highly purposeful assault on human reality," concluding that if it "is not treated both as novel *and* poem its very essence is irremediably lost." Numerous references from various sources (including Asturias himself) to support the critic's theory. Titles and quotations in Spanish.

Vázquez Amaral, José. "*El Señor Presidente* by Miguel Ángel Asturias." In his *The Contemporary Latin American Narrative*. New York: Las Américas, 1970.

A fascinating chapter which not only discusses the novel at hand, but emphasizes the reality beyond the fiction. Vázquez Amaral goes to considerable lengths to trace the history of Latin America which allows for the existence of petty tyrants, as he puts it, such as "el Señor Presidente." He states that the novel "could be written, with but a few changes, about any republic of Latin America." A bit short on in-depth literary analysis but long on political and cultural context. Helps the reader of the novel understand the harsh reality from which the work sprang. A very strong chapter. Titles and quotations in English.

JORGE LUIS BORGES
Argentina

Biography

Borges, Jorge Luis. "An Autobiographical Essay." In *Critical Essays on Jorge Luis Borges*, edited by Jaime Alazraki. Boston: G. K. Hall, 1987.

Reprinted from *The Aleph and Other Stories 1933-1969* (New York: E. P. Dutton, 1970), this piece provides a highly personal as well as personable account of Borges' life (through age seventy) by the writer himself. Very concise, the essay is divided into sections entitled "Family Childhood," "Europe," "Buenos Aires," "Maturity," and "Crowded Years," and it is full of factual information, but as important, and perhaps more so, it also contains numerous anecdotes (such as of the author's first encounter with gauchos), reflections, and personal observations by the writer concerning his family, his works, his fame, his career, and his life. Charmingly personal, nonscholarly, and highly readable. An excellent introduction to Borges' life.

———————. "A Borges Family Chronicle." In *Prose for Borges*, edited by Charles Newman and Mary Kinzie. Evanston, Ill.: Northwestern University Press, 1974.

A brief, personal, and very selective account of Borges' life through 1971. Selective because it is not a standard, fact-filled chronicle, but a sort of family album (containing sixteen captioned photographs) focusing solely on those moments captured in the photographs. Still very interesting and revealing, particularly concerning the author's background and youth.

McMurray, George R. Introduction to *Jorge Luis Borges*. New York: Frederick Ungar, 1980.

A brief (twelve-page) history of Borges' life through 1979. Includes several important biographical facts but perhaps more important, this introduction contains other information as well, such as comments on the Argentine writer's timid and modest nature, his boredom with music (except for Argentine folk music), and his skill as a conversationalist. Supplemented by a literary and biographical chronology which precedes the introduction. Titles and quotations in English.

Rodríguez Monegal, Emir. *Jorge Luis Borges: A Literary Biography*. New York: E. P. Dutton, 1978.

The definitive biography of the Argentine writer by one of Borges' (and contemporary Latin American fiction's) most prominent critics. Detailed and lengthy (502 pages). Made particularly interesting by the constant blending of facts about Borges' life and literary texts by him concerning or related to the events or personalities discussed (such as a poem about a particular childhood experience). Highly informative and very useful for anyone seeking a better understanding of Borges the writer. Provides a bibliography of Borges' works (in Spanish and English) and criticism of his works (in various languages). The bibliography even includes a separate listing of published interviews with the writer. Also includes an excellent index and photographs. Titles and quotations in English.

Stabb, Martin S. "Borges: The Man and His Times." In his *Jorge Luis Borges*. New York: Twayne, 1970.

In sections entitled "Early Life and Travels," "The Poet and His City," "The Mature Writer," and "The Man Behind the Book," Stabb provides a portrait of the life and career of Borges, a writer, the critic states, whose "biography has little significance or interest except as it marks the trajectory of his remarkable literary career." Includes useful factual information (names and dates) as well as insights into Borges' personality. An excellent fourteen-page introduction to Borges the man as well as Borges the writer. Titles and quotations in Spanish with English translations.

Commentary

Agheana, Ion T. *The Prose of Jorge Luis Borges: Existentialism and the Dynamics of Surprise*. New York: Lang, 1984.

Offering his study as a "counterpoint to established Borgesian criticism," Agheana examines the presence of existentialism and what he calls the "Dynamics of Surprise" in the Argentine writer's works. The first part of the study examines Borges' connection to existentialism and the manifestation of it in his works, particularly as it concerns the affirmation of the self, so common, the critic contends, to Borges' protagonists. The second section treats the same subject with regard to symmetry (for example, religion and philosophy) versus asymmetry (for example, individuality) in Borges' characters. A final section "deals with the rekindling of man's curiosity about himself and about the world," a curiosity which encourages "the right to raise questions and offer opinions about all matters human without pretense to conclusive objectivity." An interesting and exhaustive study. Titles and quotations in Spanish.

Aizenberg, Edna. *The Aleph Weaver: Biblical, Kabbalistic and Judaic Elements in Borges*. Potomac, Md.: Scripta Humanistica, 1984.

The first comprehensive study of the presence of Judaic and Judaic-related elements in Borges' works. Aizenberg contends that Borges "weaves and unweaves" a Judaic heritage, "using technical strategies and archetypal metaphors derived from Jewish sources." Aizenberg examines the "personal, historical and cultural circumstances" which helped develop Borges' interest in things Judaic. She then focuses on the Argentine writer's works, identifying and examining the various Judaic antecedents and elements that exist within them. An interesting and well-researched study. Contains an index. Some quotations in Spanish, some in English.

Alazraki, Jaime. "Borges and the Kabbalah." In *Prose for Borges*, edited by Charles Newman and Mary Kinzie. Evanston, Ill.: Northwestern University Press, 1974. Also appears in *TriQuarterly* 25 (Fall, 1972): 240-267.

A detailed and well-organized study of the influence of the Kabbalah on Borges' works and thought. Alazraki contends that this influence goes beyond quotations and allusions in the Argentine writer's stories. Behind Borges' "transparent texts there lies a stylistic intricacy, a certain Kabbalistic texture, a spellbinding characteristic to which Borges finds himself attracted." Alazraki studies works on the Kabbalah that have influenced Borges, as well as doctrines (those of the *Sefiroth* and the *Ibbur*), legends, and concepts which are reflected in the body of his work. Titles and quotations in English.

_____ . "Borges and the New Latin-American Novel." In *Prose for Borges*, edited by Charles Newman and Mary Kinzie. Evanston, Ill.: Northwestern University Press, 1974. Also appears in *TriQuarterly* 25 (Fall, 1972): 379-398.

Alazraki considers Borges' profound influence on the new Latin American novel, stating that though the Argentine writer has been acknowledged "as a driving force" behind this novel, very little has been written on the subject. Alazraki points out Borgesian practices (such as mixing the real with the fantastic and including characters from other writers' works) in particular Latin American novels, but emphasizes that Borges' true contributions to this novel have been freeing writers to use their imagination and a prose style (an "invisible style") the likes of which did not exist in Spanish-language prose before Borges. Titles in Spanish. Quotations in English.

Barnstone, Willis, ed. *Borges at Eighty*. Bloomington: University of Indiana Press, 1982.

Borges discusses his life, works, and thought in interviews and conversations conducted (in 1976 and 1980) at the University of Indiana, Columbia University, the University of Chicago, the Massachusetts Institute of Technology, the New York PEN Club, and on "The Dick Cavett Show." Interesting conversations covering numerous topics. Titles and quotations (very few of either) in English.

Barrenechea, Ana María. *Borges the Labyrinth Maker*. Translated by Robert Lima. New York: New York University Press, 1965.

An important study discussing both the life and the works of Borges to 1964. Emphasis on Borges' philosophies of time, infinity, the universe, reality, and literature. A good guide to understanding Borgesian thought. The bibliography (in Spanish) of Borges' works even includes a list of contents for each entry and a critical bibliography in Spanish, French, and English follows. Contains a good index. Titles and quotations in English.

Bell-Villada, Gene H. *Borges and His Fiction: A Guide to His Mind and Art*. Chapel Hill: University of North Carolina Press, 1981.

To quote critic Ronald Christ, whose comments grace the dust jacket, Bell-Villada has written this book "for readers as well as critics, for students as well as teachers," and in the process he has put together (the critic's words again) "an ideal introduction and guide" to Borges' fiction. In lengthy sections entitled "Borges's Worlds," "Borges's Fiction," and "Borges's Place in Literature," Bell-Villada provides detailed and very readable commentary concerning Borges' background, his many stories (with considerable attention paid to most), and his career, all the while downplaying the Argentine writer's role as a philosopher, an intellectual, and emphasizing his role as a storyteller. A superb study. Includes a chronology of Borges' life and career, an excellent index, and primary and secondary bibliographies in Spanish and English. Titles and quotations in English.

Bloom, Harold, ed. *Jorge Luis Borges*. New York: Chelsea House, 1986.

A wide-ranging collection of articles, many of which appear elsewhere. The editor calls the collection "a representative selection of the best criticism so far devoted" to Borges' writings. Certainly some of the most widely read and respected articles on the Argentine writer are here, such as Paul de Man's "A Modern Master" and Carter Wheelock's "Borges' New Prose." Other article titles include "Three Stories" by Louis Murillo, "The Immortal" by Ronald J. Christ, "Kabbalistic Traits in Borges' Narrative" by Jaime Alazraki, "Symbols in Borges' Work" by Emir Rodríguez Monegal, and "Borges and the Idea of Utopia" by James E. Irby. An excellent collection. Includes a chronology of Borges' life and career, a very good index, and a critical bibliography in English. Almost all titles and quotations in English.

Borges, Jorge Luis. "Simply a Man of Letters." In *Simply a Man of Letters*, edited by Carlos Cortínez. Orono: University of Maine at Orono Press, 1982.

In remarks made at a symposium held in his honor, the Argentine writer discusses his life as a man of literature, focusing on his keen interest in words, in language, and in various different languages. He also discusses his earliest published writings ("I wanted to apologize for the mistakes"), as well as how he goes about writing a story or poem. Borges' remarks are followed by a discussion session in which he responds to questions concerning his respect (or lack thereof) for literary conventions, his influence on contemporary Latin American writers, the influence of Edgar Allan Poe on his works, the presence of the mirror as a recurring symbol in his writing, and other topics. Not particularly important critically, but interesting, revealing, and personal.

Burgin, Richard. *Conversations with Jorge Luis Borges*. New York: Holt, Rinehart and Winston, 1969.
An enlightening collection of seven conversations between Borges and Burgin recorded during Borges' visit to Cambridge, Massachusetts, in 1967-1968. As Burgin points out in a rather detailed table of contents, Borges discusses everything from childhood, Nazis, and time to favorite stories, Darwin, *Don Quixote*, and Cervantes. A very personal book not as critically important as it is informative and insightful. A good introduction to Borges the man.

Christ, Ronald. "Forking Narratives." In *Simply a Man of Letters*, edited by Carlos Cortínez. Orono: University of Maine at Orono Press, 1982. Also appears in *Latin American Literary Review* 14 (Spring/Summer, 1979): 52-61.
Christ discusses the dual nature of Borges' narration, a narration which "while indicating one gesture, one action, one plot, not only does not exclude others but, rather, purposefully suggests them." Most examples are from Borges' story "The South." Christ contends that this type of narration has had a profound influence on English-speaking writers such as Robert Coover. Christ also examines (in a section which covers about half the article) the influence of this type of narration and its accompanying concept of reality on the film *Performance*. An interesting article showing Borges' influence on the English-speaking literary world. Titles and quotations in English.

_____ . *The Narrow Act: Borges' Art of Allusion*. New York: New York University Press, 1969.
Intended by the author as "an introduction to Borges' fiction by focusing on one particular device." The device in question is that of allusion, and, more specifically, allusion in Borges' works to English and American authors. Christ traces the development of this type of allusion in Borges' works, showing, as the critic puts it, "not only what Borges borrowed, but also, and more importantly, why he borrowed what he did." An exhaustive study of the topic. Provides an index and a bibliography in Spanish and English. Titles and quotations in English.

Coleman, Alexander. "Notes on Borges and American Literature." In *Prose for Borges*, edited by Charles Newman and Mary Kinzie. Evanston, Ill.: Northwestern University Press, 1974. Also appears in *TriQuarterly* 25 (Fall, 1972): 356-377.
A somewhat lengthy, detailed, and interesting study of Borges' views of American literature, answering the question asked by Coleman, "How, in fact, does Borges read us?" Using reviews, introductions, and other nonfiction sources (such as interviews), as well as poems by Borges dedicated to individual American authors, Coleman examines Borges' opinions of American writers as diverse as Jonathan Edwards, Edgar Allan Poe, Nathaniel Hawthorne, Ralph

Waldo Emerson, Walt Whitman, and Herman Melville. Titles of Borges' works in Spanish. Quotations in English.

Cortínez, Carlos, ed. *Simply a Man of Letters*. Orono: University of Maine at Orono Press, 1982.

A collection of papers, panel discussions, and other proceedings from a symposium on Borges held at the University of Maine at Orono in April, 1976. Features a title paper by Borges himself as well as numerous papers by some of the most prominent Borges scholars (such as Jaime Alazraki, Ana María Barrenechea, Emir Rodríguez Monegal, and Donald Yates). Paper titles include "Borges and Metafiction," "Jorge Luis Borges, Lover of Labyrinths: a Heideggerian Critique," and "Borges and the Symbols." Panel discussions cover such topics as "Borges and Chesterton." Collection also includes several poems both by and in homage to Borges, as well as other writings dedicated to the Argentine writer. An excellent and wide-ranging collection. Most titles and quotations in English.

de Garazalde, Giovanna. *Jorge Luis Borges: Sources and Illumination*. London: Octagon Press, 1978.

Intended as a study showing the links between Sufism and Sufi literature and the thought and works of Borges. Discusses Sufism as a "foreshadowing of Borges' thought" and then, quoting numerous sources, attempts to establish Borgesian thought. The critic then points out several thematic and technical links between Sufi literature and Borges' stories. An interesting study because it presents a different perspective on Borges' philosophical tendencies and works. Includes appendix listing references to Sufism found in the Argentine writer's works, bibliographies of works by Borges (in Spanish and English) and of Sufi literature, and a "Further Reading" section on Sufism (in English). Titles and quotations in English.

de Man, Paul. "A Modern Master." In *Critical Essays on Jorge Luis Borges*, edited by Jaime Alazraki. Boston: G. K. Hall, 1987.

An important early article originally published in *The New York Times Book Review*, November 19, 1964, just as Borges was being discovered by the North American reading public. Principally an introduction to the nature of Borges' narrative with particular emphasis throughout (in fact, from an opening quotation from William Butler Yeats) on the presence of duplicity and, more specifically, mirror-related images in all levels of the Argentine writer's prose. An interesting article on this dominant aspect of Borges' works. Titles in English.

di Giovanni, Norman Thomas. "At Work with Borges." In *The Cardinal Points of Borges*, edited by Lowell Dunham and Ivar Ivask. Norman: University of Oklahoma Press, 1971.

A fascinating article (originally presented as a paper at the International Symposium on Borges at the University of Oklahoma in 1969) by Borges' principal English-language translator on the process, problems, and joys that characterize the work he and Borges do translating the latter's works from Spanish to English. Also meant to convey "some idea of what it is like to be in daily association with Borges." Includes numerous examples and anecdotes as well as the detailed description of the translation process involved with the story "Pedro Salvadores" (the English-language text of which appears as an appendix to the article). Not an important article critically, but very insightful. Most titles and quotations in English.

di Giovanni, Norman Thomas, Daniel Halpern, and Frank MacShane, eds. *Borges on Writing*. New York: E. P. Dutton, 1973.

Three two-hour seminars given by Borges and his principal English-language translator, editor di Giovanni, to students in the graduate writing program at Columbia University in the spring of 1971. One seminar focuses on fiction, another on poetry, and another on translation. Fiction seminar features di Giovanni reading Borges' "The End of the Duel," with the Argentine writer commenting on it essentially line by line, followed by a general conversation, featuring questions and comments from students, with Borges explaining how he wrote the story. Book also includes a very short appendix entitled "The Writer's Apprenticeship," in which Borges discusses the situation and needs of a beginning writer. Revealing and personal. Contains an index. Titles and quotations in English.

Dunham, Lowell, and Ivar Ivask, eds. *The Cardinal Points of Borges*. Norman: University of Oklahoma Press, 1971.

An important collection of "scholarly articles presented by Borges specialists at the International Symposium on Borges held at the University of Oklahoma" in December, 1969. Article titles include "In the Labyrinth," "Borges and the Idea of Utopia," "A Modest Proposal for the Criticism of Borges," and the article which inspired the book's title, "The Four Cardinal Points of Borges." Contains a very good bibliography (in Spanish, French, and English) of criticism on Borges to 1969. Photographs. The language of titles and quotations varies from article to article.

Gallagher, D. P. "Jorge Luis Borges (Argentina, 1899-   )." In his *Modern Latin American Literature*. New York: Oxford University Press, 1973.

Gallagher presents a lengthy (twenty-eight-page), detailed, and very readable introduction to Borges' fictional world. The critic begins his study by calling Borges "above all the man who has restored the imagination to its proper place in Latin American literature," and then describes various aspects of Borges' writings, beginning with his tendency to present the reader "with the spectacle of men who set out to 'decipher the universe,' only to discover that they cannot even decipher an infinitesimal fragment of it, not even that which constitutes their own person." The story Gallagher uses to provide an example of this type of "spectacle," and which is discussed throughout a significant portion of the chapter as a representative Borges story, is "Death and the Compass." An excellent introduction to the nature of Borges' fiction. Titles in Spanish with English translations. Quotations in English.

Guibert, Rita. "Jorge Luis Borges." In her *Seven Voices: Seven Latin American Writers Talk to Rita Guibert*. Translated by Frances Partridge. New York: Alfred A. Knopf, 1973.

In an interview with Guibert (compiled from a series of interviews conducted in Cambridge, Massachusetts, January 15-20, 1968), Borges discusses his teaching and his students, hippies, Buenos Aires, gauchos, writers who have influenced him, contemporary Latin American literature, the need for bilingual education in both Americas, advice for young writers, and many other subjects. Informative, revealing, and very personal. Photograph included in center of book. Titles in Spanish and English.

Hangrow, Pjers, and Ted Lyon. "Heresy as Motif in the Short Stories of Borges." *Latin American Literary Review* 3 (Fall/Winter, 1974): 23-35.

In sections entitled "The Heresy of Philosophy," "Heresy as the Usurpation of Divine Power," "Heresy and Humor," and "The Heretical Character," Hangrow and Lyon examine heresy (which they define as "defiling, challenging or opposing that which is considered sacred or divine") as a "constant motif, a basic recurring element which grants thematic unity" to Borges' stories. Heresy for Borges, the two critics contend, is not meant to be antireligious, but it is used by him "as a literary device to expand his created world, to reveal basic themes of life and existence," to, as the critics conclude, "elucidate the essence of being" in the Argentine writer's prose full of "labyrinth-challenges." Titles and quotations (as numerous stories are cited) in English.

Harss, Luis, and Barbara Dohmann. "Jorge Luis Borges, or the Consolation by Philosophy." In their *Into the Mainstream: Conversations with Latin American Writers*. New York: Harper & Row, 1967.

This piece combines and intertwines biography, literary biography, commentary and interview to produce a multifaceted look at Borges' life, his works, and his philosophical beliefs, and most of all, how his philosophical beliefs are reflected in both his poetry and, more so here, his prose. A classic piece, with reference to numerous works and several quotations from Borges himself (taken from the interview conducted for and referred to in the article). A very good introduction to Borges, and particularly to his philosophies and their presence in his work. Most titles in Spanish and English. Quotations in English.

Hatlen, Burton. "Borges and Metafiction." In *Simply a Man of Letters*, edited by
Carlos Cortínez. Orono: University of Maine at Orono Press, 1982.

Contending that Borges, along with Vladimir Nabokov, John Barth, Robert
Coover, and others, is a writer of metafiction, Hatlen first offers his definition
of metafiction ("a fiction which forces us to become conscious of the nature
and significance of the 'fictioning' process itself") and then discusses the
presence of metafiction in literature. He then examines four of Borges' most
famous works ("Funes the Memorious," "The Library of Babel," "Tlön,
Uqbar, Orbis Tertius," and "The Aleph") as examples of this type of fiction.
In conclusion, he discusses "the broader social and cultural significance of the
shift from fiction to metafiction initiated by Borges and his followers." A very
readable, well-presented article on a provocative topic. Titles and quotations in
English.

Hughes, Psiche. "Love in the Abstract: The Role of Women in Borges' Literary
World." *Chasqui* 8, no. 3 (1979): 34-43.

Hughes states that her intentions in this article are: "(1) to re-examine Borges'
work in the light of his relation with his characters, the removed reticence with
which he chooses to describe their sexual/emotional experience; (2) to point
out how this same reticence is applied to the description of his own experience:
how he seeks in it the literary situation and reduces the women he introduces
in his work to abstraction; (3) to show finally how, even as abstract symbols,
they perform a vital role, in the development of the plot of destiny." She sets
out to achieve her intentions by examining several of the Argentine writer's
works. Titles and quotations in Spanish.

Irby, James E. "Borges and the Idea of Utopia." In *The Cardinal Points of Borges*,
edited by Lowell Dunham and Ivar Ivask. Norman: University of Oklahoma
Press, 1971. Also appears in *Jorge Luis Borges*, edited by Harold Bloom. New
York: Chelsea House, 1986.

In a paper presented at the International Symposium on Borges held at the
University of Oklahoma in 1969, Irby traces Borges' ideas on Utopia as expressed in the Argentine author's writings of the 1920's and 1930's and the
dramatization of these ideas in the short story/fictional essay "Tlön, Uqbar,
Orbis Tertius." Interesting not only for its discussion of Borges' ideas concerning Utopia but also for its demonstration that Borges' early writings anticipate
his later, better-known work. Titles in Spanish. Quotations in English.

Isaacs, Neil D. "The Labyrinth of Art in Four *Ficciones* by Jorge Luis Borges."
Studies in Short Fiction 6 (Summer, 1969): 383-394.

After citing several critics' opinions concerning the symbol of the labyrinth in
Borges' works, Isaacs presents his own opinion, that the labyrinth is employed
as a symbol of art. He then examines the role of the labyrinth in "The Babylon

Lottery," "The Library of Babel," "Tlön, Uqbar, Orbis Tertius," and "The Garden of Forking Paths" to substantiate his contention. His principal overall conclusion seems to be that, like Ts'ui Pên's labyrinthine novel in "The Garden of Forking Paths," Borges' works are metaphysical treatises "attempting to describe symbolically the true nature of the labyrinthine universe." Titles and quotations in English.

Kerrigan, Anthony. "Borges/Unamuno." In *Prose for Borges*, edited by Charles Newman and Mary Kinzie. Evanston, Ill.: Northwestern University Press, 1974. Through references to their lives, works, and personal comments, Kerrigan examines the similarities and differences between Borges and Miguel de Unamuno, who corresponded with each other as early as 1927. Most attention is paid to the authors' philosophical beliefs and the manifestations of these beliefs in their works. An interesting, well-documented, comparative study of two authors not normally paired together. Titles in Spanish and English. Quotations in English.

Koch, Dolores M. "Jorge Luis Borges: A Double Death as Narrative Device." *Kentucky Romance Quarterly* 30, no. 3 (1983): 293-300. Koch examines many of Borges' most famous stories (such as "The Secret Miracle," "Death and the Compass," "The Garden of Forking Paths," and "The South") to show that "Borges' tales follow the pattern of a double death: one, mimetic of reality and the other imagined within the narrative." After detailed analysis of several stories in which she believes this pattern plays a part, she concludes, in part, that the function of the "basic structural device of a double death" is "to oppose chaotic reality and man's subjection to death, mostly unexpected and often an absurd violation, with some measure of liberating, even playful, imagination." Titles and quotations in English.

Lima, Robert. "Internal Evidence on the Creativity of Borges." *Revista de Estudios Hispánicos* 1 (November, 1967): 129-156. A truly excellent article in which Lima, with many references to Borges' poems, essays, and stories, traces and comments upon the evolution and nature of the Argentine writer's art. The critic begins by discussing Borges' connection to and expression of his Argentine reality, and then focuses on his involvement in Ultraism, and his subsequent shift to fiction. Lima's discussion of Borges' stories centers first on the writer's style and then, more important, on his perceptions of reality and time, and the expression of these perceptions in his works. The critic briefly discusses several of Borges' stories: "Funes the Memorious," "The Secret Miracle," "The South," "The Circular Ruins," "Tlön, Uqbar, Orbis Tertius," "The Immortal," and "The Sect of the Phoenix." A superb introduction to Borges' art and the nature of his fiction. Titles and quotations in Spanish.

Lyons, Thomas E. "Borges and the (Somewhat) Personal Narrator." *Modern Fiction Studies* 19 (Fall, 1973): 363-372.

Lyons examines the nature, position, and function of "Borges' unique personal narrator." Citing numerous stories, the critic studies the role or place of the narrator in the text, the confusion of narrative distance, the confusion of realities, and the parody of artifice. Much attention is given to the narrator's on-again-off-again presence in the narrative, his use of footnotes, and his ambiguous statements. Lyons concludes that Borges "has created a new type of narrator in Spanish American fiction." An excellent study of a largely overlooked aspect of Borges' works. Titles and quotations in Spanish.

McMurray, George R. *Jorge Luis Borges*. New York: Frederick Ungar, 1980.

Intended by the author as "an attempt to decipher the formal and thematic aspects of a man-made universe that rivals reality in its almost overwhelming complexity," namely Borges' universe. In an effort to do this, McMurray analyzes several of Borges' stories under various sub-headings, such as "The Negation of Reason" and "The Treatment of Time," with all categorized under the general heading of "Borges and the Absurd Human Condition." He also, in separate chapters, examines various elements of Borges' aesthetics. A thoughtful if (necessarily) brief discussion of the stories analyzed as well as an in-depth analysis of Borges' technique. An informative introduction on Borges' life and a conclusion which coherently brings together the diverse elements discussed in the book. A very good and well-organized study of Borges' dominant themes and narrative devices, with many specific examples. Includes helpful notes (some even defining the literary devices discussed such as oxymoron, metonymy), an excellent index, and a well-organized bibliography in Spanish and English.

_____ . "Jorge Luis Borges." In *Latin American Literature in the Twentieth Century: A Guide*, edited by Leonard S. Klein. New York: Frederick Ungar, 1986.

Provides a brief (four-and-a-half-page) introduction to Borges' life and works. Focuses chiefly on the writer's career, writers who have influenced him, his philosophical concerns and thematic interests, and some of the main characteristics of his narrative. Very brief discussion of some of his most famous stories (such as "Death and the Compass" and "The South"). A good thumbnail sketch and starting point for the reader unfamiliar with Borges. Supplies a list of the Argentine writer's works (almost entirely in Spanish) and a short critical bibliography (mostly in English).

_____ . "New Directions." In his *Spanish American Writing Since 1941: A Critical Survey*. New York: Frederick Ungar, 1987.

McMurray devotes roughly four pages of this section of his book to an introduction to Borges' fiction. The critic offers a quick, one-paragraph overview of the Argentine author's career as a writer of fiction. This is followed by a concise description (approximately two pages) of the nature of Borges' stories, supplemented by brief comments on some of his most famous works (such as "Death and the Compass" and "The South"). A brief concluding paragraph summarizes Borges' oeuvre. A good starting point for the reader unfamiliar with Borges. Titles in Spanish with English translations. Quotations in English.

Menton, Seymour. "Jorge Luis Borges, Magic Realist." *Hispanic Review* 50 (Autumn, 1982): 411-426.
   Stating that even Borges has classified many of his stories as "fantastic," Menton differentiates between "lo fantástico" and Magic Realism (as well as what Carpentier and Asturias have called "lo real maravilloso"), concluding that while some of the Argentine writer's stories should be labeled "fantastic," many generally classified as such fit more accurately under the category of Magic Realism. The critic studies Borges' style, tone, use of oxymoron, and other factors in several stories (most notably "The South") to support his contentions. He also compares Borges' stories to the works of several Magic Realist painters. A valuable article, which provides a good definition of Magic Realism. Titles and quotations in Spanish.

Newman, Charles, and Mary Kinzie, eds. *Prose for Borges*. Evanston, Ill.: Northwestern University Press, 1974.
   A wide-ranging collection of essays by prominent Borges scholars on Borges the man and Borges the writer. Essay titles include "Borges as Reader," "The Final Creole: Borges' View of Argentine History," "Borges and the Kabbalah," and "Borges and the New Latin-American Novel." The book even includes a Borges family chronicle by the Argentine writer himself (with photographs), as well as a previously unpublished interview with his sister. Also contains a "Preface for Americans," in which editor Kinzie largely compares Borges to Ralph Waldo Emerson. An impressive and lengthy (419-page) volume. Includes a bibliography of Borges' principal works (in both Spanish and English) and English-language criticism on the writer. Titles and quotations in English.

Rodríguez Monegal, Emir. "Borges: The Intellectual Background." In *Simply a Man of Letters*, edited by Carlos Cortínez. Orono: University of Maine at Orono, 1982.
   Rodríguez Monegal recognizes Borges' reputation as a bookworm, one whose thought and works reflect more than a passing familiarity with countless books and authors. The critic declares, however, that just as important in the Argentine writer's intellectual development "was the permanent and renewed contact

with a few key persons in some of the most decisive periods of his life." The persons of influence to whom Rodríguez Monegal refers are Borges' father, his father's friend Macedonio Fernández, and Borges' collaborator and friend, Adolfo Bioy Casares. A section of the article is dedicated to each man and his role in Borges' intellectual development. Titles in Spanish and English. Quotations in English.

Sorrentino, Fernando. *Seven Conversations with Jorge Luis Borges.* Translated with additional notes by Clark M. Zlotchew. New York: Whitson, 1982.
As the translator points out in his foreword, this book has been called by one critic (Donald Yates) "the best book of its kind, the one that provides the most reliable picture of Borges derived from tape-recorded conversations with him." Termed (by the same critic) "exceptionally open and intimate" in tone. Each conversation is preceded by a summary of its contents and followed by helpful explanatory notes. Also includes an interview with Borges' chief English translator (Norman Thomas di Giovanni), a "glossary" of personalities mentioned by Borges in the course of the interviews, an index of persons quoted or mentioned, and an index of works quoted and/or mentioned. Not just informative, but an impressive package as well. Titles in various languages with most Spanish titles translated to English. Quotations in English.

Spivakorsky, Erika. "A Further Word Regarding Arabic Influences on Borges." *Hispania* 52 (September, 1969): 417-419.
Spivakorsky contends that Borges' "unusual way of integrating opposites, with its resulting multiple symbols and paradoxes, may be based on ambivalences in Arabic thought patterns." She also contends that his "concept of oneness for all men and his 'Third World of the Intellect' have their origin, perhaps indirectly, in Averroes' theory of the universal intellect." She cites several biographical facts and examples in the Argentine writer's stories (particularly "Averroes' Search") which support these contentions. A fascinating (and even controversial) article. Titles and quotations in Spanish.

Stabb, Martin S. "Borges the Writer of Fiction." In his *Jorge Luis Borges.* New York: Twayne, 1970.
A truly excellent, lengthy (forty-seven-page), and detailed guide to Borges' stories. Stabb begins his chapter with a four-page introduction in which he discusses the Argentine writer's first attempts at narrative prose (in *Universal History of Infamy*), his conscious decision in 1938 to try a new genre (the short story), and the nature of his fictional works. Dividing these works into sections entitled "Essayistic Fiction (such as "Pierre Menard, Author of the *Quixote*"), "Intermediate Fiction" (works that fall somewhere between the author's essayistic fiction and the conventional short story; works such as "Tlön, Uqbar, Orbis Tertius") and "Short Stories" (such as "The Garden of

Forking Paths"), Stabb presents an overview and analysis of some twenty of Borges' fictions. A superb, very readable introduction to this area of Borges' literary production. Titles in Spanish with English translations (when cited for first time in the book, subsequently in Spanish). Quotations in Spanish with English translations.

———————— . *Jorge Luis Borges*. New York: Twayne, 1970.
An excellent study on Borges intended by its author "to introduce the work of this fascinating and complex writer to North American readers." Focuses on "the formal aspects of Borges' literary art, as well as philosophical and esthetic concerns" as manifested in the Argentine writer's poetry, essays, and fiction. Includes an opening chapter on his life and career, followed by chapters on Borges' works in each of the three genres mentioned above (including "Borges the Writer of Fiction"), as well as a concluding chapter entitled "Borges and the Critics." A superb and very readable introduction to all aspects of Borges' literary production. Chronology of the Argentine writer's life and career through 1968. Contains an excellent index and primary and secondary bibliographies (the latter annotated) in Spanish and English. Titles and quotations in Spanish with English translations.

Wheelock, Carter. "Borges' New Prose." In *Prose for Borges*, edited by Charles Newman and Mary Kinzie. Evanston, Ill.: Northwestern University Press, 1974. Also appears in *Jorge Luis Borges*, edited by Harold Bloom. New York: Chelsea House, 1986.
A study of Borges' post-1966 prose (beginning with "The Intruder"). Carter compares the old Borges with the new by first examining the major characteristics of the writer's earlier stories (such as "The Aleph" and "The Circular Ruins") and then delineating the characteristics of his newer works. Among his conclusions are that the post-1966 stories are more straightforward, both stylistically and thematically (though some characteristics of the old Borges, such as chessmenlike characters and indifferent settings, remain). Wheelock also examines new translations of Borges' earlier stories. A lengthy and detailed article that covers the topic well. Titles and quotations in English.

Wiehe, Roger E. "Jorge Luis Borges." In *Critical Survey of Short Fiction*, edited by Frank N. Magill, vol. 3. Pasadena, Calif.: Salem Press, 1981.
A brief (six-page) introduction to Borges' life, works, and thought. Provides a short biographical sketch in addition to discussion of the major characteristics of the Argentine writer's narrative. Bulk of article is devoted to a limited analysis of some of Borges' most famous and most representative stories (such as "Pierre Menard, Author of the *Quixote*" and "The Garden of Forking Paths"). A useful introduction for the reader unfamiliar with Borges. Far more informative than its length might suggest. Includes a list of Borges' works (in Spanish and English) and a critical bibliography in English.

Yates, Donald A. "The Four Cardinal Points of Borges." In *The Cardinal Points of Borges*, edited by Lowell Dunham and Ivar Ivask. Norman: University of Oklahoma Press, 1971.

In a paper presented at the International Symposium on Borges held at the University of Oklahoma in 1969, Yates ascribes four key elements to Borges' narrative, each one corresponding to a point on the compass. The four elements are (South) Borges' Argentine nationality, (North) his interest and concern for language, particularly as it pertains to literature and literary style, (East) his deep interest in philosophical and metaphysical questions, and (West) the presence of drama. Yates puts his ideas concerning these elements to the test by briefly examining their applicability to Borges' "Pedro Salvadores," published in 1969 and considered by the Argentine writer (though few critics or readers agree) to be his best story. Yates concludes that though this story is indeed different from most of Borges' earlier, more famous works, it does, after examination of the writer's cardinal points in it, show the presence, as the critic calls it, of Borges' hand. Quotations in English.

——————— . *Jorge Luis Borges: Life, Work, and Criticism*. Fredericton, N.B., Canada: York Press, 1985.

Published in the "Authorative Studies in World Literature" series of books, which, as the publisher suggests, are intended as "succinct and inexpensive research tools . . . designed to help students and young scholars in their investigations," this work presents a thumbnail (forty-one-pages) sketch of Borges' life, work, and criticism. Chapters include "A Biography of Jorge Luis Borges," "A Chronological List of Borges' Major Works," "A Summary of Borges' Principal Writings," "An Evaluation of Borges' Achievements," and "Annotated Bibliography." Far more complete and information-filled than its length would suggest. A good handbook to Borges for the uninitiated reader. Includes an index, a well-organized list of Borges' works, and a critical bibliography in Spanish and English. Titles in English.

The Aleph

Bell-Villada, Gene H. "*El Aleph* I: Doubles and Puzzles," "*El Aleph* II: Tales of Action and Violence," and "*El Aleph* III: The Visionary Experience." In his *Borges and His Fiction: A Guide to His Mind and Art*. Chapel Hill: University of North Carolina Press, 1981.

Bell-Villada chooses to separate the stories of *The Aleph* (which he praises as a book containing "numerous masterpieces, stories of breathtaking intellectual power that are haunting in their breadth and originality and easily the equals of any of the major narratives of *Ficciones*"), into three categories, leaving the "richest and most complex" for the third chapter (such as "The Aleph" and "The Immortal"). Regardless of the chapter into which they are classified, each story benefits from the critic's meticulous and clearly expressed analysis, focusing primarily on plot description, theme, and narrative artistry. An excellent guide to the stories of this collection. Titles and quotations in English.

Ficciones

Bell-Villada, Gene H. "*Ficciones* I: Doubles, Dreamers, and Detectives" and "*Ficciones* II: The World within a Book." In his *Borges and His Fiction: A Guide to his mind and art.* Chapel Hill: University of North Carolina Press, 1981.

Bell-Villada divides his discussion of the stories of *Ficciones* into two sections, the first dealing with "Doubles, Dreamers, and Detectives" (stories such as "The South," "The Secret Miracle," "Death and the Compass," and "The Garden of Forking Paths") and the second with what the critic calls "Borges' most characteristic stories," stories that "are symbolic parables that evoke human problems and situations" (such as "The Babylon Lottery" and, most notably, "Tlön, Uqbar, Orbis Tertius"). In-depth and lucid analysis of each story, focusing primarily on plot description, theme, and narrative artistry. A superb guide to the stories of this collection. Titles and quotations in English.

"The Aleph"

Hatlen, Burton. "Borges and Metafiction." In *Simply a Man of Letters*, edited by Carlos Cortínez. Orono: University of Maine at Orono Press, 1982.

In an article concerning Borges' metafictional tendencies, Hatlen briefly (in two pages) examines "The Aleph" as an example of this type of fiction. The critic defines "metafiction" ("a fiction which forces us to become conscious of the nature and significance of the 'fictioning' process") and provides examples, followed by the analysis of "The Aleph" and three other Borges stories. A conclusion addresses the social and cultural significance of this type of fiction. Titles and quotations in English.

"The Lottery of Babylon" ("La lotería en Babilonia")

Isaacs, Neil D. "The Labyrinth of Art in Four *Ficciones* by Jorge Luis Borges." *Studies in Short Fiction* 6 (Summer, 1969): 383-394.

Contending that Borges employs the labyrinth in his works as a symbol of art, Isaacs briefly examines (in roughly one page) "The Babylon Lottery" as one of the stories which supports his claim. The critic states that "the labyrinth symbol is present in the lottery itself," which he views as "an art-form of fate—the arbitrary imposition of order or a semblance of formal order upon chaotic human experience." He concludes that Borges' labyrinth symbolism here is ironic, in this story which "describes an attempt to impose a deliberate and infinitely various disorder upon an orderly world." Titles and quotations in English.

"Death and the Compass" ("La muerte y la brújula")

Carroll, Robert C. "Borges and Bruno: The Geometry of Infinity in 'La muerte y la brújula.'" In *Simply a Man of Letters*, edited by Carlos Cortínez. Orono:

University of Maine at Orono Press, 1982. Also appears in *Modern Language Notes* 94 (March, 1979): 321-342.

Carroll contends that Borges' story "is structured by an epistemological strategy whose provenance is the Hermetist school of the European Renaissance, with its interest in the reduction of the many to the one, the complex to the simple, the location of difference in identity, and, lastly, the relationship of the concepts of infinity and finitude." Carroll focuses most of his attention on the "Dialogo Quinto" of Giordano Bruno's *De la Causa, Principio et Uno*. Numerous references to Borges' story and Bruno's work, as well as geometric diagrams, are provided to support the critic's well-researched contention. Titles and quotations in Spanish and Italian.

Gallagher, D. P. "Jorge Luis Borges (Argentina, 1899-   )." In his *Modern Latin American Literature*. New York: Oxford University Press, 1973.

In this lengthy (twenty-eight-page) chapter which serves as an introduction to Borges' fictional world, a significant portion of the chapter consists of a detailed analysis of "Death and the Compass" as a story representative of Borges' works, particularly as it concerns the tendency in the Argentine writer to present the reader "with the spectacle of men who set out to 'decipher the universe,' only to discover that they cannot even decipher an infinitesimal fragment of it, not even that which constitutes their own person." Lönnrot, the critic implies, is just such a man. Titles in Spanish with English translations. Quotations in English.

Hayes, Aden W., and Khachig Tololyan. "The Cross and the Compass in Patterns of Order in Chesterton and Borges." *Hispanic Review* 49 (Autumn, 1981): 395-405.

A study of Chesterton's "The Blue Cross" as a model for Borges' "Death and the Compass." Examines the similarities (chiefly those of "elements, patterns and devices") and differences (principally the "systems of thought which are used by the detectors from whose viewpoint these stories are told") that exist between the two works. A very readable and well-documented work. Includes a plot summary of Chesterton's story. Title and quotations from Borges' story in Spanish.

Irwin, John T. "Mysteries We Reread, Mysteries of Rereading: Poe, Borges, and the Analytic Detective Story: Also Lacan, Derrida and Johnson." *Modern Language Notes* 101 (December, 1986): 1168-1215.

A lengthy and detailed study inspired by the critic's question, "How does one write analytic detective fiction as high art when the genre's basic structure, its central mechanism, seems to discourage the unlimited rereading associated with serious writing?" In an effort to answer this question, Irwin examines Edgar Allan Poe's "The Purloined Letter" and Borges' "Death on the Compass," with considerable reference to Jacques Lacan, Jacques Derrida, and Barbara Johnson. An excellent, technical study of Borges' story. Titles and quotations in English.

"Emma Zunz"

Hall, J. B. "Deception or Self-Deception: The Essential Ambiguity of Borges' 'Emma Zunz.'" *Forum for Modern Language Studies* 18, no. 3 (1982): 258-265.
    Hall suggests that while the majority of critics have viewed "Emma Zunz" as a rather straightforward story, at most a sort of crime story with "a reversal of the usual ending," there exists another possible interpretation, one based on the evidence of ambiguity, confusion, and simple error in the narrative. Hall cites a general motif in Borges' works (that which the critic calls "worthless success") and several parts of the story in question to show that Borges clearly leaves open the possibility that the reality presented and acted upon by Emma may in fact be simply her incorrect interpretation of reality, one result of which is her killing an innocent man. An interesting perspective on the story, well documented and very readable. Titles and quotations in Spanish.

Stavans, Ilan. "'Emma Zunz': The Jewish Theodicy of Jorge Luis Borges." *Modern Fiction Studies* 32 (Autumn, 1986): 469-475.
    Stavans discusses how "Emma Zunz" is an unusual story for Borges, containing as it does a female protagonist, as well as sex, rape, and violence. He then discusses the presence of Jewish elements in Borges' works and background and examines "Emma Zunz" as a story in which these elements play a significant role. Among the critic's conclusions is that Emma and her actions are made more credible by the fact that she is Jewish than if Borges had made her character a Gentile. Some comparison of Emma, as well, to Gustave Flaubert's Emma Bovary and Thomas Hardy's Tess. Quotations in English.

"Funes the Memorious" ("Funes el emeorioso")

Hatlen, Burton. "Borges and Metafiction." In *Simply a Man of Letters*, edited by Carlos Cortínez. Orono: University of Maine at Orono Press, 1982.
    In an article concerning Borges' metafictional tendencies, Hatlen briefly (in just over a page) examines "Funes the Memorious" as an example of this type of fiction. The critic defines "metafiction" ("a fiction which forces us to become conscious of the nature and significance of the 'fictioning' process") and provides examples, followed by the analysis of "Funes the Memorious" and three other Borges stories. A conclusion addresses the social and cultural significance of this type of fiction. Titles and quotations in English.

"The Garden of Forking Paths" ("El jardín de senderos que se bifurcan")

Isaacs, Neil D. "The Labyrinth of Art in Four *Ficciones* by Jorge Luis Borges." *Studies in Short Fiction* 6 (Summer, 1969): 383-394.

Contending that Borges employs the labyrinth in his works as a symbol of art, Isaacs examines "The Garden of Forking Paths" as one of the stories which supports his claim. Stating that the "labyrinth-art metaphor is made explicit" in this work, the critic analyzes the role of this metaphor in the story and concludes, among other things, that the story shows that "the labyrinth of infinitely multiplied possibilities is *life* and it is *art*." Isaac's conclusion also discusses Ts'ui Pên's labyrinthine novel as "a metaphysical treatise attempting to describe symbolically the true nature of the labyrinthine universe," something the critic believes Borges does with the labyrinth in his works as well. Titles and quotations in English.

"The Immortal"

Ayora, Jorge. "Gnosticism and Time in 'El Inmortal.'" *Hispania* 56 (September, 1973): 593-596.

Ayora uses Gnosticism to explain the worldview of the Immortals (which the critic contends "has puzzled critics") and the "affinity between Gnostic and Borgesian revulsion toward time" to explain not only the concept of time in this story but also the "lack of use of Christian symbology" in the Argentine writer's works. Gnosticism, Ayora contends, explains both the absurd architecture of the City and the Immortals' rejection of the physical world. The Gnostics' "defiance of and rebellion against time" also, according to the critic, parallels Borges' treatment of time in his works, and this, Ayora contends, by extension, accounts for the "avoidance of Christian symbology in his works," since he could not use such symbology in works in which he does not accept the Christian concept of "linear, finite, and progressive time." Titles and quotations from Borges in Spanish. Other references in English.

"The Library of Babel" ("La Biblioteca de Babel")

Hatlen, Burton. "Borges and Metafiction." In *Simply a Man of Letters*, edited by Carlos Cortínez. Orono: University of Maine at Orono Press, 1982.

In an article concerning Borges' metafictional tendencies, Hatlen briefly (in two pages) examines "The Library of Babel" as an example of this type of fiction. The critic defines "metafiction" ("a fiction which forces us to become conscious of the nature and significance of the 'fictioning' process itself") and provides examples, followed by the analysis of "The Library of Babel" and three other Borges stories. A conclusion addresses the social and cultural significance of this type of fiction. Titles and quotations in English.

Isaacs, Neil D. "The Labyrinth of Art in Four *Ficciones* by Jorge Luis Borges." *Studies in Short Fiction* 6 (Summer, 1969): 383-394.

Contending that Borges employs the labyrinth in his works as a symbol of art, Isaacs briefly examines (in just over a page) "The Library of Babel" as one of the stories which supports his claim. Calling it "among the most clearly

Kafkaesque of Borges' stories," the critic analyzes the labyrinth symbolism present in "The Library of Babel," concluding that "Borges' library-labyrinth is at once the production and denial" of order in life. Titles and quotations in English.

"Pierre Menard, Author of the Quixote" ("Pierre Menard, autor del Quijote")

Irby, James E. "Some Notes on 'Pierre Menard.'" In *Simply a Man of Letters*, edited by Carlos Cortínez. Orono: University of Maine at Orono Press, 1982.

Just as the title suggests, and as Irby states in the first paragraph, not so much a paper (presented at a symposium on Borges) or an article as much as a collection of notes and observations on Borges' story, influenced by the critic's reading of Roland Barthes's *S/Z* and Friedrich Nietzsche's *The Will to Power*. Some fine observations and interesting answers to some potential questions concerning the Argentine writer's story. Though very readable, perhaps best suited for readers familiar with the post-structuralist theories and the extraliterary works to which he refers. Some titles (very few all together) only in original language, others in English as well. Quotations in English.

"The South" ("El Sur")

Fama, Antonio. "Desire as a Mimetic Form in 'El Sur' by Jorge Luis Borges." *Revista de Estudios Hispánicos* 16 (October, 1982): 391-397.

Stating that the narrative discourse of "The South" follows "a wish-fulfillment pattern," Fama shows how the second part of the story, in which the protagonist meets a violent yet romantic death, is actually an extrapolation of the first, in which the protagonist dies unceremoniously in the hospital. The difference, Fama contends, is that the first death is real while the second takes place only in Dahlmann's imagination in his displaced self, the second death being how he would have liked to have died in reality. The protagonist's desire to die more romantically allows him to create a second death, a second reality. A solid and very readable article. Titles and quotations in Spanish.

Menton, Seymour. "Jorge Luis Borges, Magic Realist." *Hispanic Review* 50 (Autumn, 1982): 411-426.

Contending that many of Borges' stories have been classified as "fantastic" but more accurately fit under the label of Magic Realism, Menton defines the two narrative subgenres and seeks to support his contention with several stories, "The South" being chief among them. Examining the story's style, tone, and content, and comparing it with the works of several Magic Realist painters and the major tenets of Magic Realism, Menton concludes that the story should not be read as "fantastic" (that is, he accepts Dahlmann's death at the end as real), but more directly as a work of Magic Realism. Titles and quotations in Spanish.

"Tlön, Uqbar, Orbis Tertius"

Hatlen, Burton. "Borges and Metafiction." In *Simply a Man of Letters*, edited by Carlos Cortínez. Orono: University of Maine at Orono Press, 1982.

In an article concerning Borges' metafictional tendencies, Hatlen briefly (in roughly two pages) examines "Tlön, Uqbar, Orbis Tertius" as "Borges' supreme metafiction." The critic defines "metafiction" ("a fiction which forces us to become conscious of the nature and significance of the 'fictioning' process") and provides examples, followed by the analysis of "Tlön, Uqbar, Orbis Tertius" and three other Borges stories. A conclusion addresses the social and cultural significance of this type of fiction. Titles and quotations in English.

Irby, James E. "Borges and the Idea of Utopia." In *The Cardinal Points of Borges*, edited by Lowell Dunham and Ivar Ivask. Norman: University of Oklahoma Press, 1971.

In a paper presented at the International Symposium on Borges at the University of Oklahoma in 1969. Irby discusses "Tlön, Uqbar, Orbis Tertius" as a presentation, in fictional terms, of Borges' ideas on Utopia. Irby also traces Borges' ideas on the subject as expressed in the Argentine writer's writings from the 1920's and 1930's, in which, interestingly, much of the content of the short story/fictional essay is directly anticipated. Titles in Spanish. Quotations in English.

Isaacs, Neil D. "The Labyrinth of Art in Four *Ficciones* by Jorge Luis Borges." *Studies in Short Fiction* 6 (Summer, 1969): 383-394.

Contending that Borges employs the labyrinth in his works as a symbol of art, Isaacs provides a detailed five-page study of "Tlön, Uqbar, Orbis Tertius" as one of the stories which supports his claim. Stating that "another 'solution' to the problems of life's meaninglessness and formlessness is another definition of art: the *recreation* of life," the critic analyzes the story as "a parable of that definition," concluding that "the constructions of art are labyrinthine in their intricate impositions of an order which may ultimately be seen whole by humanity." Titles and quotations in English.

Jaén, Didier T. "The Esoteric Tradition in Borges' 'Tlön, Uqbar, Orbis Tertius.'" *Studies in Short Fiction* 21 (Winter, 1984): 25-39.

Calling "Tlön, Uqbar, Orbis Tertius" perhaps the most fundamentally representative of Borges' stories." Jaén provides background on "the esoteric tradition" (a vague and variable, as he calls it, "body of doctrines whose central theme refers to the direct and secret knowledge of the origin of everything created") and then examines how this tradition and, in fact, the history of this tradition dictates "the organization and development of the narrative and gives meaning or coherence to the apparently chaotic display of erudite allusion" in

Borges' story. A thoughtful interpretation of the story and a detailed and well-researched examination of the topic. Readable even for those unfamiliar with the philosophical works and schools mentioned, though, in spite of author Jaén's fine background sketch, much better suited for those already well versed in the esoteric tradition of which the critic speaks. Quotations in English.

IGNÁCIO DE LOYOLA BRANDÃO
Brazil

Commentary

Moniz, Naomi Hoki. "Ignácio de Loyola Brandão." In *Dictionary of Brazilian Literature*, edited by Irwin Stern. Westport, Conn.: Greenwood Press, 1988.
A very brief (roughly one-page) introduction to Brandão's career. Quick mention of his early involvement in film criticism and political concerns, followed by some characteristics of his fiction and a limited discussion (one paragraph each) of *Zero* and *And Still the Earth*. A good starting point for the reader unfamiliar with Brandão. Provides a list of his works in Portuguese and a short critical bibliography in Portuguese and English.

And Still the Earth (Não verás país nenhum)

Krabbenhoft, Kenneth. "Ignácio de Loyola Brandão and the Fiction of Cognitive Estrangement." *Luso-Brazilian Review* 24 (Summer, 1987): 35-45.
Krabbenhoft begins his article contending that *And Still the Earth* "clearly belongs to the science fiction genre as defined by some of its most important theorists." The critic then examines Brandão's "achievement against the generic criteria" of two of these theorists (Darko Suvin and Patrick Parrinder) and shows how the work "fits Suvin's definition of science fiction as the literature of cognitive estrangement," and how the novel works, following Parrinder's theories, "(1) as social fable concerned with the use and abuse of power and knowledge and (2) as a vehicle for the creation of fictive language." Comparison as well of the Brazilian author's work with Mary Shelley's *Frankenstein, or The Modern Prometheus*, illustrating the place of the former "in the specifically anti-utopian current of modern science fiction." Krabbenhoft concludes, in part, that with this novel the author "deserves inclusion in the company of Aldous Huxley, Ray Bradbury and Stanislaw Lem." Titles and quotations from Brandão's works in Portuguese.

Zero

Rodríguez Monegal, Emir. "Fiction Under the Censor's Eye." *World Literature Today* 53 (Winter, 1979): 19-22.
Rodríguez Monegal begins his article by stating that "in a country where newspapers and magazines cannot print all the news that is fit to print, where radio and TV stations are heavily monitored and political meetings are scarce and controlled, literature and especially fiction have to take over tasks which are normally fulfilled by other more ephemeral media: to tell the news, to ventilate opinions, to keep the citizen informed." The specific country to which the critic refers in this article is Brazil (the Brazil of military dictatorship) and one of three novels discussed as fulfilling the tasks described above

is Brandão's *Zero*, which receives five lengthy paragraphs of discussion, chiefly concerning just how Brandão gets his point across. Brief and perhaps suited for one who has not yet read the novel. Titles throughout the article are in Portuguese with English translations.

GUILLERMO CABRERA INFANTE
Cuba

Biography

Schwartz, Ronald. "Cabrera Infante: Cuban Lyricism." In his *Nomads, Exiles, and Émigrés: The Rebirth of the Latin American Narrative, 1960-80*. Metuchen, N.J.: Scarecrow Press, 1980.

This chapter has three apparent purposes: (1) to provide a biographical sketch of Cabrera Infante, (2) to give a brief introduction to *Three Trapped Tigers*, and (3) to examine in some depth the novel *View of Dawn in the Tropics*. The biographical sketch occupies only four pages of the ten-page chapter, but it is filled with considerable information, covering, albeit briefly, the Cuban author's childhood and personal life, his career and development as a writer and film critic, and his relationship through the years with the Cuban government under both Fulgencio Batista and Fidel Castro. Concise and informative, with titles of Cabrera Infante's works in English. References to some organizations, newspapers, and magazines in Spanish.

Commentary

Guibert, Rita. "Guillermo Cabrera Infante." In her *Seven Voices: Seven Latin American Writers Talk to Rita Guibert*. Translated by Frances Partridge. New York: Alfred A. Knopf, 1973.

In an interview with Guibert (compiled from a series of interviews conducted in Cabrera Infante's London apartment, October 5-12, 1970), the Cuban author provides lengthy answers to questions concerning Cuba, Fidel Castro, the writer's association with and subsequent break from the Castro regime, exile, Ché Guevara, the Women's Liberation Movement, the United States, cinema, his novel *Three Trapped Tigers*, the Latin American novel, and many other subjects. Informative, revealing, and personal. Photograph included in center of book. Most titles (very few) in Spanish, some in English.

McMurray, George R. "Major Figures of the Boom." In his *Spanish American Writing Since 1941*. New York: Frederick Ungar, 1987.

McMurray devotes roughly six pages of this section of his book to a brief overview of Cabrera Infante's fiction. Following two introductory paragraphs, the critic offers concise commentary on each of the Cuban writer's major works of fiction, with *Three Trapped Tigers* receiving the most attention. A good starting point for the reader unfamiliar with Cabrera Infante. Titles in Spanish with English translations.

Nelson, Ardis L. *Cabrera Infante in the Menippean Tradition*. Newark, Del.: Cuesta, 1983.

A study of Cabrera Infante as a writer in the ancient Menippean tradition of satire, the tradition of Petronius' *Satyricon* and Laurence Sterne's *Tristram Shandy*. Nelson provides an excellent introduction explaining briefly the Menippean tradition itself and, more so, the features of works in this tradition and how they differ from both the novel and modern satire. Chapters examine characterization in the *Satyricon* as a model for *Three Trapped Tigers*, the influence of *Tristram Shandy* on the same novel, and, finally, the overriding theme of betrayal in the Cuban writer's work. A solid and well-presented study of an interesting topic. Entertaining prologue by Cabrera Infante. Titles and quotations in Spanish.

Peavler, Terry J. "Guillermo Cabrera Infante's Debt to Ernest Hemingway." *Hispania* 62 (May-September, 1979): 289-296.
Peavler cites Cabrera Infante's comments and references to Hemingway in interviews and reviews, as well as the two writers' similar backgrounds as reporters, "their interest in politics and sports, the mutual love for Havana, and the Cuban's predilection for reading (and writing) fragments" as evidence of a possible link of influence between Cabrera Infante and the North American writer. The critic's conclusive proof however, lies in the similarity, on several levels, between Cabrera Infante's *Así en la paz como en la guerra* (in peace as in war) and Hemingway's *In Our Time*. Peavler concludes that Hemingway was to Cabrera Infante what Gertrude Stein was to Hemingway. An excellent piece. Some reference to *Three Trapped Tigers*. Titles and quotations in Spanish.

Siemens, William. "Guillermo Cabrera Infante." In *Latin American Literature in the Twentieth Century: A Guide*, edited by Leonard S. Klein. New York: Frederick Ungar, 1986.
A brief (roughly two-page) introduction to Cabrera Infante's life and works. Some discussion (about one paragraph each) of his major works (such as *Three Trapped Tigers*) and some of the principal characteristics of his narrative. Despite its brevity, a good starting point for the reader with no prior knowledge of the writer. Includes a list of Cabrera Infante's works (in Spanish) and a short critical bibliography in Spanish and English.

World Literature Today 61 (Autumn, 1987): 509-600. Issue focusing on Cabrera Infante and his works.
Titles in this wide-ranging collection of articles include "The Mind's Isle: An Introduction to Cabrera Infante" by Mary E. Davis, "Readers, Writers, and Interpreters in Cabrera Infante's Texts" by Isabel Álvarez-Borland, "Nabokov/Cabrera Infante: True Imagery Lives" by José Miguel Oviedo, and "Cabrera Infante and the Work of Alfred Hitchcock" by Kenneth E. Hall. Also includes a chronology of the writer's life and career through 1987 (by Cabrera Infante himself) entitled "(C)ave Attemptor! A Chronology (After Laurence

Sterne's)," including such facts as when the writer first went to the movies (at twenty-nine days old). Includes numerous photographs and both a primary and secondary bibliography in various languages. Most titles and virtually all quotations in Spanish with English translations.

Three Trapped Tigers (Tres tristes tigres)

Gallagher, D. P. "Guillermo Cabrera Infante (Cuba, 1929-   )." In *Modern Latin American Literature*. New York: Oxford University Press, 1973.

The bulk of this twenty-two-page chapter is devoted to an overview and analysis of *Three Trapped Tigers*, which Gallagher calls "maybe the most original work of fiction to have been written in Latin America, and also the funniest." The critic's discussion of Cabrera Infante's novel touches on numerous aspects of the work, including its function "as a documentary of pre-revolutionary night-life," the lack of real communication between the characters, and the role of language and literature in the work. An excellent piece. Very readable. Titles in Spanish with English translations. Quotations in English.

Guibert, Rita. "Guillermo Cabrera Infante." In her *Seven Voices: Seven Latin American Writers Talk to Rita Guibert*. Translated by Frances Partridge. New York: Alfred A. Knopf, 1973.

In a brief section (pages 410-415) of a lengthy interview conducted in 1970, Cabrera Infante responds to questions concerning the difficulties of translating *Three Trapped Tigers*, the meaning of the book's title, the contention by some that it is a book for men rather than women, the nature of its characters, the Cuban author's advice that it be read aloud, and other topics concerning the work. Not of great analytical value (which is not the interview's intention) but interesting and insightful.

_____ . "The Tongue-Twisted Tiger: An Interview with Cabrera Infante." *Review 72* (Spring, 1972): 10-16.

In an excerpt for the most part identical to the one cited in the above entry (and taken from the same interview), Cabrera Infante talks about the mission of a writer, how he writes and other aspects of writing, but mostly he talks about *Three Trapped Tigers*. Concerning the novel, the Cuban writer responds to questions on the difficulty of translating it, why he did not want to call it a novel, what its title means, why it might be better suited for the male reader, whether the characters in it are real, why it should be read out loud, whether it is meant to be autobiographical, and why this novel, "written in Cuban" (as the author himself states), has been so successful in Spain and Spanish America. Titles and some terms in Spanish.

Hazera, Lydia D. "Strategies for Reader Participation in the Works of Cortázar, Cabrera Infante and Vargas Llosa." *Latin American Literary Review* 13 (July-December, 1985): 19-34.

In an excellent article on ways in which these three authors "trigger the reader's active participation," Hazera examines Cabrera Infante's *Three Trapped Tigers* to show that the Cuban writer encourages the reader to participate by employing a fragmentary structure, by means of negation (chiefly by Cabrera Infante, in his introduction to the text, informing the reader that the book is unliterary, that it is a book of spoken language, thereby "predispos[ing] the reader to counter the negation and substitute a positive view, to discover the potential of the spoken language as literature"), and through various forms and levels of parody. An interesting comparison of the issue of reader participation in the three writers' works. Titles and quotations in English.

Hussey, Barbara L. "Mirror Images in *Three Trapped Tigers*." *International Fiction Review* 2 (1975): 165-168.

Hussey states that Cabrera Infante's novel "represents the author's attempt to freeze time and space, and it is about the efforts of his counterparts in the novel to do the same." This "freezing of time and space" is achieved largely through the use of mirrors and mirror images. The critic studies various examples of such images in the novel, from the reflections of characters to the reference to the numbers "88" and "101," before concluding that the Cuban writer's work is a "word game about people playing word games, . . . a mirror of people looking in mirrors and art concerned with the nature of art," or a "self-contained" work, as she states elsewhere, in which mirrors and mirror images play a vital role. Titles and quotations in English.

Kadir, Djelal. "Stalking the Oxen of the Sun and Felling Sacred Cows: Joyce's *Ulysses* and Cabrera Infante's *Tres tristes tigres*." *Latin American Literary Review* 8 (Spring/Summer, 1976): 15-22.

Kadir begins by citing Ralph Waldo Emerson: "I am very much struck in literature by the appearance that one person wrote all the books." The critic then moves on to, as he says, "examine a rather peculiar 'self-repetition' which at various instances takes on varying appellations: Homer, Joyce, and Cabrera Infante." He refers to the three authors' works and particularly compares those of the latter two ("The ventriloquy that was *Ulysses* has now become the dummy of a new ventriloquist that is *Three Trapped Tigers*"), before concluding that Joyce and Cabrera Infante carry on the self-mocking "Spirit of Literature" found as far back as Homer, stating that "the voice of that Spirit has only changed ventriloquists." Titles (once the article begins) and quotations in English.

Merrim, Stephanie. "A Secret Idiom: The Grammar and Role of Language in *Tres tristes tigres*." *Latin American Literary Review* 8 (Spring/Summer, 1980): 96-117.

A rather technical and complete analysis of Cabrera Infante's use of language in this novel which the critic calls "a large-scale tongue-twister." She does not find the work, however, a collection of disconnected and unrelated styles and levels of grammar. Instead, she contends that the Cuban writer's use of language in the novel is consistent and orderly, creating a coherent language or "metalanguage." She offers numerous examples as proof. An interesting concept and well documented. Titles in Spanish. Most quotations in Spanish with English translations. Some (few) only in Spanish.

_____ . "Through the Film Darkly: Grade 'B' Movies and Dreamwork in *Tres tristes tigres* and *El beso de la mujer araña.*" *Modern Language Studies* 15 (Fall, 1985): 300-312.

Discusses the function and reasoning behind the presence of B movies in the two novels referred to in the title. Special attention is given to Cabrera Infante's view of such movies in a cultural context and why these movies, and not other more mainstream films, appear so frequently in his works. Particular attention is paid to the presence and significance of such movies in the "Bachata" section of *Three Trapped Tigers*. Bulk of the article, however, is devoted to Puig's use of B movies in *Kiss of the Spider Woman*. Titles and quotations in Spanish.

Mitchell, Phyllis. "The Reel Against the Real: Cinema in the Novels of Guillermo Cabrera Infante and Manuel Puig." *Latin American Literary Review* 11 (Fall/ Winter, 1977): 22-29.

An interesting study of the important role of movies in the lives of the characters found in Cabrera Infante's *Three Trapped Tigers* and in various novels by Puig. Mitchell shows that Cabrera Infante's characters are nonliterary (with one even, interestingly, selling his father's library to get money for the movies), their worldview shaped by the popular media, particularly movies. Movies even give the characters lines to speak, a common mythology, and a set of heroes, as the characters live vicariously through the films. A solid article. Titles and quotations in English.

Ortega, Julio. "An Open Novel." Translated by Mary A. Kilmer. *Review 72* (Winter/Spring, 1971-1972): 17-21.

In sections (preceded by a brief introduction) entitled "The Rules of the Game," "Memorial Rites," "Speech Replaces Reality," and "A Multiple Re-birth," Ortega discusses what he calls the "open quality" of *Three Trapped Tigers*, which, the critic contends, is found, in part, "in its anti-traditionalism which renounces plot, conventional unities, verism, drama or psychology, in its purely verbal reality, and perhaps even more so, in the fact that this verbal reality is an exclusive determination to use oral forms of expression." Ortega goes on to call Cabrera Infante "a type of Borges jolted by laughter and heat." Titles (*TTT*) and quotations in English.

Resnick, Claudia Cairo. "The Use of Jokes in Cabrera Infante's *Tres tristes tigres* [*Three Trapped Tigers*]." *Latin American Literary Review* 9 (1976): 14-21.

Resnick points out what she interprets as flaws in the criticism of other critics who have studied the presence, nature, and function of jokes in Cabrera Infante's novel, and presents her own theories, centered chiefly on Sigmund Freud's theories concerning jokes (particularly jokes involved with sexual arousal), the presence of homosexuality in the novel, and inside-joke patterns that seem to exist between the male characters and may exist between author Cabrera Infante and his male, but not his female, reader. Titles and quotations in Spanish with English translations.

Schwartz, Ronald. "Cabrera Infante: Cuban Lyricism." In his *Nomads, Exiles, and Émigrés: The Rebirth of the Latin American Narrative, 1960-80*. Metuchen, N.J.: Scarecrow Press, 1980.

This chapter has three apparent purposes: (1) to provide a biographical sketch of Cabrera Infante, (2) to give a brief introduction to *Three Trapped Tigers*, and (3) to examine in some depth the novel *View of Dawn in the Tropics*. The introduction to *Three Trapped Tigers* occupies only the first paragraph and two middle pages of the ten-page chapter, but it nonetheless serves as a good general introduction for the reader unfamiliar with this novel, which Schwartz claims "represents the synthesis of the direction most Latin American writers were taking at the peak of the literary 'boom' of the mid-1960's." Succinct and cogent. Titles in English.

Siemens, William L. "Mirrors and Metamorphosis: Lewis Carroll's Presence in *Tres tristes tigres*." *Hispania* 62 (May-September, 1979): 297-303.

Siemens examines various elements in Cabrera Infante's novel which link his work to that of Lewis Carroll. The critic begins with the novel's opening epigraph, taken from Carroll, and then moves on to the character of Bustrófedon (whom Siemens terms "a logical extension of Carroll's tendency to play with words"), the presence of mirror images in the work, the inclusion of a character similiar to Carroll's Cheshire Cat, and several other allusions to the English author and his works present in the Cuban writer's novel. Most of Siemens' analysis focuses on the two authors' wordplay and the use of mirror images. Title and quotations from Cabrera Infante's novel in Spanish.

Souza, Raymond D. "Cabrera Infante: Creation in Progress." In his *Major Cuban Novelists*. Columbia: University of Missouri Press, 1976.

An excellent overview of *Three Trapped Tigers* with emphasis on the novel's focus on the creative process. Most of Souza's attention centers on the dynamic creativity of the many characters which populate the work. The characters, the critic contends, are searching "for order in a chaotic world and for meaning in a confused society," and this search leads them to create (often spontaneously) a new reality. Emphasis as well on the creativity of author Cabrera Infante not only concerning the novel as a whole but specifically his use of language, his parodies of other Cuban writers within the novel, and, in fact, his multiple versions of the work itself (in various editions). An interesting chapter and a helpful reading aid for this novel which is, as Souza suggests, "one of Spanish America's most stimulating and creative novels," so easy to read and so difficult to understand. Titles and quotations in Spanish.

Titler, Jonathan. "Intratextual Distance in *Tres tristes tigres.*" *Modern Language Notes* 93 (March, 1978): 285-296.

A study of the relationships among the author, narrator, characters, and reader of *Three Trapped Tigers*, focusing on the space, or "intratextual distance" which exists between them (based on the model set forth in Wayne C. Booth's *The Rhetoric of Fiction*). Among other things, Titler concludes that the novel is characterized by a self-conscious author, "purposely flat and static characters," self-involved and unreliable narrators, and, as a result, a self-conscious, suspicious and distant reader, all this being the intention of the author and making the reading experience a pleasurable though certainly unconventional one. Titles and quotations in Spanish.

ALEJO CARPENTIER
Cuba

Biography

Schwartz, Ronald. "Carpentier: Cuban Cosmopolite, Baroque Stylist." In his *Nomads, Exiles, and Émigrés: The Rebirth of the Latin American Narrative, 1960-80*. Metuchen, N.J.: Scarecrow Press, 1980.

This chapter has two apparent purposes: (1) to provide a brief biographical sketch of Carpentier; and (2) to discuss through description and analysis the Cuban writer's novel *Explosion in a Cathedral*. The biographical sketch covers only two and a half pages near the beginning of the chapter, but in spite of its brevity it provides a concise and amazingly detailed picture of Carpentier's life and career, including a quick, chronological overview of his major works. Emphasis on the numerous influences, both literary and extra-literary, with which he has had contact and which have manifested themselves in his works. A good starting point for the reader unfamiliar with Carpentier. Titles and quotations in English.

Commentary

Brotherston, Gordon. "The Genesis of America: Alejo Carpentier." In his *The Emergence of the Latin American Novel*. Cambridge: Cambridge University Press, 1977.

Brotherston uses this chapter chiefly to discuss Carpentier's affinity for and concern with Latin American reality, a separate reality from that of Europe, with its own mythology and background. The critic discusses the Cuban writer's expression of this reality in various novels, such as *The Kingdom of the World* and (more so) *The Lost Steps*, though the most detailed attention is paid to the theme of Latin American reality as expressed in *Explosion in a Cathedral* and its main character, Esteban, "the one chosen to guide us through a world especially dear to the author: the 'theological archipelago of the Caribbean', as it is called, the luminous heart of America to which both author and character, as Cubans, belong." An interesting and effective overview of this basic concern of Carpentier's narrative as seen in several of his works. Titles and quotations in English.

González Echevarría, Roberto. "Alejo Carpentier." In *Critical Survey of Long Fiction* (Foreign Language Series), edited by Frank N. Magill, vol. 1. Pasadena, Calif.: 1984.

A roughly ten-page overview of Carpentier's work in long fiction. Contains a list of his principal novels (some only in Spanish), a summary of his work in other literary forms, and a rather lengthy (two-page) assessment of his achievements. This is followed by a two-and-a-half-page biographical sketch and a three-page overview and analysis of *The Lost Steps*, *Reasons of State*, and *La consagracion de la primavera* (consecration of spring). A good introduction to Carpentier for the reader unfamiliar with his work in general and his long fiction in particular. Provides a list of his other major works (almost all in Spanish) and a short critical bibliography in English. Titles of translated works in English.

——————— . *Alejo Carpentier: The Pilgrim at Home*. Ithaca, N.Y.: Cornell University Press, 1977.
A widely acclaimed study of what González Echevarría defines as the four "moments" in the evolution of Carpentier's literary career and of the works produced during each "moment." The critic establishes each of these moments in his introduction and then provides a roughly sixty-page chapter on each one. Considered by most to be the best comprehensive study of Carpentier's writings. Includes an excellent index and lengthy primary and secondary bibliographies (covering twenty-one pages in all) in various languages. Most titles and quotations in English.

Harss, Luis, and Barbara Dohmann. "Alejo Carpentier, or the Eternal Return." In their *Into the Mainstream: Conversations with Latin American Writers*. New York: Harper & Row, 1967.
An interview-based discussion of Carpentier and his works. Contains a fair amount of information on the Cuban writer's life and early career, as well as his thoughts on writing, on Latin American reality (and the Latin American novel), and on politics (particularly Cuban politics). Most of the chapter, however, is devoted to an overview of his works through the mid-1960's, consisting chiefly of the cogent observations by Harss and Dohmann, supplemented nicely with comments from Carpentier himself. A classic piece of criticism and an excellent introduction to the writer and his works. Titles of Carpentier's works in Spanish with English translations. Titles of other writers' works (very few) in Spanish only. Quotations in English.

McMurray, George R. "New Directions." In his *Spanish American Writing Since 1941: A Critical Survey*. N.Y.: Frederick Ungar, 1987.
McMurray devotes roughly four pages of this section of his book to a brief overview of Carpentier's fiction. Following an introductory paragraph, the critic offers concise commentary on each of the Cuban writer's major works, before summarizing the nature of Carpentier's fictional world in a concluding paragraph. A good starting point for the reader unfamiliar with Carpentier. Titles in Spanish with English translations.

Schwartz, Kessel. "Alejo Carpentier." In *Latin American Literature in the Twentieth Century: A Guide*, edited by Leonard S. Klein. New York: Frederick Ungar, 1986.

A brief (two-and-a-half-page) introduction to Carpentier's life and works. Some discussion (one paragraph each) of the Cuban writer's major works. Summary of the dominant characteristics of his narrative. A good starting point for the reader unfamiliar with Carpentier. Includes a list of his works (almost entirely in Spanish) and a short critical bibliography in Spanish and English.

Shaw, Donald L. *Alejo Carpentier*. Boston: Twayne, 1985.
An excellent overview of Carpentier's works. A chapter entitled "The Apprenticeship" discusses the Cuban author's early life and first works. "Discovering 'The Marvelous Real'" discusses the title concept and its manifestation in some stories and *The Kingdom of This World*. *The Lost Steps*, *Explosion in a Cathedral*, and *Reasons of State* are treated in separate individual chapters while additional chapters cover other works and offer concluding remarks. Provides a chronology of Carpentier's life and career, a very good index, and primary and secondary bibliographies (the latter annotated) in Spanish and English. Almost all titles in Spanish with English translations. Some (usually works of other authors) in Spanish only. Quotations in English.

Souza, Raymond D. "Alejo Carpentier's Timeless History." In his *Major Cuban Novelists*. Columbia: University of Missouri Press, 1976.
Souza presents a detailed overview of Carpentier's novels through *Explosion in a Cathedral*. The critic provides considerable plot description for each novel discussed, as well as analysis of characters, technique, and theme. The result is not only an analysis of individual works but a feeling for the elements, both technical and thematic, which characterize Carpentier's novels. Three of these elements are the writer's objective treatment of his characters, his particular use of language, and his extended view of history and time, a view in which, as Souza remarks at one point, "an individual lifetime is like a second in a century of time." An excellent introduction to the Cuban author's novels (again, through *Explosion in a Cathedral*). Supplemented with comments from Carpentier himself. Titles and quotations in Spanish.

Explosion in a Cathedral (El siglo de las luces)
González Echevarría, Roberto. "Memories of the Future." In his *Alejo Carpentier: The Pilgrim at Home*. Ithaca, N.Y.: Cornell University Press, 1977.
This chapter focuses on what González Echevarría calls the fourth "moment" in the evolution of Carpentier's literary career. This "moment" covers the period "from the mid-fifties to the present" and "reassesses the previous three by undermining the notions of both author and history and positing the revolutionary nature of writing, its perpetual shifting around an absent source." It is a moment "strongly inspired by the eighteenth century . . . and appears to be a reversion to the avant-garde, particularly because of its recourse to the

Kabbala and to a ludic conception of writing." *Explosion in a Cathedral* is examined as a work of this "moment." Most titles and quotations in English.

Kilmer-Tchalekian, Mary A. "Ambiguity in *El siglo de la luces.*" *Latin American Literary Review* 8 (Spring/Summer, 1976): 47-55.
Kilmer-Tchalekian contends that "Carpentier deliberately cultivates effects of ambiguity" in *Explosion in a Cathedral*, that "ambiguity is a constant feature in the molding of this novel, a principle of organization which Carpentier uses to communicate his vision of reality." She then traces the presence of ambiguity in the work beginning with the prologue and in the process shows that "suggestion, conjecture, imprecision, symbols and shifting narrative voice are Carpentier's chief means of weaving ambiguity into the narrative fabric." A detailed and very readable article on an interesting subject. Titles and quotations in Spanish with English translations.

Schwartz, Ronald. "Carpentier: Cuban Cosmopolite, Baroque Stylist." In his *Nomads, Exiles, and Émigrés: The Rebirth of the Latin American Narrative, 1960-80*. Metuchen, N.J.: Scarecrow Press, 1980.
This chapter has two apparent purposes: (1) to provide a brief biographical sketch of Carpentier and (2) to discuss through description and analysis *Explosion in a Cathedral*. Discussion of the novel occupies approximately ten-and-a-half pages of the fourteen-page chapter. Schwartz provides a fine, detailed description of the work's plot, followed by insightful commentary (from Schwartz and others) concerning, chiefly, its artistry. Schwartz concludes by calling Carpentier "a modern Chateaubriand, a master stylist, a giant among contemporary Latin American novelists." Offers a good discussion of the work in question. Titles and quotations in English.

Shaw, Donald L. "The Antilles Again." In his *Alejo Carpentier*. Boston: Twayne, 1985.
This fourteen-page chapter of Shaw's book is dedicated exclusively to an overview and analysis of *Explosion in a Cathedral*. The critic discusses various elements of the work, focusing primarily on narrative technique, the main characters (particularly Hughes and Esteban) and their presentation and function, and the work's themes and symbolism. Some comparison of the novel in question to some of the Cuban author's other works (most notably *Manhunt* and *The Lost Steps*). One of Shaw's conclusions is that *Explosion in a Cathedral* "points forward toward ever new, but ever ambiguous, attempts on man's part to strike a balance between utopian aspirations and historical conditions," and in this area it offers "a warning from Caribbean history," a warning which, says the critic, "remains Carpentier's most mature expression of his personal insight." Titles in Spanish. Quotations in English.

The Kingdom of This World (El reino de este mundo)

González Echevarría, Roberto. "Fugitive Island." In his *Alejo Carpentier: The Pilgrim at Home*. Ithaca, N.Y.: Cornell University Press, 1977.

Approximately half of this fifty-eight-page chapter is devoted to a discussion of *The Kingdom of This World*. The chapter itself, and the context within which the analysis of this novel is presented, deals with what González Echevarría terms the second "moment" in the evolution of Carpentier's literary career. This moment, "extending from about 1939 to 1949 and encompassing what has come to be known as 'magical realism,' centers on the concert of the natural fusion of Latin American history and a process of writing that excludes the conscious author." It is a moment, the critic states, that "draws heavily upon Afro-Antillian folklore." Most titles and quotations in English.

Kirk, John M. "Magic Realism and Voodoo: Alejo Carpentier's *The Kingdom of This World*." *Perspectives on Contemporary Literature* 5 (1979): 124-130.

Kirk examines the presence and significance of Voodoo in Carpentier's novel, contending that it has three main functions within the story: (1) as a source of comfort for the black slaves "in their unceasing humiliation;" (2) as a weapon of war; and, most important, (3) as "a representation of the true, indigenous spirit of the black folk culture, against which all 'foreign borrowings' are powerless." The critic cites examples from the text which illustrate each of these functions, concluding that the presence of Voodoo, as well as other elements of the work, helps illustrate the magical quality Carpentier insisted was characteristic of Latin American reality. Title of novel and quotations from text in English. Title of one other work by Carpentier and quotations from other sources in Spanish.

Shaw, Donald L. "Discovering 'The Marvelous Real.'" In his *Alejo Carpentier*. Boston: Twayne, 1985.

Roughly eight pages of this twenty-page chapter are devoted to a discussion of *The Kingdom of This World*. The bulk of this section consists of a rather detailed plot description accompanied throughout by critical commentary, with particular emphasis on, as Shaw calls it, "the much debated ending" of the novel. Separate sections of the discussion treat narrative technique and symbolism, as well as Carpentier's prologue and the effects his visit to Haiti (prior to writing the novel) had on him. Best read within the context of the entire chapter. Titles in Spanish. Quotations in English.

The Lost Steps (Los pasos perdidos)

González Echevarría, Roberto. "The Parting of the Waters." In his *Alejo Carpentier: The Pilgrim at Home*. Ithaca, N.Y.: Cornell University Press, 1977.

This chapter focuses on what González Echevarría considers the "third moment" in the evolution of Carpentier's literary career, a moment "from about

1949 to the mid-fifties [that] questions the assumptions of the preceding one by inquiring about the situation of the modern Latin American writer vis-à-vis his sources, that is to say, the natural, autochthonous tradition celebrated in *The Kingdom of This World*. It is a Sartrean moment that includes *The Lost Steps* and 'Manhunt' and in which the context of contemporary political history and the alienation of the writer corrode the assumed link between him and his project." It is within the context of this chapter that the critic presents a lengthy discussion of *The Lost Steps*. Most titles and quotations in English.

Martin, John, and Kathleen McNerney. "Carpentier and Jolivet: Magic Music in *Los pasos perdidos*." *Hispanic Review* 52 (Autumn, 1984): 491-498.
A fascinating article on the numerous parallels between the narrator of *The Lost Steps* and the twentieth century French composer, André Jolivet. These parallels include "a disenchantment with the values of modern society, the desire to return to the origins of music and to its initial magical function, the interest in primitive instruments, and, perhaps most striking, the use of an extremely esoteric musical form from ancient Greece, the threnody." These and other connections between Jolivet and Carpentier's narrator (and Carpentier himself, who, the two critics theorize, had considerable contact with Jolivet in France) are detailed in the body of this very readable article. Titles and quotations in Spanish and French.

Peavler, Terry J. "The Source for the Archtype in *Los pasos perdidos*." *Romance Notes* 15 (1974): 581-587.
Peavler cites the usefulness of criticism on the role of myth in *The Lost Steps*, though he disagrees with such criticism which ties "the temptation of the woman to the temptation to return, in the rather weak and unsatisfactory reconciliation with the father," stating that such arguments "seem forced." The purpose of his article, however, is not "to refute the clear evidence that the narrator does not fit the heroic pattern at least in an abstract sense, . . . but to establish clearly that Carpentier used a specific literary source." That source, for Peavler, is Edgar Allan Poe's *The Narrative of Arthur Gordon Pym*, which the critic compares to Carpentier's text, finding numerous similarities (include those concerning narrative structure and character relationships), similarities "too great to be mere coincidence." The critic concludes that "myth . . . is indeed the key to *Los pasos perdidos*, but the primary metal of that structural key is wrought from a specific literary source, not from a general mythic concept." An enlightening and very readable study. Titles and quotations in original language.

Shaw, Donald L. "A Journey Through Time." In his *Alejo Carpentier*. Boston: Twayne, 1985.
This fourteen-page chapter of Shaw's study of Carpentier's literary career and

works is devoted solely to *The Lost Steps*. The critic begins the chapter with a roughly three-page section entitled "The Background to *Los pasos perdidos* [The Lost Steps]," in which he discusses the approximately ten years of Carpentier's life which preceded the writing of the novel. Shaw then devotes the remainder of the chapter to an overview and analysis of the work in question. Titles in Spanish. Quotations in English.

Tusa, Bobs M. "A Detective Story: The Influence of Mircea Eliade on Alejo Carpentier's *Los pasos perdidos*." *Hispanófila* 30 (September, 1986): 41-65.

Tusa draws a connection between Mircea Eliade, the religion historian, and Carpentier, two men, the critic contends, whose works reflect their "desire to transcend historical time and to enter the stall of absolute time." Tusa then turns detective (thus the title of the article), using "internal as well as external evidence," to support his contention that Eliade's "1952 article 'Symbolisme indian de l'abolition du temps' [Indian symbolism of the abolition of time] not only determined the structure, plot, and characters of *Los pasos perdidos* but also caused Carpentier to emphasize an aspect of his philosophical position which is unique in his *oeuvre*." An interesting and well-researched piece. Titles and quotations in Spanish and French.

Vázquez Amaral, José. "The Return of the Native: Alejo Carpentier's *The Lost Steps*." In his *The Contemporary Latin American Narrative*. New York: Las Américas, 1970.

After a brief discussion of Latin American expatriate writers who brought European literary influences back with them to their native lands, Vázquez Amaral introduces Carpentier as one of these writers and one of "the great writers of our time, without having to append the usual limitation of space by calling him Latin American." He then provides a lengthy overview (twenty-two pages) of *The Lost Steps* which consists chiefly of a detailed plot summary supplemented throughout by analytical observations. An excellent, very readable introduction to Carpentier's novel. Titles and quotations in English.

Reasons of State (El recurso del método)

González Echevarría, Roberto. "Memories of the Future." In his *Alejo Carpentier: The Pilgrim at Home*. Ithaca, N.Y.: Cornell University Press, 1977.

González Echevarría examines *Reasons of State* as a work of what the critic calls the fourth "moment" in the evolution of Carpentier's literary career, a "moment" which covers "from the mid-fifties to the present," and "reassesses the previous three by undermining the notions of both author and history and positing the revolutionary nature of writing, its perpetual shifting around an absent source." This "moment," the critic also contends, is "strongly inspired by the eighteenth century . . . and appears to be a reversion to the avant-garde, particularly because of its recourse to the Kabbala and to a ludic conception of writing." Most titles and quotations in English.

Luna, Norman. "The Barbaric Dictator and the Enlightened Tyrant in *El otoño del patriarca* and *El recuso del método*." *Latin American Literary Review* 15 (Fall/ Winter, 1979): 25-32.

Luna compares the dictators and the portraits painted of them in *Reasons of State* and García Márquez' *The Autumn of the Patriarch*. The article contains numerous cogent observations concerning the two novels and their respective protagonists, one of those being found in Luna's opening claim (to paraphrase the critic): that the historicoideological outline of Latin American dictatorship in Carpentier's novel finds its mythicolegendary parallel in García Márquez' book. *The Autumn of the Patriarch*, he contends later, is "atemporal and spectral," while *Reasons of State* is "contemporary and historical." Titles and quotations in Spanish with English translations.

Peavler, Terry J. "A New Novel by Alejo Carpentier." *Latin American Literary Review* 3 (Spring/Summer, 1975): 31-36.

Essentially an overview, review, and analysis of Carpentier's *Reasons of State*. Peavler introduces the novel within the context of the Cuban author's other works (stating that, "it lacks precisely those characteristics that have established Carpentier as one of the most celebrated and distinctive voices in Latin America") and provides a short plot summary. The critic then discusses the work's relation to history, its treatment of time, and its thematic focus. The rest of the article is devoted to technical problems and other flaws ("errors" and "signs of carelessness," Peavler calls them) present in the novel. Peavler concludes, however, that in spite of its weaknesses, *Reasons of State* is a good novel, and, "were it by a lesser artist, it could well be considered a success." Provides a good introduction to the work. Titles and quotations in English.

Shaw, Donald L. "*Reasons of State*." In his *Alejo Carpentier*. Boston: Twayne, 1985.

In an opening section entitled "Return to Cuba," Shaw discusses Carpentier's life and, in particular, his role in and relation to the Castro government from the Cuban writer's return (from Venezuela) to his native land until his death in 1980. The critic then embarks on a roughly ten-page overview and analysis (with emphasis on theme and characterization of the protagonist) of *Reasons of State*, a novel the critic contends "stimulates thought rather than mere indignation," a work which "takes its place alongside García Márquez's novel [*The Autumn of the Patriarch*] and Roa Bastos' *Yo el Supremo* [*I the Supreme*] to form a memorable trio of portraits of dictators. A solid study. Titles in Spanish. Quotations in English.

JULIO CORTÁZAR
Argentina

Biography

Mac Adam, Alfred J. "Cortázar on Cortázar: A Literary Chronology." *Review 72* (Winter, 1972): 35-41.

Using several sources, Mac Adam compiles an interesting chronology of Cortázar's life and career through 1972; the bulk of almost every entry is a quotation from the Argentine writer himself, commenting on the particular period or event in his life referred to in the entry. Personal and insightful. Most titles in Spanish. One title and one quotation in French. All other quotations in English.

Commentary

Alazraki, Jaime. "Introduction: Toward the Last Square of the *Hopscotch.*" In *The Final Island: The Fiction of Julio Cortázar*, edited by Alazraki and Ivar Ivask. Norman: University of Oklahoma Press, 1978.

Serving as the introductory chapter to a book of essays on Cortázar, this piece presents a general introduction to the nature of the Argentine writer's fiction, focusing primarily on the differences and similarities between him and Borges. (For example, Alazraki writes, "If Borges' fantasies are oblique allusions to the situation of man in a world he can never fully fathom, to an order he has created as a substitute labyrinth to the one created by a divine mind, Cortázar's stories strive to transcend the schemes and constraints of culture and seek precisely to touch that order Borges finds too abstruse and complex to be understood by man.") Alazraki also discusses Cortázar's concerns with language, reality, time, and space, his place as a "neofantastic" writer, and his characters' "quest for authenticity." Supplemented with numerous quotations by Cortázar himself. A very good introduction to the nature of his fiction. Titles in Spanish. Quotations in French and English.

Alazraki, Jaime, and Ivar Ivask, eds. *The Final Island: The Fiction of Julio Cortázar*. Norman: University of Oklahoma Press, 1978.

This book is a collection of essays "by twelve Cortázar specialists who either analyze individual outstanding works or interpret certain central motifs." Essay titles include "Lying to Athena: Cortázar and the Art of Fiction," "*Eros ludens*: Games, Love and Humor in *Hopscotch*," and "The New Man (But Not the New Woman)." Includes an introduction to the nature of Cortázar's narrative, a chronology of his life and career (with emphasis on the latter), a short story and two essays by Cortázar himself, and a lengthy bibliography on works by and about the Argentine writer (in several languages, but mostly Spanish and English). Contains photographs. An excellent collection. Titles and quotations vary, but most in English.

Books Abroad 50 (Summer, 1976). Julio Cortázar issue.
This issue contains numerous pieces on Cortázar and his works, including "Lying to Athena: Cortázar and the Art of Fiction" by Gregory Rabassa, "*Los reyes*: Cortázar's Mythology of Writing" by Roberto González Echevarría, "Vampires and Vampiresses: A Reading of *62*" by Ana María Hernández, "The Ambivalence of the Hand in Cortázar's Fiction" by Malva E. Filer, and "Pursuers" by Saúl Sosnowski. Also includes a chronology of the Argentine writer's life and career through 1975 by Evelyn Picon Garfield. Selected primary and secondary bibliography in various languages by Martha Paley Francescato. Numerous photographs. Most titles and quotations in English.

Carter, E. D., Jr. *Julio Cortázar: Life, Work, and Criticism*. Fredericton, N.B., Canada: York Press, 1986.
Published in the "Authoritative Studies in World Literature" series, the intention of which is to provide "succinct and inexpensive research tools . . . designed to help students and young scholars in their investigations," this work presents a thumbnail (forty-three-page) sketch of Cortázar's life, work, and criticism. Chapters include "A Biography of Julio Cortázar," "A Chronological List of Cortázar's Works," "A Survey of Cortázar's Major Works," "Julio Cortázar in Perspective," and "Annotated Bibliography." Far more complete and information-filled than its length would suggest. Includes a well-organized list of Cortázar's works and critical bibliography in Spanish and English. Titles in English.

Filer, Malva E. "The Ambivalence of the Hand in Cortázar's Fiction." In *The Final Island: The Fiction of Julio Cortázar*, edited by Jaime Alazraki and Ivar Ivask. Norman: University of Oklahoma Press, 1978. Also appears in *Books Abroad* 50 (Summer, 1976): 595-599.
Filer studies the role of hands in Cortázar's fiction and specifically relates "the role he gives to hands to some attitudes or psychological problems, as shown particularly by his main characters." Citing several works, among them *Hopscotch* and *62: A Model Kit*, Filer concludes that hands in the Argentine writer's works "symbolize instinct, intuition, imagination and, in general, the irrational," almost always connected with a character's attempt to liberate him or herself from "reason, moral convention and the mechanization by routine," though this liberation is often negative and sometimes even violent. A valuable study of a generally ignored element of Cortázar's fiction. Titles and quotations from *Hopscotch* and *62: A Model Kit* in English. Titles and quotations from other works by Cortázar in Spanish. Limited citing of French works in original language.

Foster, David W. "Julio Cortázar." In *Critical Survey of Short Fiction*, edited by Frank N. Magill, vol. 3. Pasadena, Calif.: Salem Press, 1981.

A brief (three-and-a-half-page) introduction to Cortázar's short fiction. A list of his collections of stories (some in Spanish and English, others only in Spanish), followed by brief mention of his work in other genres, consideration of his influence as an author, a summary of the characteristics of his stories, and a very brief biographical note. Bulk of article is devoted to analysis of Cortázar's "Blow-Up" as a story "synecdochically" representative of some of the writer's best stories. A good, short introduction for the reader unfamiliar with Cortázar's work in short fiction. Provides a partial list of Cortázar's other works (in Spanish and English) and a short critical bibliography in English.

Francescato, Martha Paley. "The New Man (But Not the New Woman)." In *The Final Island: The Fiction of Julio Cortázar*, edited by Jaime Alazraki and Ivar Ivask. Norman: University of Oklahoma Press, 1978. Also appears in *Books Abroad* 50 (Summer, 1976): 589-594.
Francescato cites some of the prominent male protagonists of Cortázar's works and the Argentine writer's concept of the "new man," and asks, "But what about the woman?" Her article seeks to answer that question, and her findings (through an examination of the role of women and male-female relationships in some of Cortázar's works, chiefly *62: A Model Kit* and *A Manual for Manuel*) reveal that Cortázar's track record in the treatment of women characters is not very good, reflected mostly through the male characters' expressed attitudes toward them and their secondary role in Cortázar's fictional world. She does find some bright spots, but very few. An interesting study of a largely ignored aspect of Cortázar's fiction. Most titles and all quotations in English.

Garfield, Evelyn Picon. *Julio Cortázar*. New York: Frederick Ungar, 1975.
An excellent book-length overview of Cortázar's works and his ideas about writers, readers, the short story, and the novel. Particularly interesting because it contains numerous comments from Cortázar himself taken from interviews with critic Garfield and from the Argentine writer's notes. These comments supplement the critic's discussion of Cortázar's works. Following an opening chronology of Cortázar's life and career, and an introductory chapter entitled "An Encounter with Julio Cortázar," separate, lengthy chapters treat his short stories, his novels, and his other writings. A brief final chapter serves as a conclusion. Contains an excellent index; primary and secondary bibliographies are in Spanish and English. Titles appear first time in Spanish with English translations, subsequently in Spanish only. Quotations in English.

——————— . "Julio Cortázar." In *Latin American Literature in the Twentieth Century: A Guide*, edited by Leonard S. Klein. New York: Frederick Ungar, 1986.
A brief (four-page) introduction to Cortázar's life and works. Focuses on the chief characteristics of the Argentine writer's prose and discusses, albeit very

briefly, some of his most famous and most representative short stories, essay-istic fiction, and novels. A good thumbnail sketch and starting point for the reader unfamiliar with Cortázar. A list of some of the writer's works (most in Spanish, some in English) and a short critical bibliography in Spanish and English.

González Echevarría, Roberto. "*Los reyes*: Cortázar's Mythology of Writing." In *The Final Island: The Fiction of Julio Cortázar*, edited by Jaime Alazraki and Ivar Ivask. Norman: University of Oklahoma Press, 1978. Also appears in *Books Abroad* 50 (Summer, 1976): 548-557.

González Echevarría uses "*Los reyes* [the kings] to sketch a primal scene, to delineate what might very broadly be called Cortázar's conception of writing—conception, that is, both in its etymological sense of insemination or generation, and in its more common meaning of notion or idea." The critic determines that the monster/hero confrontation of *Los reyes* "constitutes the primal scene of Cortázar's mythology of writing: a hegemonic struggle for the center that resolves itself in a mutual cancellation and in the superimposition of beginnings and ends." He then examines "All Fires the Fire" and "The Pursuer" in regard to this finding. Familiarity with Greek mythology, Nietzsche, and Cortázar's works referred to helpful. Titles (except for *Los reyes*) and quotations (except one instance in which a passage from "The Pursuer" is quoted are in both English and Spanish, and another in which a short poem by Octavio Paz is cited in Spanish) in English.

Guibert, Rita. "Julio Cortázar." In her *Seven Voices: Seven Latin American Writers Talk to Rita Guibert*. Translated by Frances Partridge. New York: Alfred A. Knopf, 1973.

Unlike the other interviews in this volume, this one, at Cortázar's request, consists of his written rather than oral responses to questions submitted to him in writing by Guibert. The result is actually a written monologue in which the questions that inspire the shifts of topic are only referred to by the Argentine writer. The interview was to appear with Cortázar's editorial approval in *Life en español* (life in Spanish), but was instead published verbatim, causing considerable controversy, chiefly because of the political views expressed by the writer. Besides politics (which opens and to a large degree dominates the interview), Cortázar discusses authors who have influenced him, metaphysical concerns in his works, the film version of "Blow-Up," the influence of *Hopscotch* on other Latin American writers, the concept of a collective Latin American literature, the international recognition of Latin American writers, and Latin American writers in exile in Europe. Informative and revealing, but, because of the format, not as personal as the other interviews in the same volume. Photograph included in center of book. Most titles in Spanish and English.

Harss, Luis, and Barbara Dohmann. "Julio Cortázar, or the Slap in the Face." In their *Into the Mainstream: Conversations with Latin American Writers*. New York: Harper & Row, 1967.

An interview-based discussion of Cortázar and his works. Contains a fair amount of information on the Argentine writer's life and early career. Most of the chapter, however, is devoted to an overview of Cortázar's works through the mid-1960's, consisting for the most part of the cogent observations of Harss and Dohmann, but supplemented nicely with comments from Cortázar himself. A classic piece of criticism and an excellent introduction to the writer and his works. Titles of Cortázar's works in Spanish with English translations. Titles of other writers' works (very few) in Spanish only. Quotations in English.

Holsten, Ken. "Three Characters and a Theme in Cortázar." *Revista de Estudios Hispánicos* 9 (January, 1975): 119-129.

Holsten examines the theme of the search, "the metaphysical quest" which "permeates Cortázar's novels on every level," contending that the characters involved in this search seek to transcend "the psychological limitations of Western Man and experience expanded dimensions of awareness." Holsten shows how only two of Cortázar's characters—Johnny Carter of "The Pursuer" and La Maga of *Hopscotch*—are able to accomplish this, ironically without trying. The third character examined (Horacio Oliveira of *Hopscotch*), however, by contrast, is "too steeped in Western rationalism to be able to surmount its limitations." The critic makes a case for Oliveira being representative of Cortázar himself, suffering as they both do from a "hyper-intellectuality" that limits their transcendental potential. A very readable and interesting study. Titles and quotations in Spanish.

McMurray, George R. "Major Figures of the Boom." In his *Spanish American Writing Since 1941: A Critical Survey*. New York: Frederick Ungar, 1987.

McMurray devotes roughly seven pages of this section of his book to a brief overview of Cortázar's fiction. Following two introductory paragraphs, the critic offers concise commentary on the Argentine writer's major fictional works, both short stories and novels, and on the nature of his fiction. A good starting point for the reader unfamiliar with Cortázar. Titles in Spanish with English translations.

Morello-Frosch, Marta. "Julio Cortázar: From Beasts to Bolts." *Books Abroad* 44 (Winter, 1970): 22-25.

This short article presents a general overview of Cortazar's career through *62: A Model Kit*. Each of his book-length works receives some mention (from a few lines to a lengthy paragraph), with the final two paragraphs focused primarily on the mixing of the real and the fantastic in his works. A good introduction for the reader unfamiliar with Cortázar. Titles in English or in Spanish with English translations.

Pérez, Genaro J. "Julio Cortázar." In *Critical Survey of Long Fiction* (Foreign Language Series), edited by Frank Magill, vol. 1. Pasadena, Calif.: Salem Press, 1984.
A roughly ten-page overview of Cortázar's work in long fiction. Contains a list of his principal novels, a summary of his varied work in other literary forms, and a brief assessment of his literary achievements. This is followed by a short biographical sketch and an approximately six-page overview and analysis of his major novels: *The Winners*, *Hopscotch*, *62: A Model Kit*, and *A Manual for Manuel*. A good introduction to Cortázar for the reader unfamiliar with the writer's work in general and his novels in particular. Includes a list of his other works (some only in Spanish) and a short critical bibliography in English. Titles in English.

Rabassa, Gregory. "Lying to Athena: Cortázar and the Art of Fiction." In *The Final Island: The Fiction of Julio Cortázar*, edited by Jaime Alazraki and Ivar Ivask. Norman: University of Oklahoma Press, 1978. Also appears in *Books Abroad* 50 (Summer, 1978): 542-547.
An article focusing essentially on the importance of "fiction" in Cortázar's fiction, that is, elements that indeed make the Argentine writer's works imaginative fiction rather than what is commonly considered "reality" or, perhaps by extension, "reality fiction" (such as that of the nineteenth century). Reference is made to *Hopscotch* and *62: A Model Kit*, among other works. Attention is paid as well to the kind of reader Cortázar's type of fiction requires, the kind of reader the writer "pleads for and the kind that he does not always receive." Some consideration of this type of fiction in other Latin American authors. Titles (with the exception of one Borges story and a Pérez Galdos novel) and quotations in English.

Reedy, Daniel R. "Through the Looking Glass: Aspects of Cortázar's Epiphanies of Reality." *Bulletin of Hispanic Studies* 54 (1977): 125-134.
Reedy contends that the looking-glass images (whether as "a crystal ball, the porthole of an airplane, the glass wall of a formicarium, the lens of a camera, or the refracted glass of a kaleidoscope") function symbolically in several of Cortázar's works "as apertures through which other realities are disclosed or through which the pathway to the mythic centre is revealed." Reedy examines these images and their specific function (as well as the resulting entrance into the new reality) in "Bestiary," "The Secret Weapons," "Blow-Up," "Axolotl," "The Island at Noon," and *Hopscotch*. An interesting topic and a detailed study. Titles and quotations in Spanish.

Review 72 (Winter, 1972): 14-41. "Focus" section on Julio Cortázar.
This section contains six diverse pieces on Cortázar and his works: (1) "Cortázar, Borges and the Loss of Experience" by J. M. Alonso; (2) "'The Exquisite Cadaver of Surrealism'" by Evelyn Picon Garfield; (3) "Snapshots of 'Blow-Up'" by Rita Guibert, Stanley Kauffmann, and Charles Thomas Samuels; (4) "Le Fantôme of Lautréamont" by Emir Rodríguez Monegal; (5) "The Deluxe Model" by C. D. B. Bryan; and (6) "Cortázar on Cortázar: A Literary Chronology." Titles and quotations (except those in French in Rodríguez Monegal's article) provided in English.

All Fires the Fire (Todos los fuegos el fuego)

Garfield, Evelyn Picon. "A Swiss Cheese Reality." In her *Julio Cortázar*. New York: Frederick Ungar, 1975.
The final thirteen pages of this chapter on Cortázar's short fiction are dedicated to a discussion of *All Fires the Fire*. Most attention is paid to "The Southern Thruway," "Nurse Cora," "Reunion," and "The Other Heaven." Considerable plot description with some limited consideration of theme, narrative technique and style, and characters. Supplemented with comments from Cortázar himself. Most titles in Spanish with English translations. Titles translated previously in the chapter appear only in Spanish. Quotations in English.

Bestiary (Bestiario)

Garfield, Evelyn Picon. "A Swiss Cheese Reality." In her *Julio Cortázar*. New York: Frederick Ungar, 1975.
In a lengthy chapter dedicated to Cortázar's short stories, Garfield devotes approximately fifteen pages to a general discussion of *Bestiary*, a collection in which "the exceptional experiences, narrated in disarmingly simple and straightforward language, beset the characters with an urgency to act, an urgency that produces tension and uneasiness in the reader." Garfield begins by discussing Cortázar's dramatic poem *Los reyes* (the kings), which was published before *Bestiary* and which set the tone for the Argentine writer's approach to accepted reality in his stories. What follows is a brief discussion of many of the stories which comprise the collection, with Cortázar's own personal comments about the stories frequently included. Best read in tandem with the beginning of the chapter, which focuses on Cortázar's thoughts on the short story in general. Titles in Spanish with English translations. Quotations in English.

End of the Game (Final del juego)

Garfield, Evelyn Picon. "A Swiss Cheese Reality." In her *Julio Cortázar*. New York: Frederick Ungar, 1975.
Garfield devotes roughly ten pages of this chapter on Cortázar's short fiction to a general overview of *End of the Game*, a collection, she contends, which

"exhibits a wide range of themes and stylistic propensities in Cortázar's fiction." "The Night Face Up," "Continuity of Parks," "Torito," "The River," and "No One's to Blame" receive the most attention from the critic. A good overview of the collection in question. Most titles appear in Spanish with English translations. Titles translated to English earlier in the same chapter appear only in Spanish in this section. Quotations in English.

Hopscotch (Rayuela)

Boldy, Steven. "The Final Chapters of Cortázar's *Rayuela*: Madness, Suicide, Conformism." *Bulletin of Hispanic Studies* 57 (1980): 233-238.

Boldy essentially studies the duality present in Cortázar's novel, and in particular the duality and its implied flexibility in the terms "locura" (insanity) and "tirarse" (to throw oneself) of the final chapters to establish that an interpretation of these terms within the context of the novel ("Any discussion of these terms outside the novel as a whole would be meaningless") shows that to "accept Oliveira *either* goes mad, *or* commits suicide, *or* simply conforms is to ignore the very nature of the novel." A well-documented piece. Titles and quotations in Spanish.

Brotherston, Gordon. "Intellectual Geography: Julio Cortázar." In his *The Emergence of the Latin American Novel*. London: Cambridge University Press, 1977.

In large part a study of the character of Horacio Oliveira, initiated with a review of the scene in which Talita is perched on two planks over a Buenos Aires street. Several references to and comparisons made between Oliveira and characters from some of Cortázar's other works, most notably Johnny Carter of "The Pursuer" and Manuel of *A Manual for Manuel*. Emphasis is on Cortázar's self-expression through these characters, particularly Oliveira. Titles and quotations in English.

Filer, Malva E. "The Ambivalence of the Hand in Cortázar's Fiction." In *The Final Island: The Fiction of Julio Cortázar*, edited by Jaime Alazraki and Ivar Ivask. Norman: University of Oklahoma Press, 1978. Also appears in *Books Abroad* 50 (Summer, 1976): 595-599.

In an article examining the presence of hands in Cortazar's fiction and relating "the role he gives to the hand to some attitudes or psychological problems, as shown particularly by his main characters," Filer cites several works in which hands play a part, *Hopscotch* being one of these. The hand for protagonist Oliveira, Filer contends, "would intercede to provide an escape from the limits of reason and find access to the 'Center,' the object of his desperate search." The critic also examines the attention given to Pola's hands in the novel. Some comparison between the treatment and significance of Pola's hands and those of Frau Marta in *62: A Model Kit*. All references to *Hopscotch* and to *62: A*

Model Kit are in English. References to other works by Cortázar are in Spanish. Limited references to French works in the original language.

Foster, David William. "Julio Cortázar and the Intellectual as Everyman." In his *Currents in the Contemporary Argentine Novel: Arlt, Mallea, Sábato, and Cortázar*. Columbia: University of Missouri Press, 1975.

Foster begins (actually precedes) this thirty-page chapter on *Hopscotch* with a one-page synopsis on Cortázar's life and career. The context of the critic's subsequent analysis of the novel may best be summed up by a statement he makes near the end of said analysis, when he writes that "a work has no one ideal interpretation, not even for the author. It is instead what one makes of it, including what he can reasonably convince others about it." Foster's analysis of *Hopscotch* is essentially a record of "what he makes of it," of what he takes it to mean, with little concern for narrative technique or style. The result is an insightful reading of the significance and meaning of this important work. Titles and quotations in English.

Garfield, Evelyn Picon. "Figures, Searches, and Centers." In her *Julio Cortázar*. New York: Frederick Ungar, 1975.

Garfield devotes some twenty-six pages of this chapter on Cortázar's novels to *Hopscotch*. She begins her discussion with the unconventional nature of the novel's structure and the purpose for which the Argentine writer arranged the work as he did. This is followed by a very good, concise plot summary and a lengthy discussion of various prominent elements of the novel, most notably the character of Horacio Oliveira, the novel's philosophical theme, its expression of Cortázar's theories concerning both the antinovel and the "reader-accomplice," and the author's use of language. An excellent overview of the novel supported by numerous examples from the text and supplemented with enlightening comments by Cortázar himself. Titles in Spanish with English translations. Quotations in English.

Hazera, Lydia D. "Strategies for Reader Participation in the Works of Cortázar, Cabrera Infante and Vargas Llosa." *Latin American Literary Review* 13 (July-December, 1985): 19-34.

In an excellent article on ways in which these three authors "trigger the reader's active participation," Hazera examines Cortázar's *Hopscotch* to show that the Argentine author "wants the reader, in the process of reading, to go through a creative experience similar to the one the author had while writing." The critic contends that Cortázar helps the reader do this by the use of negation, (specifically Morelli's "negating the value of the traditional novel and advocating the production of a new novel, an antinovel"), the use of blanks (or gaps) in the narrative which the reader must connect or fill in, by providing a group of fictional readers in the story who are meant to serve as role models, and by employing language games that encourage reader participation. Hazera also compares the issue of reader participation in the three writers' works. Titles and quotations in English.

Holsten, Ken. "Three Characters and a Theme in Cortázar." *Revista de Estudios Hispánicos* 9 (January, 1975): 119-129.

Holsten examines the theme of the search, and, in particular, "the metaphysical quest" which "permeates Cortázar's novels on every level," contending that the characters involved in this search seek to transcend "the psychological limitations of Western Man and experience expanded dimensions of awareness." The critic examines La Maga of *Hopscotch* as one of only two characters (along with Johnny Carter of "The Pursuer") in Cortázar's works who have the ability to transcend the limitations mentioned above. Ironically, however, she (like Johnny Carter) is able to do it without trying, while Horacio Oliveira, who consciously seeks to achieve this transcendence, is "too steeped in Western rationalism to be able to surmount its limitations." Holsten also examines Cortázar's own personal connection to this theme and his parallels to Oliveira. A very readable, solid study. Titles and quotations in Spanish.

Jiménez-Fajardo, Salvador. "The Redeeming Quest: Patterns of Unification in Carpentier, Fuentes and Cortázar." *Revista de Estudios Hispánicos* 11 (January, 1977): 91-117.

Jiménez-Fajardo's lengthy (twenty-eight-page) article is intended as a detailed comparative study of the "basic coincidence" which *Hopscotch* and *The Death of Artemio Cruz* share with an earlier work, Alejo Carpentier's "Journey to the Source." Jiménez-Fajardo examines Carpentier's work and those of Fuentes and Cortázar to find, in part, that the two later works, by virtue of their similarities to "Journey to the Source," allow the reader "to go beyond the failures of the protagonists in their quest for an integrated vision and to participate in an instance of esthetic unity elaborated out of the seemingly unintegrated elements of their chaos." Titles and quotations in Spanish and French.

Reedy, Daniel R. "Through the Looking-Glass: Aspects of Cortázar's Epiphanies of Reality." *Bulletin of Hispanic Studies* 54 (1977): 125-134.

Reedy views the looking-glass images in Cortázar's works "as apertures through which other realities are disclosed or through which the pathway to the mythic centre is revealed." The critic provides a detailed analysis of *Hopscotch* with respect to its mirror images (a crystalline doorway, a kaleidoscope, a window) and the new realities for which they serve as a conduit (though the protagonist, Oliveira, is not always prepared to move through the entrance they represent). A solid study. Titles and quotations in Spanish.

Safir, Margery A. "An Erotics of Liberation: Notes of Transgressive Behavior in *Hopscotch* and *Libro de Manuel*." In *The Final Island: The Fiction of Julio Cortázar*, edited by Jaime Alazraki and Ivar Ivask. Norman: University of Oklahoma Press, 1978. Also appears in *Books Abroad* 50 (Summer, 1976): 558-569.

In a detailed study of the presence and significance of transgressive behavior in one episode each of *Hopscotch* and *A Manual for Manuel*, Safir examines chapter 36 of *Hopscotch*, the chapter which details Oliveira's sexual activities with Emmanuele. The critic examines the events described, their significance in the protagonist's life (as well as their thematic significance within the novel), the language used to present them, and the reason, with respect to writing itself, for which Cortázar may have included the chapter. She compares this chapter with the erotic Andrés/Francine scene in the Hotel Terrass in *A Manual for Manuel*. One of her conclusions, in addition to those concerning each scene, is that these scenes show that *A Manual for Manuel* is not a repetition but an extension of *Hopscotch*. Titles and quotations in English.

Valentine, Robert V. "Horacio's Mental Journey in *Rayuela*." In *Travel, Quest, and Pilgrimage as a Literary Theme: Studies in Honor of Reino Virtanen*, edited by Frans C. Amelinckx and Joyce N. Megay. Lincoln, Nebr.: Society of Spanish and Spanish-American Studies, 1978.

Valentine calls Horacio's journey in *Hopscotch* "a metaphysical voyage" and contends that the protagonist's "so-called return to Buenos Aires from his self-imposed exile is a complex mental journey, a deeply personal interior voyage into the essential features of his engagement in the creative act as an Argentine writer." He goes on to state that the voyage "is an epiphany of sorts, stimulated by an accumulation of encounters with several women in Paris, a couple of persistent recurring dreams and the chance finding in his pocket of a Buenos Aires pharmacy list." The critic cites several passages which support his claims before concluding that Horacio "probably never physically returns to Buenos Aires," but writes the novel in Paris. An intriguing reading of the work. Titles and quotations in Spanish.

_____ . "The Rhetoric of Horacio's Narration in *Rayuela*." *Bulletin of Hispanic Studies* 58 (1981): 339-344.

Contradicting other criticism on the subject, Valentine establishes Horacio as the single narrator of *Hopscotch*, stating that the "reader is confined to what Horacio can see and know." Horacio, for the critic, is a "self-conscious dramatized narrator," one who "perceives, controls and narrates for Cortázar's implied author," and it is the obviously narrow distance between narrator and author, in addition to the narrator's confusion in telling the tale, which increases the reader's interest in the story and his sympathy for the narrator of this work about "the coming into existence of a novel." An interesting perspective on Cortázar's novel. Well documented. Titles and quotations in Spanish.

Vázquez Amaral, José. "Julio Cortázar's *Hopscotch* and Argentinian Spiritual Alienation." In his *The Contemporary Latin American Narrative*. New York: Las Américas, 1970.

Vázquez Amaral discusses the characters as well as the nature of Cortázar's novel, stating that the work stands as "a summation of all the disenchantment of Western man with what he has sought, thought, or loved, that has slowly but inexorably turned to ashes." Almost half the short chapter is dedicated to a discussion of Argentina's identity crisis, caused in large part by the loss of the gaucho and the influx of immigrants. Vázquez Amaral does not view Cortázar's novel as particularly impressive from a technical standpoint (stating that "it has the ashen flavor of the déjà vu"), but he does see it, mostly through its characters, as an expression of the disenchantment of Western man, but even more so of the "frustration and total ennui" of the modern Argentine with the promises of the West. An interesting reading of the theme of Cortázar's novel. Titles in English.

A Manual for Manuel (Libro de Manuel)

Francescato, Martha Paley. "The New Man (But Not the New Woman)." In *The Final Island: The Fiction of Julio Cortázar*, edited by Jaime Alazraki and Ivar Ivask. Norman: University of Oklahoma Press, 1978. Also appears in *Books Abroad* 50 (Summer, 1976): 589-594.

Citing the importance given to Cortázar's male protagonists and referring to the Argentine writer's concept of the "new man," Francescato asks, "But what about the new woman?" To answer that question she examines the male-female relationships and the role and treatment of women in some of Cortázar's works, *A Manual for Manuel* being one of them. Her findings concerning women in this novel are overwhelmingly negative, as women, for example, are not expected to appreciate certain works of art or music, and their participation in the *Joda* is reluctantly accepted, though said participation involves making sandwiches. An interesting study. Most titles and all quotations in English.

Garfield, Evelyn Picon. "Figures, Searches, and Centers." In her *Julio Cortázar*. New York: Frederick Ungar, 1975.

In this chapter on Cortázar's novels, Garfield devotes approximately six pages to *A Manual for Manuel*, a novel, she states, which "clearly reflects the author's 'political coming of age.'" She briefly discusses Cortázar's similarities to Andrés and then offers a summary of the novel's plot. The remainder of her discussion of the work focuses primarily on the characters and the novel's political message. A good overview of the work featuring enlightening comments from Cortázar himself. Titles in Spanish with English translations. Quotations in English.

González, Alan A. "*A Manual for Manuel.*" In *Magill's Literary Annual, 1979*, edited by Frank N. Magill, vol. 1. Pasadena, Calif.: Salem Press, 1979.

González begins this four-page article with a brief introduction to the novel in question as a "political" novel and how, as such, it fits into Cortázar's oeuvre. The bulk of the article deals with the Argentine writer's political views and how these views manifest themselves in *A Manual for Manuel*. Good background information regarding this "unsettling book which leaves the reader both puzzled and enlightened," rather than an in-depth analysis or even a full-scale introduction. "Sources for Further Study" section lists reviews of the work (in English). Titles and quotations in English.

Safir, Margery A. "An Erotics of Liberation: Notes on Transgressive Behavior in *Hopscotch* and *Libro de Manuel.*" In *The Final Island: The Fiction of Julio Cortázar*, edited by Jaime Alazraki and Ivar Ivask. Norman: University of Oklahoma Press, 1978. Also appears in *Books Abroad* 50 (Summer, 1976): 558-569.

Safir presents a detailed study of the presence and significance of transgressive behavior in one episode each of *Hopscotch* and *A Manual for Manuel*. The critic examines the erotic Andrés/Francine scene in the Hotel Terrass (and two scenes leading to it) from *A Manual for Manuel*, focusing on the events described in the scene, their significance in the protagonist's life (as well as their thematic significance in the work), the language and narrative voice used to describe them, and the reason, with respect to writing, for which Cortázar says he included the scene. She compares this scene with the Oliveira/ Emmanuele scene (in chapter 36) from *Hopscotch*. One of her conclusions, in addition to those concerning each scene, is that these scenes show that *A Manual for Manuel* is not a repetition but an extension of *Hopscotch*. Titles and quotations in English.

Schwartz, Ronald. "Cortázar: Argentine Intellectual Conjurer." In his *Nomads, Exiles, and Émigrés: The Rebirth of the Latin American Narrative, 1960-80*. Metuchen, N.J.: Scarecrow Press, 1980.

This chapter largely describes and analyzes *A Manual for Manuel* and, to some degree, compares it (favorably) to *Hopscotch*. Schwartz contends that the novel "represents one of the best examples of a novel written in the 'boom' tradition," and that, even more so, it "establishes Cortázar as a political person trying to carry out his own belief in the future world of socialism without belonging to any political party." Most of the analysis focuses on the work's characters and its potential political message, as well, again, as its similarities to (and differences from) *Hopscotch*. Some consideration of the novel's problems, though the majority of the criticism is in praise of Cortázar's genius. A very interesting and readable analysis. Titles and quotations in English.

Vernon, Kathleen M. "Cortázar's 3 R's: Reading, Rhetoric and Revolution in *Libro de Manuel*." *Modern Language Studies* 16 (Summer, 1986): 264-270.

Focusing on the idea that readers are "as essential to the literary experience as authors and the books they write" and on Cortázar's own emphasis on the reader (particularly in *Hopscotch*), Vernon examines the reader and the act of reading involved in *A Manual for Manuel*. Her study shows that there are two types of reader and two types of reading for this novel, an idea supported and even encouraged by Cortázar himself, from the novel's very title, to the work's prologue, to the paradoxical political and artistic natures of the work, to the inclusion of both fictional narrative and documentary materials, and to the work's very narration. Titles and quotations in Spanish.

The Secret Weapons (Las armas secretas)

Garfield, Evelyn Picon. "A Swiss Cheese Reality." In her *Julio Cortázar*. New York: Frederick Ungar, 1975.

In this chapter dedicated to Cortázar's short fiction, Garfield provides a roughly ten-page discussion of *The Secret Weapons*. Most attention is paid to "Blow-Up" and "The Pursuer," though considerable attention is given to "At Your Service" as well. Most of the discussion of the stories is dedicated to plot description and treatment of theme, particularly themes concerning, as Garfield suggests at one point, "the two sides of the same coin," such as "the creative process and its relationship to life" (as in "Blow-Up" and "The Pursuer"). Supplemented with personal comments from Cortázar himself. Best read in tandem with the section (at the beginning of the chapter) concerning Cortázar's thoughts on the short story. Most titles in Spanish with English translations. Titles translated previously in the chapter appear in Spanish only. Quotations in English.

62: A Model Kit (62: Modelo para armar)

Filer, Malva E. "The Ambivalence of the Hand in Cortázar's Fiction." In *The Final Island: The Fiction of Julio Cortázar*, edited by Jaime Alazraki and Ivar Ivask. Norman: University of Oklahoma Press, 1978. Also appears in *Books Abroad* 50 (Summer, 1976): 595-599.

Filer studies the presence of hands in Cortázar's fiction and relates "the role he gives to the hand to attitudes or psychological problems, as shown particularly by his main characters." One of the works examined is *62: A Model Kit*. Filer cites the attention given to Frau Marta's hands, which as the critic states, are "related to her 'arachnoid ways' and altogether sinister appearance." Some comparison made between Frau Marta's hands and those of Pola in *Hopscotch*. All references to *62: A Model Kit* and to *Hopscotch* are in

English. Other works by Cortázar are cited in Spanish. Limited reference to
French works in the original language.

Francescato, Martha Paley. "The New Man (But Not the New Woman)." In *The
    Final Island: The Fiction of Julio Cortázar*, edited by Jaime Alazraki and Ivar
    Ivask. Norman: University of Oklahoma Press, 1978. Also appears in *Books
    Abroad* (Summer, 1976): 589-594.
    In an article recognizing the importance accorded Cortázar's male protago-
    nists, and citing the Argentine author's concept of the "new man," Francescato
    asks, "But what about the woman?" She seeks an answer to this question by
    studying male-female relationships and the role and treatment of women in
    some of Cortázar's works, one of which is *62: A Model Kit*. Her findings
    concerning women in this novel are negative, as they are treated as objects,
    with condescension, and with what borders on misogyny. These findings are
    supported by numerous quotations from the text. An interesting study. Most
    titles and all quotations in English.

Garfield, Evelyn Picon. "Figures, Searches, and Centers." In her *Julio Cortázar*.
    New York: Frederick Ungar, 1975.
    This chapter on Cortázar's long fiction contains a sixteen-page section devoted
    to *62: A Model Kit*. Garfield discusses the genesis of the work, its characters
    and character portrayal, its structure, its message, and its language. Her obser-
    vations are supported by numerous examples from the text and supplemented
    with comments from Cortázar himself. An excellent overview of the novel in
    question. Title in Spanish with English translation. Quotations in English.

Hernández, Ana María. "Vampires and Vampiresses: A Reading of *62*." In *The
    Final Island: The Fiction of Julio Cortázar*, edited by Jaime Alazraki and Ivar
    Ivask. Norman: University of Oklahoma Press, 1978. Also appears in *Books
    Abroad* 50 (Summer, 1976): 570-575.
    An interesting and detailed study of the "very complex system of cross-
    references and allusions, functioning on different levels but with the central
    theme of vampirism as a common basis" in *62: A Model Kit*. Some of the
    many vampire-related elements examined in the study include the presence
    and significance of mirrors and mirror images, references to "the Countess,"
    and the behavior of Helene and others. Title and most quotations from Cor-
    tázar's novel are in English, some in Spanish, one in French. Titles and
    quotations from other sources in English.

Jones, Julie. "*62*: Cortázar's *Novela Pastoril*." *Inti* 21 (Spring, 1985): 27-35.
    A fascinating article viewing Cortazar's novel from an interesting perspective,
    showing how the "involved entanglement between a series of lovers, the tend-
    ency to see love as a form of enslavement, the *otium* which allows the charac-

ters to wander about in groups pursuing their love interests, cultivating their art and playing games, the shared nostalgia for the Golden Age," all suggest that *62: A Model Kit* is, in fact, a twentieth century version of the Spanish pastoral novel of the sixteenth century. Numerous references to the sixteenth century works and their characteristics help the reader unfamiliar with the genre. Well-drawn parallels between Cortázar's novel and the original pastoral novels. Titles and quotations in Spanish.

The Winners (Los premios)

Brown, James Franklin. "Cortázar and the Minotaur in *Los premios.*" *Romance Notes* 23 (Spring, 1983): 199-203.

Brown traces Cortázar's interest in the Greek myth of Theseus and the Minotaur from his poem *Los reyes* (the kings) to other works (such as *Bestiary*) and contends that the motif of this myth is present in *The Winners* as well. Citing other critics' views of the Minotaur in Cortázar's works, and drawing heavily from the novel's text, Brown concludes that a group of the passengers comprise a collective Theseus and that each passenger's interior struggle and self-confrontation (symbolized by their struggle to reach the ship's poop) is his or her own personal minotaur. An interesting reading of the novel in question. Titles and quotations in Spanish.

Callan, Richard J. "Cortázar's *Los premios*: A Journey of Discovery." *Revista de Estudios Hispánicos* 15 (October, 1981): 365-375.

Callan calls *The Winners* a novel in which, "on the occasion of a cruise and within the context of a war game, Cortázar depicts the initiation into manhood of one of the passengers according to the psychology of Carl Jung." That character, according to the critic, is Gabriel Medrano. Callan studies Medrano's behavior, his relationships with the other passengers (particularly Claudia), his dream, and his trip to the ship's poop to proclaim him "a prototype of the ego who has freed himself from the grip of the unconscious." Titles and quotations in Spanish.

Garfield, Evelyn Picon. "Figures, Searches, and Centers." In her *Julio Cortázar*. New York: Frederick Ungar, 1975.

In a chapter dedicated to Cortázar's novels, Garfield devotes approximately nine pages to a discussion of *The Winners*. Most attention is given to the novel's plot, its cast of characters (and Cortázar's portrayal of them), its unconventional structure, the points of view from which it is told, and its theme. Supplemented with comments from Cortázar himself. Titles in Spanish with English translations. Quotations in English.

Valentine, Robert V. "The Meaning of Persio's Monologues in *The Winners.*" *Latin American Literary Review* 13 (Fall/Winter, 1978): 10-19.

Valentine begins by pointing out that a common feature of the contemporary Spanish American novel is that they are novels about the writing of a novel. *The Winners*, according to the critic, fits into this category, and he believes that as an aspect of Cortázar's "concern with the literary creative act, Persio's monologues, interspersed among the events on the ship, attempt a poetic overview of the creative process undergone in the composition of the novel." The critic examines the monologues from this perspective, concluding that the "reader willing to come to grips with the monologues discovers their relationship to the rest of the novel," and in so doing, Valentine appears to suggest, discovers the work's "central meaning: the dramatization by the novelist of the emergence of his novel." Titles and quotations in English.

"All Fires the Fire" ("Todos los fuegos el fuego")

González Echevarría, Roberto. *"Los reyes*: Cortázar's Mythology of Writing." In *The Final Island: The Fiction of Julio Cortázar*, edited by Jaime Alazraki and Ivar Ivask. Norman: University of Oklahoma Press, 1978. (Also appears in *Books Abroad* 50 [Summer, 1976]: 548-557.)

González Echevarría uses *Los reyes* (the kings) to establish the monster/hero confrontation as the primal scene in what he calls "Cortázar's mythology of writing." He views this scene as "a hegemonic struggle for the center that resolves itself in a mutual cancellation and in the superimposition of beginnings and ends," and states that scenes similar to it and with similar results occur frequently in the Argentine writer's fiction. He then examines "All Fires the Fire," with its "mutual annihilation," as a prime example of this. "The Pursuer" is also examined. Familiarity with Greek mythology, Nietzsche, and Cortázar's works referred to helpful. Titles (except *Los reyes*) and quotations (except in one instance in which a passage from "The Pursuer" is quoted in both English and Spanish, and another in which a short poem by Octavio Paz is cited in Spanish) in English.

"Axolotl"

Bennett, Maurice J. "A Dialogue of Gazes: Metamorphosis and Epiphany in Julio Cortázar's 'Axolotl.'" *Studies in Short Fiction* 23 (Winter, 1986): 57-62.

Relying heavily on (and quoting) Carl Jung, and with considerable reference to Cortázar's use of the myth of Theseus and the Minotaur, Bennett examines "Axolotl," a story the critic believes "recasts this ancient myth as an account of the mysterious transformation of a man into a kind of an aquatic lizard." Bennett believes that in the union of the man and the axolotl, in fact, in their union as coauthors, so to speak, of the story, Cortázar "retrieves the ancient idea of a fully sentient universe, where consciousness is not limited to man alone but is an essential attribute of the creation." An interesting piece. Titles and quotations in English.

Reedy, Daniel R. "Through the Looking Glass: Aspects of Cortázar's Epiphanies of Reality." *Bulletin of Hispanic Studies* 54 (1977): 125-134.

Reedy views the looking-glass images in Cortázar's works "as apertures through which other realities are disclosed or through which the pathway to the mythic centre is revealed." The critic provides a detailed study of "Axolotl" (among other works) with respect to its looking-glass image (the aquarium) and the new reality for which it serves as a conduit. A solid study. Titles and quotations in Spanish.

Rosser, Harry L. "The Voice of the Salamander: Cortázar's 'Axolotl' and the Transformation of the Self." *Kentucky Romance Quarterly* 30, no. 4 (1983): 419-427.

After a brief discussion of Cortázar's views on the fantastic, Rosser states that the purpose of his study of "Axolotl" is "to offer an interpretation of Cortázar's narrative within the context of his unusual view of reality." He then presents a summary of the story's plot and the narrative techniques employed by the Argentine writer to communicate the story. The rest of the article provides an essentially Jungian interpretation of the transformation of the narrator-protagonist, which is seen as an attainment of consciousness, an "inner rebirth," as he, among other things, becomes "consciously aware of the effects of an instinctual side that he had neglected or suppressed." Considerable reference to Jung, but well explained within the context of the article. A thought-provoking reading of Cortázar's story. Titles and quotations in English.

Sánchez, Marta E. "A View From Inside the Fishbowl: Julio Cortázar's 'Axolotl.'" In *Bridges to Fantasy*, edited by George E. Slusser, Eric S. Rabkin, and Robert E. Scholes. Carbondale: Southern Illinois University Press, 1982.

A fascinating article in which Sánchez refutes Tzvetan Todorov's assertion that the twentieth century has produced no fantastic literature. She uses Cortázar's story as proof that "the fantastic in the twentieth century has not disappeared, but has undergone a transformation." The critic first establishes that in Cortázar's story, ambiguity (a requirement of fantastic literature for Todorov) does not concern *what* the man sees but *who* relates it. She further examines Cortázar's deliberate use of ambiguity in sections entitled "It's All in the Pronouns: The Problem of *Énonciation*," "Man-Fish Duality: The Binary Opposition," and "Ambiguity Resolved: Axolotl Speaks." An excellent analysis of the intentional ambiguity in Cortázar's story, both from the perspective of how it is used and its effect on the reader. Quotations in Spanish with English translations or simply in English.

"Bestiary" ("Bestiario")
Reedy, Daniel R. "Through the Looking Glass: Aspects of Cortázar's Epiphanies of Reality." *Bulletin of Hispanic Studies* 54 (1977): 125-134.

In this article in which Reedy shows how looking-glass images function symbolically as gateways to other realities, the critic examines several of Cortázar's works, including "Bestiary," a story in which "the symbolism of images mirrored in the glass pane of a formicarium provides an unconscious awareness of the nature of the conflict" in which the protagonist, Isabel, finds herself. Reedy presents a detailed analysis of the specific function of the formicarium and how it is presented in the story as well as the new reality, so to speak, achieved by the protagonist. Titles and quotations in Spanish.

"Blow-Up" ("Las babas del diablo")
Guibert, Rita, Stanley Kauffmann, and Charles Thomas Samuels. "Snapshots of *Blow-Up*." *Review 72* (Winter, 1972): 22-25.
Three brief essays, entitled "Cortázar Defends Antonioni" (which consists entirely of Cortázar's response to a question by Guibert concerning his story and Michelangelo Antonioni's film), "The Invisible Immanence of Evil" (by Kauffmann), and "Sorting Things Out in *Blow-Up*" (by Samuels), which, in some way or another, address the similarities and differences between Cortázar's "Blow-Up" and Antonioni's film of the same name. Not in-depth, but interesting. Titles in English.

Peavler, Terry J. "*Blow-Up*: A Reconsideration of Antonioni's Infidelity to Cortázar." *Publications of the Modern Language Association of America* 94 (October, 1979): 887-893.
Peavler provides a brief overview of the criticism on Cortázar's story and Michelangelo Antonioni's film, concentrating on the majority of said criticism's lack of ability to point out more than the most obvious connections, both similarities and differences, between the two works. The critic then examines the similarities, many beneath the surface, which tie the two works together, such as both protagonists' ability to fictionalize, the enigmatic nature of reality concerning the supposed crime in each work, the opening of the creative act by both Cortázar and Antonioni, and the struggle each artist has with "the medium itself and with the relationship between reality and the results of his artistic effort." Peavler's conclusion is that despite critics' (of both works) appraisals that the works are largely dissimilar, much more connects the story and the film than lies on the surface. An interesting, very readable, and well-documented piece. Title of Cortázar's work in Spanish. Quotations in Spanish with English translations.

Reedy, Daniel R. "Through the Looking Glass: Aspects of Cortázar's Epiphanies of Reality." *Bulletin of Hispanic Studies* 54 (1977): 125-134.
In this article in which Reedy contends that the looking-glass images function symbolically in Cortázar's works "as apertures through which other realities are disclosed or through which the pathway to the mythic centre is revealed,"

Reedy provides a detailed analysis of "Blow-Up" (among other works) with respect to its looking-glass image (the lens of a camera) and the "other" reality it introduces. A solid study. Titles and quotations in Spanish.

"House Taken Over" ("Casa tomada")

Gyurko, Lanin A. "Hallucination and Nightmare in Two Stories by Cortázar." *Modern Language Review* 67 (July, 1972): 550-562.

Gyurko studies "House Taken Over" and "Cefalea" (also of *Bestiary*) as two stories in which hallucinations and nightmares play a significant role. Gyurko contends that the brother and sister in "House Taken Over" are not plagued by nor driven from their home by any actual presence in their house, but they are instead tortured by "an invasion of the mind," insomnia and nightmares spawned by their guilty consciences for maintaining an incestuous relationship in their ancestral home. During the day they can occupy themselves and largely ignore the invading feelings of guilt. But at night their minds are more open to the feelings which plague them and ultimately drive them from the house. An interesting reading of the story. Titles and quotations in Spanish.

"The Island at Noon" ("La isla a mediodía")

Reedy, Daniel R. "Through the Looking Glass: Aspects of Cortázar's Epiphanies of Reality." *Bulletin of Hispanic Studies* 54 (1977): 125-134.

Reedy contends that the looking-glass images function symbolically in Cortázar's works "as apertures through which other realities are disclosed or through which the pathway to the mythic centre is revealed." The critic analyzes "The Island at Noon" (among other works) with respect to its looking-glass image (the porthole of an airplane) and the new reality for which this image serves as a conduit. A solid study. Titles and quotations in Spanish.

"The Pursuer" ("El perseguidor")

Felkel, Robert W. "The Historical Dimension in Julio Cortázar's 'The Pursuer.'" *Latin American Literary Review* 14 (Spring/Summer, 1979): 20-27.

Felkel studies Cortázar's story in relation to the real characters and events on which it is based. Felkel states that his study goes beyond simply identifying Johnny Carter as Charlie Parker. The critic identifies the four main characters with their real counterparts and, using both Cortázar's descriptions and those of a witness to the real events, examines the relationship to reality of the recording session which appears in the story. He also discusses the death of both Johnny Carter and Charlie Parker, and other similar events or traits (such as each one's reaction to his daughter's death and their concept of time), as well as a few elements of the story which differ from reality. A valuable study of this story, which Felkel says "needs to be placed in historical context in order to divulge its full meaning." Titles and quotations in English.

González Echevarría, Roberto. "*Los reyes*: Cortázar's Mythology of Writing." In
The Final Island: The Fiction of Julio Cortázar, edited by Jaime Alazraki and
Ivar Ivask. Norman: University of Oklahoma Press, 1978. Also appears in
Books Abroad (Summer, 1976): 548-557.

González Echevarría uses *Los reyes* (the kings) to establish the monster/hero
confrontation as the primal scene in what he calls "Cortázar's mythology of
writing." The critic views this scene as "a hegemonic struggle for the center
that resolves itself in a mutual cancellation and in the superimposition of
beginnings and ends," and states that scenes similar to it, and with similar
results, occur frequently in Cortázar's fiction. He then examines "The Pursuer" (and "All Fires the Fire") in relation to his contentions. Familiarity with
Greek mythology, Nietzsche, and Cortázar's works referred to helpful. Titles
(except *Los reyes*) and quotations (except in one instance in which a passage
from "The Pursuer" is quoted in both English and Spanish, and another in
which a short poem by Octavio Paz is cited in Spanish) are in English.

Holsten, Ken. "Three Characters and a Theme in Cortázar." *Revista de Estudios
Hispánicos* 9 (January, 1975): 119-129.

Holsten examines the theme of the search, and, in particular, "the metaphysical quest" which "permeates Cortázar's novels on every level," contending
that the characters involved in this search seek to transcend "the psychological
limitations of Western Man and experience expanded dimensions of awareness." One of the characters examined by the critic in relation to this theme is
Johnny Carter, who Holsten shows to be one of only two characters in Cortázar's works who have the ability to transcend the limitations mentioned
above, though he, ironically, is able to do it without trying. The other characters examined are La Maga and Horacio Oliveira, both of *Hopscotch*. Holsten
also studies Cortázar's own personal connection to the theme in question. A
very readable, solid study. Titles and quotations in Spanish.

"The Secret Weapons" ("Las armas secretas")

Reedy, Daniel R. "Through the Looking Glass: Aspects of Cortázar's Epiphanies of
Reality." *Bulletin of Hispanic Studies* 54 (1977): 125-134.

Reedy states that the looking-glass images function symbolically in Cortázar's
works "as apertures through which other realities are disclosed or through
which the pathway to the mythic centre is revealed." "The Secret Weapons" is
one of several works for which Reedy provides detailed analysis of the
looking-glass image (a glass ball in this story) and the "other" reality it introduces. Titles and quotations in Spanish.

JOSÉ DONOSO
Chile

Biography

McMurray, George R. "The Man and His Times." In his *José Donoso*. Boston: Twayne, 1979.

Serving as the introductory chapter to McMurray's book on the Chilean writer, this chapter is divided into sections. The first section, entitled "Literary Backgrounds," summarizes (in considerable detail) "the broad framework of twentieth century Chilean and Latin American letters" through the 1950's and early 1960's. The "Biography" section provides information of Donoso's life and career. A final section, entitled "Donoso and the 'Boom' " (the longest section of the chapter—some nine pages), discusses a history of the "Boom" and Donoso's role in it (with much of the information coming from Donoso's *The Boom in Spanish American Literature: A Personal History*). A chronology of Donoso's life and career (through 1977) precedes the chapter. An excellent introduction to the Chilean writer. Titles and quotations in English.

Schwartz, Ronald. "Donoso: Chilean Phantasmagoria." In his *Nomads, Exiles, and Émigrés: The Rebirth of the Latin American Narrative, 1960-80*. Metuchen, N.J.: Scarecrow Press, 1980.

This chapter has three purposes: (1) to provide a biographical sketch of Donoso, (2) to give a brief introduction to *The Obscene Bird of Night*, and (3) to examine in some depth the novel *Sacred Families*. The biographical sketch occupies a little over four pages of this twelve-page chapter, but in spite of its brevity it is filled with information about Donoso's life and career (as both writer and teacher). In fact, it progresses almost year by year from 1946. Full of nonstatistical details (such as how Donoso wrote *Hell Without Limits* in Carlos Fuentes' garden while the Mexican writer wrote *A Change of Skin* in the study). Interesting and amazingly concise. Titles in English.

Commentary

Coleman, Alexander. "Some Thoughts on José Donoso's Traditionalism." *Studies in Short Fiction* 8 (Winter, 1971): 155-158.

In this brief article, Coleman chides critics who have called Donoso a traditional and even *costumbrista* writer, stating that to notice only the superficial traditional, realist nature of the Chilean author's narrative "is to hide their insidious and quite beautifully disguised thematics." Concentrating on two short stories and briefly referring to *Coronation*, *Hell Has No Limits*, and *This Sunday*, the critic discusses the violent thematics that lie below the surface of Donoso's works, works in which "daily life has rarely taken on such traumatic resonances. . . ." Titles in Spanish. One reference quotation in English.

McMurray, George R. "Interview with José Donoso." *Hispania* 58 (May, 1975): 391-393.
In this rather brief interview conducted in Calaceite, Teruel, Spain, in June, 1973, Donoso responds to questions concerning metaphysics, the lack of meaningful communication among his characters, the difference between *The Obscene Bird of Night* and his other works, the role of symbols in his narrative, the role of masks and disguises, writers and painters who have influenced his writing, and other topics. Informative and insightful. Titles in Spanish.

_____ . *José Donoso*. Boston: Twayne, 1979.
An excellent book-length study of Donoso's life and works. Chapter titles include "The Man and His Times," "The Short Stories," "A Period of Transition (1957-1966)" (examining *Coronation* and *This Sunday*), "Myth and the Absurd: *Hell Has No Limits*," "*The Obscene Bird of Night*: A Tribute to Consciousness," and "*Sacred Families*: A Middle-Class Reality and Fantasy." A final chapter presents critic McMurray's conclusions concerning Donoso's literary production. Chronology of the Chilean writer's life and career through 1977. Provides an excellent index, a bibliography of Donoso's works in Spanish and English, and an annotated critical bibliography in Spanish and English. Titles and quotations in English. One of the best volumes in the Twayne series.

_____ . "José Donoso." In *Latin American Literature in the Twentieth Century: A Guide*, edited by Leonard S. Klein. New York: Frederick Ungar, 1986.
A brief (roughly three-page) introduction to Donoso's life and works. Some discussion of his major themes, his short stories, and his principal novels, particularly *The Obscene Bird of Night*. A good starting point for the reader unfamiliar with Donoso. List of the Chilean writer's works (most in Spanish only). Includes a short critical bibliography in Spanish and English.

_____ . "Major Figures of the Boom." In his *Spanish American Writing Since 1941: A Critical Survey*. New York: Frederick Ungar, 1987.
McMurray devotes approximately six pages of this section of his book to a brief overview of Donoso's fiction. Following two paragraphs of introduction, the critic offers concise commentary on the Chilean writer's major works, both short stories and novels, before offering a concluding paragraph which summarizes the nature of Donoso's fictional world. A good starting point for the reader unfamiliar with Donoso. Titles in Spanish with English translations.

Martínez, Z. Nelly. "José Donoso: A Short Study of His Works." *Books Abroad* 49 (Spring, 1975): 249-255.
After a brief introduction to Donoso and his career (through 1973), Martínez delivers just what she promises in the title of her article, a short study of the

Chilean author's works, beginning with his earliest stories and following through to *The Obscene Bird of Night*. Emphasis is primarily on Donoso's characters (which the critic contends "emerge from three distinct social classes: the senile aristocracy, the manipulative maids, and the amoral pariahs of society") and the mad, chaotic worlds in which they find themselves. A good introduction to the Chilean writer's works. Titles and quotations in English.

Nigro, Kirsten F. "From Criollismo to the Grotesque: Approaches to José Donoso." In *Tradition and Renewal: Essays on Twentieth-Century Latin American Literature and Culture*, edited by Merlin H. Forster. Urbana: University of Illinois Press, 1975.
At the end of a nine-page section concerning the nature (particularly the regional nature) of the Chilean novel into the 1950's, Nigro states that though many critics have praised Donoso, "some have done so for all the wrong reasons," viewing him (amazingly, the critic seems to indicate) as a realist writer primarily concerned with the decay of Chilean society. Nigro concedes that the writer's works do deal with Chilean society on one level, but she contends as well that Donoso's "so-called realism is a mask, a disguise which has fooled many of his critics." His works are in reality, she suggests, full of chaos, presenting a grotesque (the key word here) reflection of reality, one characterized by "monstrous visions of diseased and withered souls." Almost half the article is devoted to an analysis of the presence and function of the grotesque in *Hell Has No Limits*. A solid and very reasonable study. Titles and quotations in Spanish.

Pérez, Janet. "José Donoso." In *Critical Surveys of Long Fiction* (Foreign Language Series), edited by Frank N. Magill, vol. 2. Pasadena, Calif.: Salem Press, 1984.
A thirteen-and-a-half page overview of Donoso's work in long fiction. Contains a list of his major novels (most in Spanish with English translations), a summary of his work in other literary forms, and an assessment of his achievements. This is followed by a biographical sketch and a roughly ten-page overview/analysis of his principal novels: *This Sunday*, *Coronation*, *The Obscene Bird of Night*, *Hell Has No Limits*, and *A House in the Country*. A good introduction for the reader unfamiliar with Donoso's work in general and his novels in particular. Provides a list of the Chilean writer's other major works (some only in Spanish) and a short critical bibliography in English. Titles of translated works in English.

Coronation (Coronación)
McMurray, George R. "A Period of Transition (1957-1966)." In his *José Donoso*. Boston: Twayne, 1979.
In this thirty-page chapter which examines both *Coronation* and *This Sunday*

as transitional works in Donoso's literary production, McMurray dedicates
some twelve pages to the first novel, which the critic calls "one of the best
Chilean novels published during the 1950's." The study, as is the case with all
studies in this volume, is comprehensive, treating plot, characters, theme,
symbolism, technique, and style. A conclusion at the end of the chapter compares *Coronation* to *This Sunday* and finds the latter work to be "a more
satisfactory novel than *Coronation*." An excellent study. Titles and quotations
(of which there are many) in English.

A House in the Country (Casa de campo)

Bacarisse, Pamela. "Donoso and Social Commitment: *Casa de Campo*." *Bulletin of
Hispanic Studies* 60 (October, 1983): 319-332.

Bacarisse discusses and rebukes (as has the Chilean author himself) some
critics' claim that Donoso's early novels were significantly concerned with
social issues. *A House in the Country*, however, does send a social and political
message, the critic states, and Donoso has admitted as much. She studies in
detail the social and political overtones of this work, finding, for example,
parallels not only to Donoso's Chile but to prerevolutionary Cuba. She also
identifies more traditional Donoso concerns present in the novel, such as
"individual identity, personal relationships, survival and threats of annihilation," and examines their role in the novel as well. Titles and quotations in
Spanish.

Hell Has No Limits (El lugar sin límites)

McMurray, George R. "Myth and the Absurd: *Hell Has No Limits*." In his *José
Donoso*. Boston: Twayne, 1979.

A comprehensive study of this novel which, McMurray contends, presents a
"concept of reality based primarily on myth, pervasive ambiguity, and elements of the absurd in the human experience." The critic begins by reviewing
the novel's plot and by treating its mythical allusions. This is followed by a
study of the absurd in *Hell Has No Limits* (including a somewhat lengthy
introduction to the absurdist concepts of Jean-Paul Sartre and Albert Camus).
McMurray also examines the work's structure and technique before presenting
his conclusions on this novel which he calls "one of Donoso's two masterpieces, the other being *The Obscene Bird of Night*." Titles and quotations in
English.

Nigro, Kirsten F. "From Criollismo to the Grotesque: Approaches to José Donoso."
In *Tradition and Renewal: Essays on Twentieth-Century Latin American Liter-
ature and Culture*, edited by Merlin H. Forster. Urbana: University of Illinois
Press, 1975.

Nigro traces the evolution of the Chilean novel (with emphasis on its regionalist nature) from the mid-nineteenth century into the 1950's, before declaring

that those who view Donoso as a writer primarily in the realist tradition are missing the true nature and significance of this author for whom realism is only a mask. The true face of Donoso's narrative, she contends, is characterized by a grotesque depiction of reality. The last ten pages of the article are devoted to an analysis of *Hell Has No Limits* in order to "show how and to what extent the grotesque functions as an inexorable force in Donoso's narrative world." Emphasis is on the characters and their "intricate web of interpersonal relationships." An excellent study. Title and quotations in Spanish.

The Obscene Bird of Night (El obsceno pájaro de la noche)

Bacarisse, Pamela. "*El obsceno pájaro de la noche*: A Willed Process of Evasion." In *Contemporary Latin American Fiction*, edited by Salvador Bacarisse. Edinburgh: Scottish Academic Press, 1980.

Concerning herself with the "I" of *The Obscene Bird of Night*, the, as she calls it, "surface 'autobiographer,'" Bacarisse comes to the early conclusion that the narrator, Mudito (the Little Deaf Mute), "makes a desperate attempt to escape and hide," to avoid communication, to seek not to be understood. The critic examines why (and how) he does this and, since he does it, why the reader should care enough to continue reading such evasive narration. The answer to the first part comes, primarily, from an examination of Mudito as an ontologically insecure person, while the answer to the second part is found in Donoso's rich though difficult narrative. An interesting piece. Titles and quotations in Spanish.

Caviglia, John. "Tradition and Monstrosity in *El obsceno pájaro de la noche*." *Publications of the Modern Language Association of America* 93 (January, 1978): 33-45.

Following a rather lengthy introduction, Caviglia divides his analysis of what he calls and explains as "the existential taxonomy" of *The Obscene Bird of Night* into sections entitled "The Mask: Identity as Norm," "The Monster: Identity as Normlessness," "The Old Woman: Language as Being," "The Imbunche: Language as Annihilation," and "Narcissus: The Myth as a Model for Narrative," before concluding, in part, that this novel "is normal only that it may exist. Its aberrations are the relative manifestations of a strangeness that is desired as absolute." A detailed and in-depth study. Titles in Spanish. Quotations in Spanish with English translations.

Gertel, Zunilda. "Metemorphosis as a Metaphor of the World." *Review 73* (Fall, 1973): 20-23.

Gertel cites *The Obscene Bird of Night* as one of three novels (along with Cabrera Infante's *Three Trapped Tigers* and Severo Sarduy's *From Cuba with a Song*) that "have reaffirmed the destruction of conventional reality by installing the grotesque in order to depict most effectively a shapeless world that cannot find its center." In these novels, she contends, "fragmentation is used as an expressive unit of the irrational, implying an ever-changing structure." The critic finds Donoso's novel to be a singular work within this new type of fiction, as it "portrays the universe in a continuous metamorphosis where ambiguity is an all-encompassing passing principle that reflects a world of contradiction." The characters in *The Obscene Bird of Night*, she contends, "are transformed by constant mutation into metaphor figures." She studies the "constant mutation" of these characters, with considerable reference and comparison to Hieronymous Bosch's *Garden of Earthly Delights*, "to which," the critic contends, "Donoso's cosmos is cleary related." Titles (except for one in French) and quotations in English.

Hassett, John J. "*The Obscene Bird of Night*." *Review 73* (Fall, 1973): 27-30.
Early in his article, Hassett calls *The Obscene Bird of Night* the culmination of a process of internalization on the part of Donoso in the evolution of his writing. The result of this process is a novel which "poses an unending source of difficulty and frustration for the reader accustomed to traditional fiction." The critic contends that "any attempt to understand and appreciate this novel must take into consideration two of its principal features: the peculiar nature of its fictional characters and the use of a highly complex narrative structure." The rest (and the bulk) of Hassett's article is devoted to a discussion of these two features, before he concludes that in this novel Donoso does not offer "a novel to simply read, but one to experience in which we are continuously called upon to give the text some order by discovering its unities and repetitions." Titles and quotations in English.

McMurray, George R. "*The Obscene Bird of Night*: A Tribute to Consciousness." In his *José Donoso*. Boston: Twayne, 1979.
An excellent and wide-ranging thirty-page analysis of Donoso's novel. Divided into sections entitled "Plot," "Schizophrenia and Surrealism," "Existentialist Elements," "Time, Space and Aesthetic Unity," and "Conclusions," this chapter presents a comprehensive and amazingly detailed study of the Chilean writer's "monumental, masterfully orchestrated tribute to consciousness." A superb and very readable guide to this complex novel. Essential for anyone seeking insight into Donoso's complex plot, artistry, and thematics. Titles and quotations in English.

Magnarelli, Sharon. "The Baroque, the Picaresque, and *El obsceno pájaro de la noche*." *Hispanic Journal* 2 (Spring, 1981): 81-93.
A fascinating article in which Magnarelli presents a detailed study intended to show "what is Baroque in the picaresque novel and that these same characteristics have carried over into the twentieth century, as dramatized" in Donoso's novel. Her study of the topic includes consideration of audience, struc-

ture, language (particularly the rhetorical use thereof), and narrative voice in *The Obscene Bird of Night* and its Baroque and picaresque antecedents. An interesting and well-supported contention. Titles and quotations in English.

Oberhelman, Harley D. "José Donoso and the 'Nueva narrativa.'" *Revista de Estudios Hispánicos* 9 (January, 1975): 107-117.

Oberhelman studies *The Obscene Bird of Night* as an example of Latin America's "new narrative," focusing on the work's interior reality as a reflection of and commentary on the exterior reality of Chile during the time the novel was being written. He views La Rinconada, for example, as "a copy of Chilean society," and calls Donoso's creation of it "a direct attack on a system of government which exploits the unfortunate masses as a foundation for its power." He also views the new home to which the women move as "symbolic of the new social and economic systems which must replace the decadent past." Interesting reading of the novel. Titles and quotations in Spanish.

Review 73 (Fall, 1973): 12-39. A "Focus" section devoted to Donoso and *The Obscene Bird of Night*.

This section presents six diverse pieces on Donoso and *The Obscene Bird of Night*: (1) "Chronology" by Donoso himself, (2) "Metamorphosis as a Metaphor of the World" by Zunilda Gertel, (3) "A Conflict of Themes" by Francisco Rivera, (4) *"The Obscene Bird of Night"* by John J. Hassett, (5) "Writing/Transvestism" by Severo Sarduy, and (6) "The Novel as Happening: An Interview with José Donoso" by Emir Rodríguez Monegal. Most titles (except for one in French) and quotations (with the exception of a few Spanish terms) in English.

Rodríguez Monegal, Emir. "The Novel as Happening: an Interview with José Donoso." Translated by Suzanne Jill Levine. *Review 73* (Fall, 1973): 34-39.

In an interview taped in Barcelona in August, 1970, just before the publication of *The Obscene Bird of Night* in the original Spanish, Donoso provides lengthy responses to questions concerning various aspects of his novel and the writing of it, such as the origin of its title, the novel as a "happening," the point of departure for writing it, the world of monsters and the novel, how the convent became involved in the work, how the author invented Mudito (the Little Deaf Mute), where Donoso got the "yellow bitch" legend, the work's narrative structure, how the text "forces the reader into a search for identities," and why the author keeps referring to Henry James in his answers to the questions. An informative and insightful piece. Titles and quotations in English.

Schwartz, Ronald. "Donoso: Chilean Phantasmagoria." In his *Nomads, Exiles, and Émigrés: The Rebirth of the Latin American Narrative, 1960-80*. Metuchen, N.J.: Scarecrow Press, 1980.

This chapter has three purposes: (1) to provide a biographical sketch of Donoso, (2) to give a brief introduction to *The Obscene Bird of Night*, and (3) to
examine in some depth the novel *Sacred Families*. The introduction to *The
Obscene Bird of Night* occupies the first two pages and roughly one middle
page of the twelve-page chapter. Not a detailed introduction and not, apparently, intended as such, but instead a collection of concise observations, both
from critic Schwartz and others, concerning the nature of this novel known, as
Schwartz states, "for its nightmarish, surrealistic images, its diffuse and hap-
hazard stylistics, its ambiguities and jagged, asymmetrical structural design."
Good for the reader unfamiliar with Donoso's novel. Titles in English.

Scott, Robert. "Heroic Illusion and Death Denial in Donoso's *El obsceno pájaro de
la noche*." *Symposium* 32 (Summer, 1978): 133-146.
Scott contends that "the theme of heroic illusion as a denial of death" (in
which man seeks to be a hero or at least clings to such an illusion and in so
doing manages to repress "both the terror and the reality of death"), presented
in *The Obscene Bird of Night*, has been ignored by critics. He identifies four
heroic myths or fictions in the novel (concerning, respectively, Jerónimo de
Azcoitía, the *beata*, Iris' child, and, most important, Humberto, who, in
addition to being the protagonist of his own heroic myth, plays a part in the
other three as well), all of which are established, maintained, and ultimately
destroyed by the end of the work. Interesting and detailed piece. Titles and
quotations in Spanish.

Stabb, Martin S. "The Erotic Mask: Notes on Donoso and the New Novel." *Symposium* 30 (Summer, 1976): 170-179.
Stabb begins his study with a discussion of the presence of erotic material in
Western prose fiction (particularly since World War I), its role in literature in
general, and its emergence in contemporary Spanish American fiction. He
then turns his attention to the erotic motif in Donoso's *The Obscene Bird of
Night*, focusing primarily on its relation to the work's character "triads," as he
terms them (Humberto-Mudito [the Little Deaf Mute]-Jerónimo and Inés-Iris-
Peta Ponce), the concept and use of masks, and the significance of the erotic in
Donoso's thematic intentions. Stabb concludes, in part, that the erotic for
Donoso, "is a dark force, tinged with the satanic and leading only to obsessive
desire and a fruitless quest for pleasure or release." It is, he continues, "clearly
a defining characteristic of that *obscene* nightbird chattering in the 'unsubdued
forest.'" An interesting perspective on this aspect of Donoso's novel. Titles and
quotations in Spanish.

This Sunday (Este domingo)
McMurray, George R. "A Period of Transition (1957-1966)." In his *José Donoso*.
Boston: Twayne, 1979.

In a thirty-page chapter examining *Coronation* and *This Sunday* as transitional works in Donoso's literary production, McMurray dedicates roughly seventeen pages to the latter novel, which, according to the critic, "indicates a new phase in the author's career, characterized by a tendency to explore in greater depth the unconscious realm of his protagonists and the skillful integration of form and content." A comprehensive study treating the novel's plot, characters, theme, structure, and technique. In a conclusion, McMurray compares the novel favorably to its predecessor *Coronation*, calling *This Sunday* "a finely wrought work of art exhibiting a firm equilibrium of authorial compulsion and control." An excellent study. Titles and quotations in English.

CARLOS FUENTES
Mexico

Biography

Faris, Wendy B. "Biographical Introduction." In her *Carlos Fuentes*. New York: Frederick Ungar, 1983.

A fourteen-page chapter on Fuentes' life and career, with emphasis on the latter. Includes commentary on Fuentes' political inclinations and his expression of them through his writings, and, to a lesser degree, his lifestyle. ("Though he lives very comfortably, Fuentes affirms his opposition to the capitalist system by owning no major property other than books and paintings.") The chapter also provides an overview of the Mexican author's works, with limited commentary on each. A good introduction to Fuentes the man and the writer. A fairly detailed chronology precedes the chapter. Titles and quotations in English.

Guzmán, Daniel de. "Personal Formation." In his *Carlos Fuentes*. New York: Twayne, 1972.

A twelve-page chapter that is not so much a biographical sketch of the Mexican writer as it is a portrait of the man based largely on his past in general and, in particular, various circumstances, events, decisions, and influences (such as his life as a diplomat's son, his decision to be a writer, his association with Marxists, and his decision to leave Mexico) which have had an effect on him. An interesting chapter, but short on biographical facts (such as dates) for the reader interested in such information. Titles in English or in Spanish with English translations.

Schwartz, Ronald. "Fuentes: Mexican Roots, Myths, Images." In his *Nomads, Exiles, and Émigrés: The Rebirth of the Latin American Narrative, 1960-80*. Metuchen, N.J.: Scarecrow Press, 1980.

This chapter appears to have three purposes: (1) to provide a biographical sketch of Fuentes, (2) to make some critical comments concerning *Terra Nostra*, and (3) to examine to some degree the novel *The Hydra Head*. The biographical sketch occupies approximately five pages of the ten-page chapter, and, in spite of its brevity, provides considerable information on the Mexican writer's life and career, including a chronological overview of his fiction, essays, theater, and screenplays. Informative. Titles in English.

Commentary

Davis, Mary E. "The Haunted Voice: Echoes of William Faulkner in García Márquez, Fuentes, and Vargas Llosa." *World Literature Today* 59 (Autumn, 1985): 531-535.

Davis devotes considerable space in her study to the nature and development of

Faulkner's unique voice and to how and why that voice has played so well in Latin America. When she focuses on the presence of Faulkner in Fuentes' works, she compares *Terra Nostra* to *A Fable*; Fuentes' female characters to Faulkner's Caddy Compson, Dilsey, Granny, and Drusilla of *The Unvanquished*; and *The Death of Artemio Cruz* to *As I Lay Dying*. An interesting article. Titles and quotations in English.

Doezema, Herman P. "An Interview with Carlos Fuentes." *Modern Fiction Studies* 18 (Winter, 1972-1973): 491-503.

In an interview conducted at his home in February of 1972, Fuentes responds to a series of questions, many of which focus on his novel *A Change of Skin* (chiefly concerning this novel in the evolution of the novel genre in general, its relation to his other works, the role of its narrator and reader, the role of its reader compared to that of Cortázar's *Hopscotch*, and the social purpose of the work). Other topics discussed include Fuentes' ideas on the novel genre, his audience, his thoughts on using literature as a vehicle for political messages, his work and interest in film, his fascination with *Citizen Kane*, and how this film compares to *The Death of Artemio Cruz*. Insightful interview. Frank discussion. Titles in Spanish.

Durán, Gloria B. *The Archetypes of Carlos Fuentes: From Witch to Androgyne.* Hamden, Ct.: Shoe String Press, 1980.

This book is based on Durán's claim that "there is at least one sorceress, implicit or explicit, who dominates nearly every one of Fuentes' novels." According to the critic, the "sorceress or witch stands as a guide to the subterranean world of the unconscious, which is the world that has increasingly preoccupied Fuentes." Her study officially begins with a brief examination of the importance of mythology for Fuentes, followed by a chapter entitled "The Witch as a Historical, Psychological and Social Theme," and chapters such as "*Aura* and Its Precedents in Fuentes' Earlier Works," with individual chapters dedicated to *Holy Place*, *A Change of Skin*, *Birthday*, *Terra Nostra*, and *The Hydra Head*. An interesting study of an essentially ignored aspect of Fuentes' works. Contains an excellent index, an appendix (two letters from Fuentes to Durán, one in English, the other in Spanish), and a primary and secondary bibliography in Spanish and English. Titles and quotations in English.

Dwyer, John P. "Conversation with a Blue Novelist." *Review 74* (Fall, 1974): 54-58.

In an interesting interview conducted in New York in October of 1973, Fuentes responds to questions concerning the nature of *Terra Nostra* (which he was writing at the time, though no title is mentioned here), whether he would rewrite any of his earlier works, the influence of poetry on the Latin American novel, the problem of translation, José Donoso's *The Boom in Spanish Ameri-*

can Literature: A Personal History, the "Boom" itself, and other topics. Most titles in Spanish with English translations.

Faris, Wendy B. *Carlos Fuentes*. New York: Frederick Ungar, 1983.
A fine book-length study of Fuentes' life and works (particularly the latter). A "Biographical Introduction" is followed by lengthy chapters entitled "Early Novels: Ancestral Presences, Modern Quests"; "Short Fiction and Theatre: Magical Realism, Symbolic Action"; "Poetics and Politics: The Essays"; "Later Novels: Psychology, Pop, and the Past"; and "Conclusion: The Multivocal Text." Individual works are treated in separate sections within these chapters, sections in which the critic provides "essentially self-contained analysis of individual works so that the reader may consult sections of this study individually." A fine overview of Fuentes' works with considerable detailed analysis. Should help the reader better understand the Mexican writer's works. Includes a chronology of Fuentes' life and career and an excellent index. Primary and secondary bibliography in Spanish and English. Quotations in English.

Fraser, Howard. "Carlos Fuentes." In *Critical Surveys of Long Fiction* (Foreign Language Series), edited by Frank N. Magill, vol. 2. Pasadena, Calif.: Salem Press, 1984.
An eleven-page overview of Fuentes' work in long fiction. Contains a list of his major novels (all with English translations), a summary of his work in other literary forms, and an assessment of his achievements. This is followed by a biographical sketch and a eight-page overview and analysis of his major novels, most notably *Terra Nostra*, *Aura*, *Distant Relations*, and *The Death of Artemio Cruz*. A good introduction to Fuentes for the reader unfamiliar with his work in general and his novels in particular. Includes a list of his other major works (some only in Spanish) and a short critical bibliography in English. Titles of translated works in English.

Guzmán, Daniel de. *Carlos Fuentes*. New York: Twayne, 1972.
An excellent overview of Fuentes' life and career through the late 1960's. Considerable attention (five rather short chapters) paid to the literary, cultural, and political environment of which Fuentes is a product. Provides a biographically oriented chapter as well as a chapter on the Mexican writer's short stories and another lengthy (forty-page) chapter (entitled "The Novels") on his novels through *A Change of Skin*. A chapter on Fuentes' "Other Writings" and a conclusion (bearing the title "Appraisal"). A solid and very readable guide to Fuentes' works. Includes a chronology of Mexican history (chiefly concerning the Mexican Revolution) and Fuentes' life and career through 1967, a very good index, and primary and secondary bibliographies (the latter annotated) in Spanish and English. Titles and quotations in English.

Harss, Luis, and Barbara Dohmann. "Carlos Fuentes, or the New Heresy." In their *Into the Mainstream: Conversations with Latin American Writers*. New York: Harper & Row, 1967.

An interview-based discussion of Fuentes and his works. Contains considerable background on postrevolutionary Mexican literature and society, the literary and social environment into which Fuentes was born and in which he began to write. Includes a fair amount of information on his life and early career. The section in which the beginning of the interview is related even contains a description of Fuentes' home in the Mexico City suburbs. Most of the chapter, however, is devoted to an overview of Fuentes' novels (through the mid-1960's), consisting chiefly of the cogent observations of Harss and Dohmann, but supplemented nicely with comments from Fuentes himself. A classic piece of criticism and a fine, at times up-close, introduction to the writer and his works. Titles in Spanish with English translations. Quotations in English.

Leal, Luis. "History and Myth in the Narrative of Carlos Fuentes." In *Carlos Fuentes: A Critical View*, edited by Robert Brody and Charles Rossman. Austin: University of Texas Press, 1982.

Fuentes, Leal contends, has created a fiction "that gives a mythified version of history without sacrificing the aesthetic elements so essential in the new novel." Leal's article traces the presence of history and myth in Fuentes' works and the technical skill with which the Mexican author has incorporated these elements into the text while producing works of high artistic quality. Among the numerous conclusions the critic draws from his detailed investigation of the subject is that Fuentes "swerved strongly at the beginning toward the historical, and strongly after 1969 toward the mythical, but never in a pure form." Most titles in Spanish, others in English. Quotations in English.

McMurray, George R. "Carlos Fuentes." In *Latin American Literature in the Twentieth Century: A Guide*, edited by Leonard S. Klein. New York: Frederick Ungar, 1986.

A brief (two-and-a-half-page) introduction to Fuentes' life and works. Very short discussion of his major narrative fiction as well as his work in theater, essay, and literary criticism. A paragraph dedicated to his place in both the North and Latin American novel. A good starting point for the reader unfamiliar with the Mexican writer. Contains a list of Fuentes' works (some titles in Spanish with English translations, others only in Spanish). Short critical bibliography in Spanish and English.

_____ . "Major Figures of the Boom." In his *Spanish American Writing Since 1941: A Critical Survey*. New York: Frederick Ungar, 1987.

McMurray devotes approximately eight pages of this section of his book to a brief overview of Fuentes' fiction. Following an introductory paragraph, the critic offers concise commentary on each of the Mexican author's major fictional works, including his short stories. A good starting point for the reader unfamiliar with Fuentes. Titles in Spanish with English translations.

World Literature Today 57 (Autumn, 1983): 529-598. Issue focusing on Carlos Fuentes.

This issue contains a wide-ranging collection of pieces on Carlos Fuentes and his works. Titles include "*Terra Nostra*: Coming to Grips with History by Jaime Alazraki, "Carlos Fuentes: The Burden of History" by Alfred J. Mac Adam, "The End of *Terra Nostra*" by Allen Josephs, "Carlos Fuentes: A Permanent Bedazzlement" by Gustavo Sainz, and "The Return of the Past: Chiasmus in the Texts of Carlos Fuentes" by Margaret Sayers Peden. Also includes an essay by Fuentes himself, entitled "On Reading and Writing Myself: How I Wrote *Aura*." Contains a chronology of Fuentes'life and career and numerous photographs. Primary and secondary bibliography in various languages. Most titles and virtually all quotations in Spanish with English translations.

Aura

Alazraki, Jaime. "Theme and System in Carlos Fuentes' *Aura*." In *Carlos Fuentes: A Critical View*, edited by Robert Brody and Charles Rossman. Austin: University of Texas Press, 1982.

Alazraki begins by comparing *Aura* to the Gothic novel and by attempting, as well, to establish sources for the work, focusing finally on Jules Michelet's *La Sorcière*. The critic cites several similarities between the two works, contending that "the ingredients of Fuentes' narrative . . . come mostly from" Michelet's work. He adds later that "one must look for *Aura*'s originality more in its expression than its content." This expression, Alazraki shows in his detailed analysis of the text, is characterized by various dualities (often superimposed), concerning everything from the nature of the characters themselves, to the use of dark and light images, to the use of a narrator-protagonist, even to the presence of two languages (Spanish and French). By virtue of these dualities in the novel's system of expression, Alazraki contends, "theme and system shake hands." Titles and quotations in English.

Ciccone, Anthony. "The Artistic Depiction of the Element of Fantasy-Reality in *Aura* (1962) by Carlos Fuentes." *Kentucky Romance Quarterly* 24 (1977): 47-54.

Ciccone examines Fuentes' employment of narrative person (chiefly concerning Felipe's "multi-dimensional role and the reliability of his perception"); space (focusing on the house and the other houses on the street, with their varied architectural styles); and time (an "alternate time possess[ing] a stationary and unchanging element of past, present, and future"), "in an effort to demonstrate the efficacy of these techniques in artistically portraying the element of reality-irreality present in the novella." A detailed, well-documented study. Titles and quotations in Spanish.

Dauster, Frank. "The Wounded Vision: *Aura, Zona sagrada*, and *Cumpleaños*." In *Carlos Fuentes: A Critical View*, edited by Robert Brody and Charles Rossman. Austin: University of Texas Press, 1982.

In sections entitled, "*Aura*: The Disordered Vision," "*Zona sagrada*: The Descent into Madness," and "*Cumpleaños*: The Vision Disturbed," Dauster examines the "implications of the unreliable narrator" in the three works, contending that the resemblances among them "are so strong that the novels appear to be three stages in a process of psychotic breakdown and healing." Montero, of *Aura*, Dauster concludes, enters into the delusion; Mito, of *Holy Place*, suffers "psychotic destruction"; and George, of *Birthday*, experiences a "return to life, scarred but healed." Interesting reading of the three works together. Titles in Spanish. Quotations in English.

Durán, Gloria. "*Aura* and Its Precedents in Fuentes' Earlier Works." In her *The Archtypes of Carlos Fuentes: From Witch to Androgyne*. Hamden, Ct.: Shoe String Press, 1980.

In a book-length study of the presence and role of the witch archetype in Fuentes' major works, Durán dedicates this thirty-two page chapter to, as the title indicates, *Aura* and its precedents in Fuentes' earlier works. The critic examines the plot, archetypal patterns, and themes of *Aura*, and then devotes individual sections of the chapter to a study of the witches present in *The Death of Artemio Cruz* and *Where the Air Is Clear*, with a final section entitled "Types of Witches in Fuentes up to 1962." An interesting perspective on the works in question. Titles and quotations in English.

Faris, Wendy B. "The Witches of Desire: *Aura*." In her *Carlos Fuentes*. New York: Frederick Ungar, 1983.

In a chapter on Fuentes' short fiction and theater, Faris devotes a short section (six pages) to a discussion of *Aura*, which, she contends at one point, "seems to be a classic example of magical realism, where the magical grows out of the real." In the course of her discussion of the work, Faris treats the novella's plot, its second-person narration, its many details which "suggest that mysterious forces may be at work," its thematic connection to Mexican history, and its similarity to Henry James's *The Aspern Papers* and Nathaniel Hawthorne's "Rappaccini's Daughter." Provides a good overview. Concise and informative. Titles and quotations in English.

Guzmán, Daniel de. "The Novels." In his *Carlos Fuentes*. New York: Twayne, 1972. A discussion of *Aura* occupies approximately eight pages of this forty-page chapter on Fuentes' novels through *A Change of Skin*. The critic treats the mix of reality and fantasy (and the role of dreams) in the work as well as its narrative voice (and its effect), before moving on to a lengthy summary of the plot. The critic finally considers the opinion of both Fuentes and others concerning this short novel. A very good overview and analysis of the work in question. Titles and quotations in English.

Rojas, Nelson. "Time and Sense in Carlos Fuentes' *Aura*." *Hispania* 61 (December, 1978): 859-864.

Rojas explores "the interrelationship between the Spanish verbal system and the narrator's very special conception of time in which, by means of a skillful manipulation of the verbal system, the 'present' is seen as a fleeting instant which is replaced by another fleeting instant which is in turn replaced by yet another fleeting instant, *ad infinitum*." The critic contends that the narrator creates the "illusion of a continuously moving narration" through the use of enumeration and active, rather than static, verbs. Rojas also discusses the extensive and special use of the future tense in the chiefly present-tense narration. Includes numerous examples. Titles and quotations in Spanish.

A Change of Skin (Cambio de piel)

Doezema, Herman P. "An Interview with Carlos Fuentes." *Modern Fiction Studies* 18 (1972-1973): 491-503.

In an interview conducted at his home in February of 1972, Fuentes responds to a series of questions, many of which concern *A Change of Skin*. Questions with regard to this novel touch on *A Change of Skin* as, to use Doezema's words, "an attempt to break through a crisis that . . . the novel [genre] faces today," as well as this work in relation to Fuentes' other novels, his narrative technique, the role of the novel's narrator and its reader, the role of the reader of Fuentes' novel and that of Cortázar's *Hopscotch*, the story behind Freddy Lambert's name, and the social purpose of the novel. An insightful and frank interview. Titles in English.

Durán, Gloria. "*Change of Skin*." In her *The Archtypes of Carlos Fuentes: From Witch to Androgyne*. Hamden, Conn. Shoe String Press, 1980.

In sections (and subsections) entitled "The Theme of Woman as Witch"; "Ophelia, the Mother"; "Elizabeth, Dragona-Ligera"; "The Characters: Real and Unreal"; "Sacrifice: The Witch as Sacrificial Victim"; "Witches and Nazis"; "The Monks"; "The Narrative Precedent in Ixca Cienfuegos"; "Intellectualism and Archtypes"; "The Archtypal Mask"; and others, Durán presents a detailed and lengthy (thirty-four-page) study focusing primarily on the influence, presence, and significance of the witch archetype in *A Change of Skin*. Titles and quotations in English.

_____ . "Dolls and Puppets as Wish Fulfillment Symbols in Carlos Fuentes." In *Carlos Fuentes: A Critical View*, edited by Robert Brody and Charles Rossman. Austin: University of Texas Press, 1982.

Durán examines the role of dolls in Fuentes' *A Change of Skin*, "The Doll Queen," and *Holy Place*. The critic's analysis of dolls in *A Change of Skin* centers on Herr Urs. Durán concludes, in part, that dolls in Fuentes' works "can satisfy a craving for love which is divorced from reality (as in "The Doll Queen"); they can substitute for the real object of our desire (as Bela does in *Zona sagrada* [*Holy Place*]); they can serve as the sadomasochistic feelings of the relatively powerless (as was the case of Herr Urs and of Mito and Giancarlo [these last two from *Holy Place*]). Most titles in Spanish. Quotations in English.

Faris, Wendy B. "Breaking Mental Habits: *A Change of Skin*." In her *Carlos Fuentes*. New York: Frederick Ungar, 1983.

In this fourteen-page section of a lengthy chapter entitled "Later Novels: Psychology, Pop, and the Past," Faris presents an analysis of *A Change of Skin* in which she examines the novel's plot, its structure, its treatment of time (a novel in which the "rules of temporal logic do not apply"), its characters and their connection to a mythic past, the "changing of skin" or switching of not only the characters but also of the narrator(s), the mixing of classic and traditional with current and pop, and the link between the novel's violent present and the Spanish Conquest and the Nazi campaign against the Jews. An excellent overall analysis of the work in question. Very readable. Should help the reader of this difficult novel. Titles and quotations in English.

Filer, Malva E. "*A Change of Skin* and the Shaping of Mexican Time." In *Carlos Fuentes: A Critical View*, edited by Robert Brody and Charles Rossman. Austin: University of Texas Press, 1982.

Filer begins by citing the contention of Octavio Paz that Mexicans are "contemporaries of all mankind," a concept which, the critic believes, lies at the center of Fuentes' writings, including *A Change of Skin*. The purpose of her article is to "analyze some aspects of this novel as they relate to the author's view of Mexico and that country's possible role in a culturally pluralistic world." After an examination of these aspects, she concludes, in part, that in this novel, "not only are Mexicans the contemporaries of all mankind, but all mankind has been made to participate in the exorcism and the shaping, of a Mexican time." Titles (with only one exception) and quotations in English.

Guzmán, Daniel de. "The Novels." In his *Carlos Fuentes*. New York: Twayne, 1972.

Approximately five pages of this chapter on Fuentes' novels are devoted to a discussion of *A Change of Skin*, the last (in chronological order) of the works treated in the chapter. Brief mention of the difficulties surrounding the publication of the novel (censured in Spain and eventually published in Mexico) and its plot. Most attention (though only in the manner of a general overview) paid to the nature of the novel's narrative, concentrating on technique, as well as the novel's "themes of myth-reality-fantasy." Titles in English.

Knight, Thomas J. "The Setting of *Cambio de piel.*" *Romance Notes* 24 (Spring, 1984): 229-232.

Precisely as the title indicates, this is an article about the setting of *A Change of Skin*, and, specifically, the Pyramid of Cholula, the setting, as Knight states, of the novel's "imagined deaths and resurrections." This is not an article of in-depth literary analysis, however. It is, instead, a detailed, almost step-by-step travelogue of what one sees, and what Fuentes' characters see, when visiting the pyramid. The critic/"guide" places what is seen in both historical and literary contexts. An interesting article that brings Fuentes' setting to life and into a rather clear context or focus. Title of Fuentes' novel, as indicated in the title of the article, in Spanish. No quotations.

The Death of Artemio Cruz (La muerte de Artemio Cruz)

Boldy, Steven. "Fathers and Sons in Fuentes' *La muerte de Artemio Cruz.*" *Bulletin of Hispanic Studies* 61 (January, 1984): 31-40.

Boldy contends that beneath the superficial structure of *The Death of Artemio Cruz* there is "a deeper structure," one characterized by "an archetypal structure of father, legitimate son and illegitimate son or symbolic heir which occurs three times in the novel." The critic goes on to suggest that "the two 'sons' are opposites, representing dual alternative forces in the Mexican history and psyche." He provides an in-depth examination of the text to support his contentions and in the process presents a fascinating study of Fuentes' work from an unusual perspective. Titles and quotations in Spanish.

Faris, Wendy B. "Fragmenting Forces in the Revolution and the Self: *The Death of Artemio Cruz.*" In her *Carlos Fuentes*. New York: Frederick Ungar, 1983.

Divided into an introductory section as well as sections entitled "Central Events and Images"; "The Revolution—And After: History and the Land"; "Social Criticism"; "Private Power"; "The Self: 'Memory Is Desire Satisfied'"; "Narrative Technique"; and "Style and Language"; this twenty-two-page discussion of Fuentes' novel treats numerous elements of the work, from its plot to its theme, to its presentation. A fine, wide-ranging overview of the work. Very readable. Titles and quotations in English.

Guzmán, Daniel de. "The Novels." In his *Carlos Fuentes*. New York: Twayne, 1972.

Roughly ten pages of this forty-page chapter are devoted to a discussion of *The Death of Artemio Cruz*. The critic chronicles the critical reception the novel received on publication, followed by a description of the narrative and a rather detailed plot summary (with commentary on characters, theme, and the reader's experience throughout). Considerable space is dedicated to other critics' views of the novel, the literary influences apparent in it, and, finally, the significance of this work within the context of Fuentes' evolution (and career) as a writer. Excellent overview and analysis of the novel in question. Titles and quotations in English.

Gyurko, Lanin A. "*La muerte de Artemio Cruz* and *Citizen Kane*: A Comparative Analysis." In *Carlos Fuentes: A Critical View*, edited by Robert Brody and Charles Rossman. Austin: University of Texas Press, 1982.
Gyurko cites the influence of Orson Welles's film *Citizen Kane* on Fuentes in general and on his *The Death of Artemio Cruz* in particular, claiming that the influence of the film on the novel begins with the protagonist but continues with "the structure of Fuentes' novel, with its multiple and constantly shifting points of view on the protagonist, its evocation of Cruz's life not as a chronological progression from birth to death but as a series of fragments that shift rapidly in time, from Cruz's early career to his old age and back to his childhood in response to the associational flux of his stricken consciousness, and in its style—its dramatic intensity, its mannered delivery, and its baroque pyramiding of images." Gyurko presents a detailed examination of these and other similarities of influence between the film and the novel. Titles of Fuentes' works in Spanish. Quotations in English.

_____ . "Structure and Theme in Fuentes' *La muerte de Artemio Cruz*." *Symposium* 34 (Spring, 1980): 29-41.
Gyurko presents a detailed analysis of the structure of *The Death of Artemio Cruz* and how it relates to the presentation and nature of the protagonist and in turn how it relates to the novel's theme. The critic makes numerous cogent observations concerning the triadic structure of the narrative, which Gyurko contends "convey[s] Cruz's negative states, his permanent isolation, alienation, and disintegration," but which also shows a positive side in that the "creation of multiple selves constitutes an attempt by the failing Cruz to revivify himself and thereby to score a victory over death." The critic's analysis leads him to conclude, in part, that if the protagonist is viewed "as a symbol of modern Mexico, then the permanent splitting in his identity mounts the stinging attack that Fuentes makes . . . in this novel . . . an indictment of a country whose idealists . . . are continually sacrificed, just as is the idealistic center of Cruz himself." Titles and quotations in Spanish.

Hellerman, M. Kasey. "The Coatlicue-Malinche Conflict: A Mother and Son Identity Crisis in the Writings of Carlos Fuentes." *Hispania* 57 (December, 1974): 868-875.
Hellerman first explains the nature of the Coatlicue-Malinche conflict and then

discusses its presence in four of Fuentes' works, including *The Death of Artemio Cruz*. The critic finds two manifestations of the conflict in this work. First, Catalina seeks comfort, "a surrogate protector and lover," in her son, Lorenzo. He is physically far from her influence, however, and later goes to Spain where he dies, Fuentes' example of a son of the Malinche who "fulfills his life mission because he is unhindered by maternal fantasies and aspirations." In the same work, Regina uses the Coatlicue myth to convince herself that she and Cruz met by chance on the beach rather than through the kidnapping and violent rape which actually took place. A fascinating article. Titles and quotations in Spanish.

Jiménez-Fajardo, Salvador. "The Redeeming Quest: Patterns of Unification in Carpentier, Fuentes and Cortázar." *Revista de Estudios Hispánicos* 11 (January, 1987): 91-117.

Jiménez-Fajardo's lengthy (twenty-eight-page) article is intended as a detailed comparative study of the "basic coincidence" which *The Death of Artemio Cruz* and *Hopscotch* share with an earlier work, Alejo Carpentier's "Journey to the Source." He examines Carpentier's work and those of Fuentes and Cortázar to find, in part, that *The Death of Artemio Cruz* and *Hopscotch*, through their similarities to "Journey to the Source," allow the reader "to go beyond the failures of the protagonists in their quest for an integrated vision and to participate in an instance of esthetic unity elaborated out of the seemingly unintegrated elements of their chaos." Titles and quotations in Spanish and French.

Shaw, Donald L. "Narrative Arrangement in *La muerte de Artemio Cruz*." In *Contemporary Latin American Fiction*, edited by Salvador Bacarisse. Edinburgh: Scottish Academic Press, 1980.

A truly excellent article in which Shaw meticulously examines the narrative arrangement of Fuentes' novel to prove that the work, "far from an arbitrary jumble, or merely bodying forth a mechanical relationship between private objection and public success, represents the triumph of a conscious artistic intention over a conventional arrangement of episodes." The critic not only discusses the intentional and meaningful arrangement of events (an arrangement with chapters which deliberately complement or contrast one another and a clearly marked structural center), but he considers in the process of his explanation of the novel's structure why the Mexican author arranges his work as he does, the advantage that such an unconventional narrative organization has over a purely chronological one. Interesting, enlightening, and very readable. Titles and quotations in Spanish.

Sommers, Joseph. "The Field of Choice: Carlos Fuentes." In his *After the Storm: Landmarks of the Modern Mexican Novel*. Albuquerque: University of New Mexico Press, 1968.

A somewhat brief (twelve-page) discussion of *The Death of Artemio Cruz*. Sommers briefly treats the novel's tone, structure, point of view, and treatment of time. Considerably more space is devoted to the work's theme and an overall assessment of its literary quality. Some comparison throughout between the novel in question and *Where the Air Is Clear*. Detailed and with numerous examples despite its brevity. A good overview and introduction to the work. Very readable. Titles and quotations in English.

Vázquez Amaral, José. *"The Death of Artemio Cruz* by Carlos Fuentes." In his *The Contemporary Latin American Narrative*. New York: Las Américas, 1970.
In a short (seven-page) chapter which is part overview and part review, Vázquez Amaral discusses various aspects of Fuentes' novel. A considerable portion of the chapter, for example, is devoted to a comparison between Fuentes' work (and the characters therein) and Mariano Azuela's *The Underdogs* as two novels of the Mexican Revolution. The critic also places Fuentes' novel within the context of the Mexican writer's career, particularly as it compares to *Where the Air Is Clear*. Finally, Vázquez Amaral criticizes Fuentes for including what the critic calls "Lorenzo Cruz's misfortunes in Spain," which the critic views as "a very ugly blemish in a very well written and a very good novel." Contains interesting observations. Titles in English.

Walter, Richard J. "Literature and History in Contemporary Latin America." *Latin American Literary Review* 15 (January-June, 1987): 173-182.
Walter calls *The Death of Artemio Cruz*, García Márquez' *One Hundred Years of Solitude*, and Vargas Llosa's *The War of the End of the World* "essential reading for any historian of Latin America." He contends as well that any reader, historian or not, would better appreciate these works if said reader knew and understood "the historical context in which they are set." Walter provides this context for each novel (in the case of Fuentes' novel, the Mexican Revolution and its legacy), before assessing the value of each one for the historian (Fuentes, in part, the critic contends, brings "great events and the large sweep of history down to the personal and individual level") and concluding that all three authors deal with "the consequences of modernization for traditional societies," the problem of revolution (and its accompanying violence and "ideological confusion"), the role of charismatic leaders, and eventual frustration with the revolution. Particularly useful for the reader unfamiliar with Latin American history. All titles (except one in Portuguese with an English translation) and quotations in English.

Distant Relations (Una familia lejana)

Faris, Wendy B. " 'Proustitution' ? ? Distant Relations." In her *Carlos Fuentes*. New York: Frederick Ungar, 1983.
A roughly eleven-page section dedicated to an analytical overview of the novel

in question. Faris discusses the nature of the novel, its similarities to Fuentes' other works, its plot, the significance of its title (citing the original Spanish title as well to provide an even more accurate interpretation of Fuentes' choice of words), its potential connection to Latin American literary history (with possible references to Carpentier and Borges, for example), and, most of all, as indicated in the title, the similarities between Fuentes' work and that of Marcel Proust, specifically *Remembrance of Things Past*. A considerable portion of Faris' discussion of the work focuses on the thematic significance of memory and the past. Titles and quotations in English.

Smith, Gilbert. *"Distant Relations."* In *Magill's Literary Annual*, 1983, edited by Frank N. Magill, vol. 1. Pasadena, Calif.: Salem Press, 1983.
   Smith begins his four-page overview of *Distant Relations* by briefly discussing its similarities to *The Death of Artemio Cruz* and *Terra Nostra*. This is followed by a discussion of the nature of the novel's story, Fuentes' incorporation of the supernatural into the work, the "personal" aspect of the work based on the "very strong identification between the fictional narrator and the 'real' novelist," the thematic question concerning the nature of the narrative, and the theme concerning "the complex cultural milieu of the New World manipulated and distorted by the European tradition, transformed into what it is today." "Sources for Further Study" section lists reviews of the work (in English). Titles and quotations in English.

The Good Conscience (Las buenas conciencias)

Faris, Wendy B. "Tradition, Repression, and Independence: *The Good Conscience*." In her *Carlos Fuentes*. New York: Frederick Ungar, 1983.
   A very brief (roughly six-page) treatment of the novel in question. Very short on analysis, this section of a much longer chapter on Fuentes' early novels focuses on the plot of *The Good Conscience* with some consideration of the work's theme interspersed in the summary of its plot. A good, general introduction for the reader unfamiliar with the novel. Title and quotations in English.

Guzmán, Daniel de. "The Novels." In his *Carlos Fuentes*. New York: Twayne, 1972.
   Guzmán devotes roughly six pages of this forty-page chapter to *The Good Conscience*. The critic discusses the nature of the novel's narrative (particularly as it relates to the novels by Fuentes which both precede and follow it) and the thematic significance of the title. This is followed by a lengthy and detailed plot summary. The section concludes with consideration of the work's autobiographical content, the various literary influences present in it, and its style. An excellent overview and analysis of the work. Very readable. Titles and quotations in English.

Gyurko, Lanin A. "The Stifling of Identity in Fuentes' *Las buenas conciencias.*" *Hispania* 59 (May, 1976): 225-238.

Gyurko states that in *The Good Conscience* "there is a contrast between the efforts made by the characters to construct an independent identity and the repressive forces that thwart those attempts." The critic claims that these constrictions are both external (society and family tradition) and internal (the individual's lack of will and courage to break out of his "privileged class and family structure"). Gyurko provides a thorough examination of this aspect of the novel by studying the characters, their actions and interactions, and more technical aspects of the narrative, all of which reflect the "stifling of identity" to which the critic refers. Titles and quotations in Spanish.

Hellerman, M. Kasey. "The Coatlicue-Malinche Conflict: A Mother and Son Identity Crisis in the Writings of Carlos Fuentes." *Hispania* 57 (December, 1974): 868-875.

After beginning his article with a concise background sketch of the information necessary to understand the Coatlicue-Malinche conflict, Hellerman moves on to an examination of this conflict in four of Fuentes' works, including *The Good Conscience*. The critic targets Asunción Balcárcel as a "victim" of the conflict by being, in effect, a mother without conception (or birth, for that matter). Her role as Jaime's mother and her denial and rejection of his real mother (the Malinche figure in this arrangement), in addition to the attraction that exists between Asunción and Jaime, create confusion in the boy, an identity crisis. "Stifled by Asunción's fantasies," Hellerman writes, "Jaime is unaware of his heritage" as a son of the Malinche, and as a result follows the false side of his lineage. A fascinating article. Titles and quotations in Spanish.

Holy Place (Zona sagrada)

Dauster, Frank. "The Wounded Vision: *Aura*, *Zona sagrada*, and *Cumpleaños.*" In *Carlos Fuentes: A Critical View*, edited by Robert Brody and Charles Rossman. Austin: University of Texas Press, 1982.

Dauster divides his article into three sections, "*Aura*: The Disordered Vision"; "*Zona sagrada*: The Descent into Madness"; and "*Cumpleaños*: The Vision Disturbed" to examine the "implications of the unreliable narrator" in the three works, contending that the resemblances among them "are so strong that the novels appear to be three stages in a process of psychotic breakdown and healing." While Montero, of *Aura*, Dauster concludes, enters into the delusion; Mito, of *Holy Place*, suffers "psychotic destruction"; and George, of *Birthday*, experiences a "return to life, scarred but healed." Interesting reading of the three works together. Titles in Spanish. Quotations in English.

Durán, Gloria. "Dolls and Puppets as Wish Fulfillment Symbols in Carlos Fuentes." In *Carlos Fuentes: A Critical View*, edited by Robert Brody and

Charles Rossman. Austin: University of Texas Press, 1982.

Durán examines the role of dolls in Fuentes' *Holy Place*, "The Doll Queen," and *A Change of Skin*. The critic's analysis of dolls in *Holy Place* centers on Claudia, Bela, Mito, and Giancarlo. She contends that dolls in Fuentes' works "can satisfy a craving for love which is divorced from reality (as in 'The Doll Queen'); they can substitute for the real object of our desire (as Bela does in *Zona sagrada* [*Holy Place*]); they can serve as the sadomasochistic feelings of the relatively powerless (as was the case of Herr Urs [of *A Change of Skin*] or Mito and Giancarlo). . . . They can also . . . be sacrificed and tortured with impunity . . . as the characters in *Zona sagrada* treat both living beings and objects or animals under their control." Most titles in Spanish. Quotations in English.

_____ . "*Holy Place*: The Consummate Witch." In her *The Archtypes of Carlos Fuentes: From Witch to Androgyne*. Hamden, Conn.: Shoe String Press, 1980.

In various sections, the titles of which include "The Central Character: Circe," "The Witch as Hermaphrodite," "Mexican Mythology and its Analogy to the Ulysses of Apolodorus (the Interpretation of Octavio Paz), "Claudia as 'La Chingadora,' " "Claudia as Witch," "Other Hermaphrodites," and "The Metaphysical Goal," Durán presents a detailed and lengthy (twenty-two-page) study focusing primarily on the influence, presence, and significance of the witch archetype in *Holy Place*. Titles and quotations in English.

Faris, Wendy B. "A Modern Idol: *Holy Place*." In her *Carlos Fuentes*. New York: Frederick Ungar, 1983.

This treatment of *Holy Place* appears within the context of a lengthy chapter entitled "Later Novels: Psychology, Pop, and the Past." Faris examines this novel, "an intensely focused work," in considerable detail, focusing on the work's plot, its characters and their interrelationships, references to mythology (both Greek and Aztec), and the significance of so-called "sacred spaces" in the work. Some reference as well to Franz Kafka's *The Metamorphosis*. A fine analysis and a solid overview of the work in question. Titles and quotations in English.

Guzmán, Daniel de. "The Novels." In his *Carlos Fuentes*. New York: Twayne, 1972.

Guzmán devotes only a little more than a page of this forty-page chapter to *Holy Place*, calling it a "great disappointment" and later stating that "we need not go into more detail because it cannot by any means be called an important work," and that the principal question concerning the work is why Fuentes wrote it in the first place. In a footnote, the critic goes even further, saying that there "is general embarrassment over this work in Mexico amongst Fuentes' friends and critics because the work is considered a transparent novelization of the life of the famous actress, María Félix, and her relationship with her son." Some mention of what the novel is about, but most of the roughly one-page essay (in addition to the lengthy footnote) is a condemnation of the work on various levels. Titles in English.

Gyurko, Lanin A. "The Myths of Ulysses in Fuente's *Zona sagrada.*" *Modern Language Review* 69 (April, 1974): 316-324.
Gyurko examines the many parallels to the Ulysses myth found in *Holy Place*. One of these has to do with Guillermo's relationship with his mother and its connection to a corruption of the Ulysses myth in which Ulysses' son kills him and marries Penelope. This is just one "alternate version of the myth" present in the novel, according to the critic, who states that the "members of the protagonist's family constitute either an inversion or an ironic deflation of the heroic personages of the *Odyssey.*" An interesting reading of the novel. Titles and quotations in Spanish.

Hellerman, M. Kasey. "The Coatlicue-Malinche Conflict: A Mother and Son Identity Crisis in the Writings of Carlos Fuentes." *Hispania* 57 (December, 1974): 868-875.
Hellerman provides a concise explanation of the Coatlicue-Malinche conflict and discusses its presence in four of Fuentes' novels, including *Holy Place*. The critic finds the conflict to be both strong and particularly complicated in this work as Claudia Nervo not only takes on the role of Coatlicue, but of Coatlicue's companion Aztec goddesses, Cihuacoatl and Tlazoltéotl as well, as she plays the part of both the good mother and the bad mother to son Guillermo. The result is that Guillermo, reared without his father's influence, and given the strong influence of his mother, "faces an identity problem caused by a dominant matriarchal environment." A fascinating article. Titles and quotations in Spanish.

The Hydra Head (La cabeza de hidra)
Davis, Mary E. "On Becoming Velázquez: Carlos Fuentes' *The Hydra Head.*" In *Carlos Fuentes: A Critical View*, edited by Robert Brody and Charles Rossman. Austin: University of Texas Press, 1982.
Davis traces the influence, presence, and significance of the seventeenth century Spanish painter Diego Velázquez and allusions to him and his works in *The Hydra Head*. Most attention is paid to the relationship between Félix and the painter, though some consideration is given as well to other signs of Velázquez' presence in the novel, most notably (and still related to Félix) the prominent presence of "Las meninas" ("The Ladies in Waiting"), which Davis calls "the warp and woof of the text." Titles and quotations in English.

Durán, Gloria. "The Hydra Head and the Tale." In her *The Archtypes of Carlos Fuentes: From Witch to Androgyne*. Hamden, Conn.: Shoe String Press, 1980.

In sections entitled "A Heroine of Three Parts"; "Appraisal of the Novel as Spy Thriller"; "Fuentes as Journalist"; "The Mythological Theme"; "Trevor/ Mann, the Wise Old Man"; "The Snare of Sex in Fuentes's Works"; "Fuentes's Fatalism"; "The Danger of Timelessness"; "Other Problems in the Mythical Approach"; and "The Genuine Fairy Tale" Durán presents a detailed and lengthy (eighteen-page) study of *The Hydra Head*, focusing primarily on the influence, presence, and significance of the witch archetype in the novel. Titles and quotations in English.

Faris, Wendy B. "New Resources, Familiar Patterns: *The Hydra Head*." In her *Carlos Fuentes*. New York: Frederick Ungar, 1983.
In her long chapter, "Later Novels: Psychology, Pop, and the Past," Faris dedicates some eight pages to *The Hydra Head*, a work in which "Fuentes reverses the habitual positions of popular and serious literature in many modern texts." She discusses the nature of this work, which she views as one of the Mexican author's "less ambitious" works, but "nevertheless an amusing, sometimes even an impassioned, narrative." She focuses chiefly on plot, the questions of identity, individuality, and the double in the work. She contends early on and supports throughout that though the novel is in an overall sense uncharacteristic of Fuentes' usual work, it nevertheless contains many Fuentes constants particularly regarding theme. Titles and quotations in English.

Schwartz, Ronald. "Fuentes: Mexican Roots, Myths, Images." In his *Nomads, Exiles, and Émigrés: The Rebirth of the Latin American Narrative, 1960-80*. Metuchen, N.J.: Scarecrow Press, 1980.
This chapter appears to have three purposes: (1) to provide a biographical sketch of Fuentes, (2) to make some critical and introductory comments concerning *Terra Nostra*, and (3) to examine to some degree the novel *The Hydra Head*. This final purpose occupies almost half of the ten-page chapter as the critic examines the plot, themes, technique, and overall nature of this "gutsy novel written with fun, verve, Kafka-esque plots, preposterous coincidences, and betrayals." Schwartz's conclusion is that while the novel is not up to Fuentes' usual standards it does represent "a new polarity for him." Titles and quotations in English.

The Old Gringo (El gringo viejo)

D'Lugo, Marvin. "*The Old Gringo*." In *Magill's Literary Annual*, 1986, edited by Frank N. Magill, vol. 2. Pasadena, Calif.: Salem Press, 1986.
D'Lugo provides an excellent five-page introduction to *The Old Gringo*, a novel, the critic contends, that "addresses readers from both countries [Mexico and the United States] and asks them to ponder the question of personal and national identity that artificial borders have constructed for them." D'Lugo's

discussion of the novel touches on (among other things) the work's basic plot, the use of memory (Harriet's) and historical fact in its telling, the nature and symbolism of its characters, and the novel's theme (returning in part to the critic's comments above): "destiny, identity, and the need to transcend the borders that confine individuals and communities." "Sources for Further Study" section lists reviews of the work (in English). Titles and quotations in English.

Terra Nostra

Chávez, John R. *"Terra Nostra."* In *Magill's Literary Annual*, 1977, edited by Frank N. Magill, vol. 2. Pasadena, Calif.: Salem Press, 1977.

Chávez introduces *Terra Nostra* and then spends roughly the first four pages of his five-page article providing a plot summary of the complex novel, a plot summary punctuated by critical comments and observations that both point out aspects of Fuentes' artistry and help explain certain elements of the narrative. A final lengthy paragraph discusses the nature (and what Chávez views as the defects—chiefly concerning the novel's complexity and the lack of psychological depth with respect to its characters) of the narrative, which the critic contends, "challenges the intellect, but leaves the emotions unmoved." Should definitely help the reader decipher the complex work. "Sources for Further Study" lists review articles of the novel (in English). Title in Latin.

Durán, Gloria. *"Terra Nostra*, The Witch and the Apocalypse" and *"Terra Nostra* and the Androgyne." In her *The Archtypes of Carlos Fuentes: From Witch to Androgyne*. Hamden, Conn.: Shoe String Press, 1980.

In sections entitled "The Great Mother before *Terra Nostra*," "Thirty-three: The Importance of Numbers," "The Aztec Heritage," "The Androgynous Ideal," "The Androgyne and the Hermaphrodite," "The Archetype of the Circle," "The Mandala," and others spread out over these two chapters (covering forty-six pages), Durán presents a detailed study of *Terra Nostra* focusing primarily on the influence, presence, and significance of the witch archetype in the novel. Titles and quotations in English.

Faris, Wendy B. "Old and New Worlds: *Terra Nostra*." In her *Carlos Fuentes*. New York: Frederick Ungar, 1983.

Faris' seventeen-page discussion of Fuentes' novel focuses first (in a brief introductory section) on the general nature of this complex work and then on its plot (including interpretation of events), followed by treatment of the novel's narrative voice. Most of the discussion of narrative voice focuses on the reader's frustrated experience in seeking control over the narrative. Reference is also made to "Fuentes' theory of multivocal reading and writing" as exposed in his *Cervantes or the Critique of Reading*, and how that theory may explain both the complex voice of his work and its similarities to *Don Quixote*.

A very good introduction to and overview of the work in question. Titles and quotations in English.

González Echevarría, Roberto. *"Terra Nostra*: Theory and Practice." In *Carlos Fuentes: A Critical View*, edited by Robert Brody and Charles Rossman. Austin: University of Texas Press, 1982.
   González Echevarría compares the theory present in Fuentes' essay *Cervantes o la crítica de la lectura* (*Cervantes or the Critique of Reading*) to the practice found in his novel *Terra Nostra*. To do this he pries "apart that relationship [between the essay and the novel] to see how the impulse to intelligibility and knowledge present in that essay is thwarted in the fiction; how, against the explicit and implicit intentions of both the essay and the novel, the latter renders the link between cultural specificity and literature questionable." This also affords the critic the opportunity "to make some observations about the recent history of the Latin American novel." Most titles in Spanish only. Quotations in English.

Kerr, Lucille. "The Paradox of Power and Mystery: Carlos Fuentes' *Terra nostra.*" *Publications of the Modern Language Association* 95 (January, 1980): 91-102.
   Kerr states that "it is primarily the power of the mystery that sustains Fuentes' readers through the 783 pages" of *Terra Nostra*, though the Mexican author's text creates more mysteries that it solves, all in an effort to have the reader continue reading though at the same time not master the text. The critic suggests that "Fuentes' authorial power play replicates the thematic paradox" of the novel, as Fuentes, like El Señor, in his efforts "to exercise control and create a univocal, and even linear reality, betrays himself while striving to create a simultaneous and perpetually multiple text that would contradict El Señor's linear and univocal reality." Kerr presents considerable examples to support and illustrate her contentions. Title in Spanish. Quotations in Spanish with English translations.

Peden, Margaret Sayers. "A Reader's Guide to *Terra Nostra.*" *Review 31* (January-April, 1982): 42-48.
   Just as the title indicates, this article is intended as a reader's guide to Fuentes' complex novel which, as Peden states, "poses, but does not answer questions." The critic approaches the novel in sections entitled "Sources and Resources"; "Voice and the Written Word"; "Time and Space"; "Character"; "Theme, Symbol, and Device"; and, finally, "Reading *Terra Nostra.*" In the process she suggests other works one might read before reading Fuentes' novel (most notably Fuentes' *Cervantes o la crítica de la lectura*, translated as Cervantes or the critique of reading) and otherwise, as much as simplify the text of the novel (which she indeed does), prepares the reader for the reading experience.

An excellent and very readable guide to the novel. Supplemented by a list of suggested further reading. Titles and quotations in English.

Where the Air Is Clear (La región más transparente)

Faris, Wendy B. "The Development of a Collective Voice: *Where the Air Is Clear*." In her *Carlos Fuentes*. New York: Frederick Ungar, 1983.

In a thirty-five-page chapter, Faris examines various elements of Fuentes' novel. Her principal contention is that *Where the Air Is Clear* is an urban novel in which Mexico City functions as the chief protagonist. But it is also a novel, she contends, which celebrates the mestizo, a work which juxtaposes ancient and modern cultures, a novel "built around the dualities that structure urban society in Mexico," dualities created in large part by the very juxtaposition emphasized by Fuentes and maintained in the nation's search for identity. She examines elements of the work which illustrate her contentions. Titles and quotations in English.

Guzmán, Daniel de. "The Novels." In his *Carlos Fuentes*. New York: Twayne, 1972.

In a forty-page chapter on Fuentes' novels through 1967, Guzmán devotes approximately seven pages to *Where the Air Is Clear*. The critic begins with the novel's title and its (and Fuentes') connection to Alfonso Reyes, and then moves on to a discussion of the work's Mexican theme and to some degree its structure, characters, and style. The critic concludes that the novel is "a contrived book, an artificial elaboration, modelled deliberately on successful predecessors," but he adds that "the road to originality is through imitation" and supports Fuentes' right to experiment, especially when he does it so well. Importance of knowledge of the Mexican Revolution emphasized. A good introduction to the novel in question. Titles and quotations in English.

Hellerman, M. Kasey. "The Coatlicue-Malinche Conflict: A Mother and Son Identity Crisis in the Writings of Carlos Fuentes." *Hispania* 57 (December, 1974): 868-875.

Hellerman begins his article by explaining the background information necessary to understand the Coatlicue-Malinche conflict and then examines it in four of Fuentes' novels, including *Where the Air Is Clear*. The critic examines Rosenda Pola's assumption of divine conception and her attempts to find in her son's personality what she had not found in his father's. This action is in the Coatlicue tradition and creates an identity problem for the son. Hellerman finds this typical behavior of Fuentes' mother characters who "try to impose the destiny of Huitzilopochtli on their *hijos de la chingada*" or the Malinche. A fascinating article. Titles and quotations in Spanish.

Reeve, Richard M. "The Making of *La región más transparente*: 1949-1974." In *Carlos Fuentes: A Critical View*, edited by Robert Brody and Charles Rossman. Austin: University of Texas Press, 1982.

In a brief introduction and sections entitled "Mexico in the 1950's," "Fore-shadowing of *La región más transparente* in Fuentes' Early Writings," "Real Life Sources," "Pre-Publication Fragments of *La región más transparente*," "First Reactions to the Novel," "Translations and Critical Reaction from Abroad," and "*La región más transparente* Today," Reeve traces *Where the Air Is Clear* from 1949, when the critic contends Fuentes began the novel, to 1974, when it was published in the Aguilar edition of the Mexican author's *Obras completas* (complete works) with its final revisions. Titles in Spanish. Quotations in English.

Sommers, Joseph. "The Quest for Identity: Carlos Fuentes." In his *After the Storm: Landmarks of the Modern Mexican Novel*. Albuquerque: University of New Mexico Press, 1968.

An excellent fifty-five page analysis of *Where the Air Is Clear*. Preceded by a brief two-page introduction to Fuentes and his career (through 1966), this chapter contains a detailed discussion of the novel's plot, a section on its structure, another on the modes of narration employed by Fuentes in this work, and another on the Mexican writer's style. Other sections (some twenty-five pages) treat the potential literary influences (much as those of John Dos Passos, D. H. Lawrence, and Octavio Paz) to be found in the work and the novel's "World View," as Sommers puts it. Example-filled and very readable. A landmark study. Titles and quotations in English.

GABRIEL GARCÍA MÁRQUEZ
Colombia

Biography

Williams, Raymond L. "Introduction and Biography." In his *Gabriel García Márquez*. Boston: Twayne, 1984.

Just as the title indicates, this thirteen-page chapter presents an introduction to and the biography of the Colombian author. A short opening section deals with, as Williams puts it, "The Phenomenon of García Márquez." A second section discusses "The Rise of the New Novel and the Right of Invention in Spanish America." A third section, entitled "García Márquez and the Colombian Tradition," completes the introduction portion of the chapter. The remainder of the chapter (roughly eight pages) is devoted to "A Biographical Overview," interesting not only because it chronicles the writer's career, but also because it provides considerable information on García Márquez' familial and cultural background, which explains much of the reason for which the Colombian author writes as he does and about what he does. An excellent introduction to García Márquez the man and the writer. A chronology precedes the chapter. Titles and quotations in English.

Commentary

Bell-Villada, Gene H. "García Márquez and the Novel." *Latin American Literary Review* 13 (January-June, 1985): 15-23.

Bell-Villada claims that the success of *One Hundred Years of Solitude* and (less so) *The Autumn of the Patriarch* marked a new phase in the development of the novel genre on a world scale. In fact, he states that García Márquez is the writer "who has done the most so far to save the novel from itself." To support this contention, the critic describes the world situation of the novel in 1967 and shows how "fertile commingling of the fantastical with the realistic" in the Colombian writer's landmark novels helped revolutionize and revitalize the genre. Considerable space is devoted to a detailed and example-filled discussion of this commingling. A fascinating article. Titles and quotations in English.

Books Abroad 47 (Summer, 1973). Gabriel García Márquez issue.

This issue contains numerous articles on García Márquez and his works, including "Beyond Magic Realism: Thoughts on the Art of Gabriel García Márquez" by Gregory Rabassa, "The Short Stories of García Márquez" by Frank Dauster, "Lampooning Literature: *La mala hora*" by Wolfgang A. Luchting, "*One Hundred Years of Solitude* and *Pedro Páramo*: A Parallel" by Suzanne Jill Levine, and "The Common Wonders of García Márquez's Recent Fiction" by Marta Morello Frosch. Includes a detailed chronology of the

Colombian writer's life and career through 1973 and numerous photographs. Most titles and quotations in English.

Brushwood, John S. "Reality and Imagination in the Novels of García Márquez." *Latin American Literary Review* 13 (January-June, 1985): 9-14.

Brushwood examines García Márquez' ability to create an extraordinary reality chiefly by taking reality and making it seem larger than life (in part by "treating the commonplace as if it were exceptional and the exceptional as if it were commonplace"), by following certain literary influences (such as Carpentier, William Faulkner, and José Félix Fuenmayor) and, to a lesser degree, by exploiting the "marvellous reality" of Latin America. A solid article. Titles in English.

Davis, Mary E. "The Haunted Voice: Echoes of William Faulkner in García Márquez, Fuentes, and Vargas Llosa." *World Literature Today* 59 (Autumn, 1985): 531-535.

Davis devotes considerable space in her interesting study to the nature and development of Faulkner's unique voice and to how and why that voice has been so well accepted in Latin America. When she turns to the presence of Faulkner in García Márquez' works, she compares Macondo to Yoknapatawpha; *One Hundred Years of Solitude* to various works by the North American writer; *Leaf Storm* to *As I Lay Dying* and *Absalom, Absalom!*; *The Autumn of the Patriarch* to *Light in August*; and *Chronicle of a Death Foretold* to *Sanctuary*. Titles and quotations in English.

Harss, Luis, and Barbara Dohmann. "Gabriel García Márquez, or the Lost Chord." In their *Into the Mainstream: Conversations with Latin American Writers*. New York: Harper & Row, 1967.

An interview-based discussion of García Márquez and his works. Contains brief comments on the legacy of Colombian literature inherited by García Márquez and lengthier observations on the writer's famous setting of Macondo. Includes a fair amount of information about his life and early career. Most of the chapter, however, is devoted to an overview of his works through the mid-1960's, consisting principally of the cogent observations of Harss and Dohmann, but supplemented nicely with comments from the writer himself. Perhaps the best part about the chapter is that, because of the date of the interview (presumably sometime in 1966), it catches the Colombian writer just prior to the publication of *One Hundred Years of Solitude*. This gives the comments related to the novel (near the end of the chapter) a special air, a particular immediacy. Interesting comments also on *The Autumn of the Patriarch* several years before its publication. A classic piece of criticism and an excellent introduction to the writer and his works. Titles in Spanish with English translations. Quotations in English.

Latin American Literary Review 13 (January-June, 1985). Gabriel García Márquez issue.
This issue contains fifteen articles by some of the most prominent critics of contemporary Latin American fiction. Includes articles on such wide-ranging topics as "Reality and Imagination in the Novels of García Márquez" by John S. Brushwood, "García Márquez and the Novel" by Gene H. Bell-Villada, " 'The Aleph' and *One Hundred Years of Solitude*: Two Microcosmic Worlds" by George R. McMurray, and "An Introduction of the Early Journalism of García Márquez: 1948-1958" by Raymond Williams. Titles in Spanish and English. Quotations in English or in Spanish with English translations.

Luchting, Wolfgang A. "Gabriel García Márquez: The Boom and the Whimper." *Books Abroad* 44 (Winter, 1970): 26-30.
An article apparently intended to introduce García Márquez to the North American reading public and to encourage readers not to miss the opportunity to read *One Hundred Years of Solitude* (which, at the time, had not yet appeared in English). Luchting chronicles the reaction in Latin America and France to the novel's publication and provides a short biography of the Colombian writer with emphasis on his family background, his struggles as a writer, and the writing of his masterpiece. The rest of the article is devoted to an introduction to the nature of García Márquez' narrative, focusing on and recounting magical occurrences found in it. The critic suggests reasons for which magical elements are so prevalent in García Márquez' work, at one point quoting the writer as saying, "The irreality of Latin America is something so real and so commonplace." A good introduction to the writer. Titles in Spanish. Quotations in English.

McMurray, George R. *Gabriel García Márquez*. New York: Frederick Ungar, 1977.
A truly excellent and extremely readable overview and analysis of García Márquez' fiction through *The Autumn of the Patriarch* (1975). A brief introduction to the Colombian writer's career, followed by an opening chapter on his early writings. Subsequent chapters include "The Threat of 'La Violencia' " (covering *No One Writes to the Colonel* and *In Evil Hour*), "Myth and Reality: The Perfect Synthesis" (*One Hundred Years of Solitude*), and "Power, Solitude, and Decadence" (*The Autumn of the Patriarch*). Two other chapters cover the writer's short stories. Provides a chronology of García Márquez' life and career and a very good index. Primary and secondary bibliographies in Spanish and English. Titles and quotations in English.

_____ . "Gabriel García Márquez." In *Latin American Literature in the Twentieth Century: A Guide*, edited by Leonard S. Klein. New York: Frederick Ungar, 1986.
A brief (roughly four-page) introduction to García Márquez' life and works.

Some discussion of his major works, particularly those dealing with the fictional town of Macondo. Two somewhat lengthy paragraphs dedicated to *One Hundred Years of Solitude*. A good starting point for the reader unfamiliar with García Márquez. Includes a list of the Colombian writer's works (almost all in Spanish) and a short critical bibliography in English.

————————. "Major Figures of the Boom." In his *Spanish American Writing Since 1941: A Critical Survey*. New York: Frederick Ungar, 1987.
McMurray devotes roughly six pages of this section of his book to a brief overview of García Márquez' fiction. Following an introductory paragraph, the critic offers concise commentary on each of the Colombian writer's major works, before providing a concluding paragraph which summarizes the nature of García Márquez' fictional world. A good starting point for the reader unfamiliar with García Márquez. Titles in Spanish with English translations.

Oberhelman, Harley D. "García Márquez and the American South." *Chasqui* 5, no. 1 (1975): 29-38.
Oberhelman contends that there is in García Márquez' works "a persistent, mordant view of the American South which runs as a leitmotif parallel to his vision of decay and underdevelopment in his fictional Macondo and in the lands washed by the Caribbean." The critic traces the influence of the American South in the Colombian writer's works to García Márquez' childhood contacts with American Southerners (working for the United Fruit Company), his reading of William Faulkner, and his bus trip through the American South "in homage to Faulkner" (García Márquez' words, my translation) in 1961. Oberhelman then examines how this influence manifests itself in the Colombian's works (with most attention paid to *One Hundred Years of Solitude*). The critic concludes that wherever this influence occurs, it concerns "decay, decline, and exploitation." Titles and quotations in Spanish.

————————. *The Presence of Faulkner in the Writings of García Márquez*. Lubbock: Texas Tech Press, 1980.
A brief (forty-three pages in all) book-length study focusing on "García Márquez, his literary world, and on those moments when the presence of Faulkner is clearly evident in his thoughts and writings." Chapters include "Faulkner and the Spanish-Speaking World," "García Márquez' First Contacts with Faulkner," "Resonances of the Mind," and "Confluences of Myth and Style." Well documented from both a literary and extraliterary standpoint. A concise and detailed examination of this interesting aspect of the Colombian writer's work. Bibliographies of Faulkner's works (in English) and of García Márquez' works (in Spanish) as well. Contains a critical bibliography in Spanish, French, and English. Titles and quotations from García Márquez' works in Spanish.

Schwartz, Ronald. "García Márquez: A New Colombian Cosmology." In his *Nomads, Exiles, and Émigrés: The Rebirth of the Latin American Narrative, 1960-80*. Metuchen, N.J.: Scarecrow Press, 1980.

A chapter with two purposes: (1) to provide a brief biographical sketch of García Márquez and (2) to discuss one of his principal works, *The Autumn of the Patriarch*. The biographical sketch occupies approximately five pages of this twelve-page chapter. In spite of its brevity, it provides considerable information concerning the Colombian writer's life and career, including mention of not only his work in fiction but in journalism and screenwriting as well. Concise, interesting, and informative. A good starting point for the reader unfamiliar with the writer. Titles of García Márquez' works in English. Titles of Spanish-language organizations, newspapers, and magazines in Spanish.

Sims, Robert L. "Narrating Violence and the Permutable Violence of Narration: The Evolution of Focalization in the Works of Gabriel García Márquez from 1947 to 1981." *Hispanic Journal* 10 (Fall, 1988): 53-65.

Using (and defining for the reader) theories and terminology from Gérard Genette's *Narrative Discourse: An Essay in Method* and from paleontology, Sims presents a detailed and well-documented study of García Márquez' "narration of violence and focalization" to find that it passes through four phases, ranging from zero focalization with an omniscient narrator in the first phase to the type of focalization found in *Chronicle of a Death Foretold*, in which "violence becomes a shared experience between the retrospective narrator, the narrator-character and the reader." An interesting and well-presented topic. Titles and quotations in English.

Williams, Raymond L. *Gabriel García Márquez*. Boston: Twayne, 1984.

An excellent book-length introduction to García Márquez' life and works. The first chapter assesses the writer's place in Latin American and Colombian letters and presents a history of his life and career (through 1982). Subsequent chapters treat his earliest works (early stories and *Leafstorm*), the works of the late 1950's and early 1960's (*Big Mama's Funeral, No One Writes to the Colonel,* and *In Evil Hour*), *One Hundred Years of Solitude, The Autumn of the Patriarch,* and *Chronicles of a Death Foretold* (along with his work in journalism). A final chapter presents some generalizations concerning García Márquez' writing and assesses the Colombian author's place in Latin American and world literature. Contains an excellent index, a chronology of García Márquez' life and career, and primary and secondary bibliographies (the latter annotated) in Spanish and English. Titles in English. Quotations in Spanish with English translations.

_____ . "Gabriel García Márquez." In *Critical Survey of Long Fiction* (Foreign Language Series), edited by Frank N. Magill, vol. 2. Pasadena, Calif.: Salem Press, 1984.

A nine-page overview of García Márquez' work in long fiction. Contains a list of his principal novels (all with English translations), a summary of his work in other literary forms, and an assessment of his achievements. This is followed by a biographical sketch and an overview and analysis of his major novels. A good introduction to García Márquez for the reader unfamiliar with the Colombian writer's work in general and his novels in particular. Includes a list of his other major works (some in Spanish only) and a short critical bibliography in English. Titles in English.

The Autumn of the Patriarch (El otoño del patriarca)

Atchity, Kenneth John. *"The Autumn of the Patriarch."* In *Magill's Literary Annual*, 1977, edited by Frank N. Magill, vol. 1. Pasadena, Calif.: Salem Press, 1977.

Atchity begins his roughly four-page overview of the novel in question by briefly discussing the nature of García Márquez' writing leading up to *The Autumn of the Patriarch*. This is followed by a description of the novel's fictional world, a portrait of its protagonist, a consideration of its style, and a discussion of its themes. An excellent introduction to the work. "Sources for Further Study" lists a review article on the work (in English). Titles and quotations in English.

Brotherston, Gordon. "García Márquez and the Secrets of Saturno Santos." In *Contemporary Latin American Fiction*, edited by Salvador Bacarisse. Edinburgh: Scottish Academic Press, 1980.

Though Brotherston briefly discusses the presence of Indians in *One Hundred Years of Solitude*, the main focus of this article is the presence (and the significance) of Indians in *The Autumn of the Patriarch*, focusing chiefly, though not exclusively, on Santos Saturno and his relationship with the patriarch. Through numerous examples, Brotherston demonstrates a significant Indian presence in this work which shows, in part, "that Latin America's patriarchs owe their most intimate support to their victims of longest standing," and that "America's revolution is inconceivable without the Indian." Titles and quotations in Spanish.

Janes, Regina. "The End of Time in *Cien años de soledad* and *El otoño del patriarca*." *Chasqui* 7 (February, 1978): 28-35.

Janes compares the treatment of time in *One Hundred Years of Solitude* and *The Autumn of the Patriarch*. In the process of her study, she observes, for example, that the idea of repetition implied in both novels, while providing, as the critic puts it, a consolation for the reader of *One Hundred Years of Solitude*, constitutes the (again, the critic's term) nightmare for the reader of *The Autumn of the Patriarch*. Interesting piece. Titles and quotations in Spanish.

Lipski, John M. "Embedded Dialogue in *El otoño del patriarca*." *The American Hispanist* 2, no. 14 (1977): 9-12.

For Lipski, embedded dialogue in *The Autumn of the Patriarch* is the rapid change of narrative perspective in the course of the narration, a change (signaled only by a shift in speech style or a change of verbal reference) which allows up to four voices, "four interrelated levels of discourse," to speak in succession. This "intersection of narrative personalities," based in large part on interchangeability, along with other factors in the work, supports an interpretation of the novel's theme as one in which "the General is in fact the sum total of the individuals of which the country is comprised." Knowledge of semiotics very helpful. Titles and quotations in Spanish.

Luna, Norman. "The Barbaric Dictator and the Enlightened Tyrant in *El otoño del patriarca* and *El recurso del método.*" *Latin American Literary Review* 15 (Fall/Winter, 1979): 25-32.
Luna compares the dictators and the portraits painted of them in *The Autumn of the Patriarch* and Carpentier's *Reasons of State*. The article contains numerous cogent observations concerning the two novels and their respective protagonists, one of those being found in Luna's opening claim (to paraphrase the critic): that the historicoideological outline of Latin American dictatorship in Carpentier's novel finds its mythicolegendery parallel in García Márquez' book. *The Autumn of the Patriarch*, Luna concludes, is "atemporal and spectral," while *Reasons of State* is "contemporary and historical." Titles and quotations in Spanish with English translations.

McMurray, George R. "Power, Solitude, and Decadence: A Lyrical Portrait." In his *Gabriel García Márquez*. New York: Frederick Ungar, 1977.
This lengthy (thirty-eight-page) chapter presents an excellent and extremely readable overview and analysis of *The Autumn of the Patriarch*. McMurray provides cogent observations on numerous aspects of this novel, such as its characters, its classification (according to the critic) as essentially a lyrical work, its spiral structure, its "archetypal patterns and universal tensions reminiscent of biblical and heroic myths," its treatment of time, its plot, its symbolic motifs, and its "absurd incidents." Titles and quotations in English.

Richards, Timothy A. B. "Grotesque Realism in *El otoño del patriarca.*" In *Selected Proceedings of the Mid-America Conference on Hispanic Literature*, edited by Luis T. González-del-Valle and Catherine Nickel. Lincoln, Nebr.: Society of Spanish and Spanish-American Studies, 1986.
Richards devotes considerable space to a definition of the grotesque before presenting his claim that in *The Autumn of the Patriarch* "three interdependent major textual components are conducive to the comprehensive application of the grotesque: the narrative perspective, the concept of time and the concept of space." The remainder of the article is used to support the critic's claim and to

establish the role of the grotesque in the work in question. Titles and quotations in Spanish.

Schwartz, Ronald. "García Márquez: A New Colombian Cosmology." In his *Nomads, Exiles, and Émigrés: The Rebirth of the Latin American Narrative, 1960-80*. Metuchen, N.J.: Scarecrow Press, 1980.

A chapter with two purposes: (1) to provide a brief biographical sketch of García Márquez; and (2) to discuss one of his principal works, *The Autumn of the Patriarch*. Discussion of the novel covers roughly six pages of this twelve-page chapter. A fine plot description. The entire discussion of the work is punctuated by comments from several critics (including Schwartz himself) concerning the nature and artistry of this "novel of excesses," as Schwartz calls it. Many of the comments are negative concerning this work which unfortunately followed the Colombian writer's masterpiece, *One Hundred Years of Solitude*. *The Autumn of the Patriarch* still, according to Schwartz, shows García Márquez to be "perhaps the most gifted, innovative, and creative writer of his generation." A very good and very readable introduction to the novel in question. Titles and quotations in English.

Sims, Robert L. "Narrating Violence and the Permutable Violence of Narration: The Evolution of Focalization in the Works of Gabriel García Márquez from 1947 to 1981." *Hispanic Journal* 10 (Fall, 1988): 53-65.

In this article tracing the evolution of García Márquez' "narration of violence and focalization" (employing theories and terminology from Gérard Genette's *Narrative Discourse: An Essay in Method* and from paleontology), Sims examines *The Autumn of the Patriarch* (and specifically "the destruction of the master torturer José Ignacio Saenz de la Barra"), finding that the novel falls into the third of a four-phase evolution, characterized here by an "extreme form of variable internal focalization." Must be read within the context of the entire article. Titles and quotations in English.

Tobin, Patricia. "The Autumn of the Signifier: The Deconstructionist Moment of García Márquez." *Latin American Literary Review* 13 (January-June, 1985): 65-78.

Tobin essentially calls *One Hundred Years of Solitude* a book for the heart and *The Autumn of the Patriarch* a book for the head, a book with which the author "perpetuates a creative outrageousness fully compatible in its decentering effects with the systematic deviancy of post-structuralist deconstruction." She then presents a study of the Patriarch as the Signifier in the work. Best suited for readers with a working knowledge of structuralist and deconstructionist theories. Titles and quotations in English.

Williams, Raymond L. "*The Autumn of the Patriarch*." In his *Gabriel García Márquez*. Boston: Twayne, 1984.

This thirty-three-page chapter dedicated to García Márquez' most difficult novel is divided into two sections. The first section, "Introduction and Plot" (which occupies roughly four pages), concerns itself with The *Autumn of the Patriarch* in the context of the writer's other works and, in particular, the tradition of dictatorships and dictatorship novels in the Hispanic world before turning its attention to the novel's plot. The second section, "Structure, Theme, and Narrative Technique," provides a fairly detailed and example-filled discussion of the work's technical elements, a discussion which not only describes and analyzes García Márquez' complex technical maneuvers, but should help the reader decipher this difficult work. Titles in English. Quotations in Spanish with English translations.

Chronicle of a Death Foretold (Crónica de una muerte anunciada)

Álvarez-Borland, Isabel. "From Mystery to Parody: (Re)Readings of García Márquez's *Crónica de una muerte anunciada*." *Symposium* 38 (Winter, 1984-1985): 278-286.

Álvarez-Borland states that she views *Chronicle of a Death Foretold* "as a questioning structure rather than as an answer-providing construct." She analyzes the work's "detective conventions as well as their aesthetic effects" on her way to concluding that García Márquez' novel is not about what happened but why it happened, and given the nature of both its story and its narrative discourse, it can be viewed as an ironic parody on two levels: "as a parody of the institutions and morals on a textual level, and as a parody of the classic detective structure at the artistic level." A solid study with an interesting perspective. Titles and quotations in Spanish.

Conlon, John J. "*Chronicle of a Death Foretold*." In *Magill's Literary Annual*, 1984, edited by Frank N. Magill, vol. 1. Pasadena, Calif.: Salem Press, 1984.

Conlon begins his roughly five-page overview of *Chronicle of a Death Foretold* by providing background on García Márquez' career and by placing the novel in question within the context of that career. This is followed by a discussion of various elements of the novel, including its intriguing mixture of fact and fiction, its story, the techniques used in the telling of the story, the work's humor, and its thematic concerns. An excellent introduction to the work. "Sources for Further Study" section lists review articles on the novel (in English). Titles in Spanish with English translations. Quotations in English.

Grossman, Edith. "Truth Is Stranger Than Fact." *Review* 30 (December, 1981): 71-73.

Grossman is concerned chiefly with the relationship between the story of *Chronicle of a Death Foretold* and the actual events on which it is based. She first discusses the tendency in fiction to imitate reality from the theories of Aristotle to the works of Truman Capote and Norman Mailer. She then turns her attention to an examination of the two stories (complete with pictures from the real-life case). What she finds, in general, is that García Márquez "expands, heightens and enlarges the panorama of figures and events so that potential legend seems to hover in the background," as he "dazzles the reader with uncommon blendings of fantasy, fable and fact." Interesting perspective on the work. Titles in Spanish with English translations. Quotations in English.

Rabassa, Gregory. "García Márquez's New Book: Literature or Journalism?" *World Literature Today* 56 (Winter, 1982): 48-51.
    Rabassa begins his article recalling García Márquez' comments in the late 1970's that he would "abandon literature for journalism until the Pinochet dictatorship disappeared in Chile." The critic contends that with *Chronicle of a Death Foretold*, at least according to the Colombian author's definition of journalism (embellishing the story when it might become boring), García Márquez has not deviated from his previous statement. The remainder of the article (with the exception of a short section concerning the concept of the chronicle as a genre) is essentially an overview of the novella in question. Good introduction to the work. Titles and quotations in English.

Sims, Robert L. "Narrating Violence and the Permutable Violence of Narration: The Evolution of Focalization in the Works of Gabriel García Márquez from 1947 to 1981." *Hispanic Journal* 10 (Fall, 1988): 53-65.
    In the process of tracing the evolution of García Márquez' "narration of violence and focalization" (employing theories and terminology from Gérard Genette's *Narrative Discourse: An Essay in Method* and from paleontology), Sims examines *Chronicle of a Death Foretold* to find that it falls in the fourth phase of a four-phase evolution, characterized in part here by a double narrator who "oscillates between the poles of zero and internal focalization," using "interpolated narration" when narrating finally, in the last few pages, the scene of violence. Must be read within the context of the entire article. Titles and quotations in English.

Williams, Raymond L. "*Chronicle of a Death Foretold* (1981) and Journalism." In his *Gabriel García Márquez*. Boston: Twayne, 1984.
    In a twenty-page chapter dedicated primarily to García Márquez' career as a journalist and the journalistic traits in his fiction writing, Williams devotes a roughly six-page section to *Chronicle of a Death Foretold*, the only novel so treated in this chapter. The critic briefly discusses the novel's plot but focuses primarily on the journalistic characteristics of the work, from the real-life story on which the novel is based, to the multiple and often-quoted sources of García Márquez' narrator. Williams contends that the real focus of the novel is not Santiago's death, but "the story's coming into being, the author's placing the

numerous pieces together." The critic also compares the characteristics of the novel in question with some of García Márquez' previous works. Titles in English. Quotations in Spanish with English translations.

In Evil Hour (La mala hora)
Chávez, John R. *"In Evil Hour."* In *Magill's Literary Annual*, 1980, edited by Frank N. Magill, vol. 1. Pasadena, Calif.: Salem Press, 1980.
Chávez begins his roughly four-page article on *In Evil Hour* by setting the environment of the story and presenting a thumbnail sketch of the nature of the novel's plot and a definition of its central theme (each character's reaction, "especially their political reaction" to the public shame of the lampoons). This is followed by a discussion of various other aspects of the work, including the presentation of the story and the characters and their actions (and reactions to the lampoons), the discussion of which becomes a summary of the novel's plot. A very good introduction to the work. Titles in English.

McMurray, George R. "The Threat of 'La Violencia.' " In his *Gabriel García Márquez*. New York: Frederick Ungar, 1977.
The final fourteen pages of this chapter are devoted to an overview and analysis of *In Evil Hour* (the first eleven pages treat *No One Writes to the Colonel*). McMurray presents an extremely readable discussion of several aspects of this work: its plot, its characters, the role of the lampoons in the novel, the work's structure, the presentation of time, the tone of the narrative, the role of irony, and other topics. A thorough and concise introduction to the work in question. Titles and quotations in English.

Sims, Robert L. "Narrating Violence and the Permutable Violence of Narration: The Evolution of Focalization in the Works of Gabriel García Márquez from 1947 to 1981." *Hispanic Journal* 10 (Fall, 1988): 53-65.
In this article tracing the evolution of García Márquez' "narration of violence and focalization" (employing theories and terminology from Gérard Genette's *Narrative Discourse: An Essay in Method* and from paleontology), Sims examines *In Evil Hour* (and specifically the scene in which César Montero decides to kill Pastor) and concludes that it falls within the second phase of a four-phase evolution, this second phase being characterized, at least in this work, by external focalization, which, among other things, "tends to reduce the narrator-character to a series of precise, mechanical actions and the reader to an anxious spectator trying to decipher them." Must be read within the context of the entire article. Titles and quotations in English.

Williams, Raymond L. "The Middle Years (1956-1962)." In his *Gabriel García Márquez*. Boston: Twayne, 1984.
In this chapter devoted to the Colombian author's fiction between *Leafstorm*

and *One Hundred Years of Solitude*, Williams dedicates roughly nine pages to *In Evil Hour*. He begins by discussing the work's most fundamental differences (expression of political protest) from and similarities (characters) to *No One Writes to the Colonel* (also examined in this chapter), and then treats the novel's structure and plot, the narrative technique employed by García Márquez, and the Colombian writer's use of language (particularly concerning the concept of heteroglossia) in the work. A final paragraph renews the comparison between this novel and *No One Writes to the Colonel*. An excellent study of the work. Titles in English. Quotations in Spanish with English translations.

Leafstorm (La hojarasca)

McMurray, George R. "Early Gropings and Success." In his *Gabriel García Márquez*. New York: Frederick Ungar, 1977.

McMurray devotes roughly thirteen (out of fourteen) pages of this chapter on García Márquez' early writings to *Leafstorm*. The critic presents an excellent and extremely readable overview and analysis of the novel, covering the work's plot, the narrative techniques with which it is written, the treatment of time in the narrative, the work's themes, its imagery, its characters, and even some of its defects. A superb introduction to the novel. Titles and quotations in English.

Williams, Raymond L. "The Early Fiction (1948-55)." In his *Gabriel García Márquez*. Boston: Twayne, 1984.

In a twenty-six-page chapter dedicated to García Márquez' early writings, Williams devotes the final eight pages to the Colombian author's first novel, *Leafstorm*. The critic traces the work's connection to the story "Monologue of Isabel Watching It Rain in Macondo" (discussed earlier in the chapter), and examines the novel's plot, its structure, its various narrative points of view, its depiction of reality, and its language (particularly in regard to the creation of an odd or "different" reality). An excellent overview and analysis of García Márquez' "initial novel-length voyage into the land of Macondo." Titles and quotations in English.

Love in the Time of Cholera (El amor en los tiempos del cólera)

Brower, Keith H. "*Love in the Time of Cholera*." In *Magill's Literary Annual*, 1989, edited by Frank N. Magill, vol. 2. Pasadena, Calif.: Salem Press, 1989.

This article opens with an brief introduction to García Márquez' career and reputation as a writer, followed by a rather detailed summary of the plot of the novel in question. What follows is an analysis of the principal as well as some of the secondary characters, the manipulation of time in the novel, and the novel's theme. A final section provides an overview of the nature of the novel's narrative. An excellent introduction to the work. "Sources for Further Study" section lists review articles of the novel (in English). Titles and quotations in English.

Swook, Margaret L. "The Motif of Voyage as Mythical Symbol in *El amor en los tiempos del cólera* by Gabriel García Márquez." *Hispanic Journal* 10 (Fall, 1988): 85-91.

Swook cites the significance of the voyage in ancient mythologies and contends that García Márquez uses the voyage and images associated with it in *Love in the Time of Cholera* to "characterize critical stages or passages in the lives of his protagonists as well as to depict the setting in which they are placed." The critic cites several voyages or trips undertaken by Fermina and Florentino, both separately and together, and shows how in each case the voyage occurs at a critical stage in their development and that the voyage (be it in carriage, ship, or even hot-air balloon) is always more important and afforded more attention than the destination. Interesting comments as well concerning voyage-related images (Florentino, for example, during his stagnant existence as he waits for Fermina, is associated first with a docked ship and then with a sunken galleon) and the significance of the voyage motif concerning the "underlying question of predetermined destiny which these patterns present" (particularly concerning the final voyage). A fascinating and enlightening study. Very readable. Titles and quotations (very few) in Spanish.

No One Writes to the Colonel (El coronel no tiene quien le escriba)

McMurray, George R. "The Threat of 'La Violencia.'" In his *Gabriel García Márquez*. New York: Frederick Ungar, 1977.

The first eleven pages of this chapter are devoted to an overview and analysis of *No One Writes to the Colonel* (the final fourteen pages treat *In Evil Hour*). McMurray presents an extremely readable discussion of many aspects of this short novel: its plot, its array of characters, its treatment of political themes, its protagonist as an absurd hero (as well as his sense of humor), the symbol of the rooster, the significance of the final dialogue (particularly the final word of the story), and the narrative techniques and artistry used in telling the story. Concise and enlightening. Titles and quotations in English.

Pontiero, Giovanni. "Art and Commitment in Gabriel García Márquez's *El coronel no tiene quien le escriba*." *Kentucky Romance Quarterly* 22 (1975): 443-457.

Pontiero examines the array of characters that populate *No One Writes to the Colonel*, with emphasis on their personalities, their circumstances, their actions, and their thematic significance, before concluding from his analysis that the sociopolitical aspect of Garcia Marquez' narrative is different from that of the fiction which preceded him in Colombia, as the writer "aims at an imaginative and intense account of human experience of striking concision within the framework of Colombia's history. All that is peculiar to the Colombian scene is faithfully observed with its social consequences, but the human drama of this provincial community 'pudriendo vivos' [rotting alive] . . . is conceived in universal terms with the forcefulness and truth of the classical Greek tragedies."

Williams, Raymond L. "The Middle Years (1956-62)." In his *Gabriel García Márquez*. Boston: Twayne, 1984.
In a chapter dedicated to García Márquez' fiction between *Leafstorm* and *One Hundred Years of Solitude*, Williams includes a brief discussion (roughly three pages) of *No One Writes to the Colonel*. The critic deals chiefly with the work's plot, its humor in the face of despair, and its "constant but subtle references to the political situation," which Williams believes "make the book above all one about politics." At various points in his discussion of the work he emphasizes that the short novel is, in fact, "a discourse in silence," that it is "the portrayal of people reduced to silence" because of the political repression which surrounds them. The novel, he concludes, however, is not without optimism, making it, in spite of its generally negative ambiance, "an early example of the basic affirmation of humanity found in García Márquez's later work." Titles and quotations in English.

Woods, Richard D. "Time and Futility in the Novel *El coronel no tiene quien le escriba*." *Kentucky Romance Quarterly* 17 (1970): 287-295.
Woods calls García Márquez' manipulation of time in his works "deceptively simple" and goes on to point out numerous ways (such as by "resuscitating the past," the repetition of Friday and October, the presence of death, and the image of the clock—particularly the stopped clock) in which the Colombian writer effectively "utilizes time as the scaffolding on which to construct the theme of futility" in *No One Writes to the Colonel*. Very readable and interesting. Titles and quotations in Spanish.

One Hundred Years of Solitude (Cien años de soledad)
Bell-Villada, Gene H. "Names and Narrative Pattern in *One Hundred Years of Solitude*." *Latin American Literary Review* 9 (Spring/Summer, 1981): 37-46.
Bell-Villada first discusses the difficulty even "the most seasoned literary critics" have had with the names of characters in *One Hundred Years of Solitude*. He then goes on to state that the "names present a lucid, rigorously consistent and fairly simple pattern of character traits and biological trajectories." He shows, for example, that all the various Aurelianos are similar in intellect, personality, sex drive, and, even, in the manner in which they die. The José Arcadios are similar to one another in these areas as well. The critic also examines the names of the female characters and of others, before drawing his conclusions. Interesting piece on a potentially confusing element of García Márquez' novel. Titles and quotations in English.

Brotherston, Gordon. "An End to Secular Solitude: Gabriel García Márquez." In his *The Emergence of the Latin American Novel*. London: Cambridge University Press, 1977.

This chapter serves essentially as an introduction to García Márquez' fictional world, with emphasis on *One Hundred Years of Solitude*. The chapter opens with a lengthy quote taken from the very beginning of the novel, followed by an analysis that concentrates less on stylistic and technical elements of the work and more on the world the Colombian author creates and the meaning of that world. A very good introduction to *One Hundred Years of Solitude* in particular and to the nature of García Márquez' fictional world in general. Titles in Spanish with English translations (or vice versa). Quotations in English.

_____ . "García Márquez and the Secrets of Saturno Santos." In *Contemporary Latin American Fiction*, edited by Salvador Bacarisse. Edinburgh: Scottish Academic Press, 1980.

In an article focusing chiefly on the Indian presence and its significance in *The Autumn of the Patriarch*, Brotherston briefly discusses the Indian presence (though not really its significance) in *One Hundred Years of Solitude*. The critic cites several instances in which Indians play a significant part: the presence of Cataure and his sister, the children learning Arawak before Spanish, and the role played by the Indians in the amnesia plague. Brotherston states that García Márquez' inclusion of Indians in the two works discussed in this article "deserves attention if nothing else because of the tight-lipped treatment received by Indians in Colombian literature." Titles and quotations in Spanish.

Dixon, Paul B. "Joke Formulas in *Cien años de soledad*." *Chasqui* 15 (February-May, 1986): 15-22.

Dixon contends that *One Hundred Years of Solitude*, in spite of the seriousness critics have attached to it, is not to be taken seriously but as a joke. He sets out to show that, "structurally speaking, there are many similarities between motifs of *CAS* [*One Hundred Years of Solitude*](or even the novel as a whole) and jokes." In the process of his study, the critic examines "the predominant joke structures of the novel," these being "Multiplication Jokes," "Expectation Jokes," and "Unmasking Jokes." References to theories of the joke (citing Freud, for example) and several examples from the text. An interesting perspective and written with a sense of humor. Titles and quotations from García Márquez' novel in Spanish.

Faris, Wendy B. "Magic and Violence in Macondo and San Lorenzo." *Latin American Literary Review* 13 (January-June, 1985): 44-54.

Faris compares, with emphasis on the elements of magic and violence, *One Hundred Years of Solitude* and Kurt Vonnegut's *Cat's Cradle*. She begins by discussing the presence and function of ice in the two novels and then moves on to consider, among other points, the two works' similar beginning styles, their apocalyptic endings, "their concept of insularity," and their magical realism (*One Hundred Years of Solitude*) and satirical fantasy (*Cat's Cradle*). An interesting study of two works not usually paired together. Titles and quotations in English.

Gallagher, D. P. "Gabriel García Márquez (Columbia, 1928-   )." In his *Modern Latin American Literature*. New York: Oxford University Press, 1973.

Gallagher begins by stating that García Márquez "is a man who has so far [as of the time this chapter was written] dedicated his entire literary career to the writing of one novel," though the critic adds, this "is not to say that he has written only one book." Gallagher then briefly mentions the other books of García Márquez, but the "one novel" the critic refers to is *One Hundred Years of Solitude*, the work to which this entire twenty-page chapter is devoted. Gallagher discusses numerous aspects of the work and in the process presents an excellent and very readable overview and analysis of the novel. Titles in Spanish with English translations. Quotations in English.

Janes, Regina. "The End of Time in *Cien años de soledad* and *El otono del patriarca*." *Chasqui* 7 (February, 1978): 28-35.

Janes compares the treatment of time and, in particular, its end in *One Hundred Years of Solitude* and *The Autumn of the Patriarch*. In the process, she observes, for example, that in the first novel, the end of the work implies that there "is a narrator behind the narrator Melquíades; there is a reader behind the reader Aureliano, ourselves. The double time element creates a hall of mirrors, reflections of reflections, infinitely receding." This suggestion of repetition is a consolation for the reader of *One Hundred Years of Solitude*. The same idea, expressed in another way, but expressed nonetheless, in *The Autumn of the Patriarch* is the nightmare of the work, the possibility of a repetition of the patriarch. Titles and quotations in Spanish.

Levine, Suzanne J. "*One Hundred Years of Solitude* and *Pedro Páramo*: A Parallel." *Books Abroad* 47 (Summer, 1973): 490-495.

Levine studies the many similarities and some of the differences that exist between García Márquez' novel and Juan Rulfo's *Pedro Páramo*. The critic finds that both novels: deal with "social and political problems common to most Latin American countries," are stories of intricate rural society, (with the focus on one family in a small town), make use of Biblical and Greek myth, question machismo and feudalism, and superimpose different moments of time. The novels differ, however, in the personalities and behavior of their female characters, in the fact that *Pedro Páramo* is more Faulknerian than *One Hundred Years of Solitude*, and, most important, that Rulfo's novel leaves the reader with a final affirmation of death, while García Márquez' work leaves the reader with a final affirmation of life. An interesting piece on two works rarely compared to each other. Titles and quotations in English.

McMurray, George R. " 'The Aleph' and *One Hundred Years of Solitude*: Two Microscopic Worlds." *Latin American Literary Review* 13 (January-June, 1985): 55-64.
McMurray compares Borges' story to García Márquez' novel, stating that both "strive to depict a total fictional universe," and both end in oblivion, though before they do, "what remains in the reader's mind, however, is an intuitively grasped, total image of Beatriz [from "The Aleph"], on the one hand, and, on the other, a poetic compendium of Western civilization [*One Hundred Years of Solitude*]." The critic describes in detail how each writer attempts to convey this "total fictional universe," concluding that had Borges' story never been published, Garcia Marquez' novel "would be different from what it is and not as good as the masterpiece we know." Interesting and very readable. Titles and quotations in English.

——————— . "Myth and Reality: The Perfect Synthesis." In his *Gabriel García Márquez*. New York: Frederick Ungar, 1977.
McMurray uses this entire forty-page chapter to present an excellent and extremely readable overview and analysis of *One Hundred Years of Solitude*. The critic manages to discuss concisely numerous and diverse aspects of García Márquez' novel, such as its plot, its structure, its story's connection to Colombian history, the author's use of cyclical and mythical time (which provides "a temporary escape from the harsh realities of history"), the mythical and historical functions of the work's characters, the significance of the final three pages, the style employed by the Colombian author and its relationship to the "fusion of reality and fantasy" in the novel, and the humor found in the text. Titles and quotations in English.

Oberhelman, Harley D. "García Márquez and the American South." *Chasqui* 5, no. 1 (1975): 29-38.
In this article examining what Oberhelman considers "a persistent, mordant view of the American South" in García Márquez' works, a view forged by the Colombian author's childhood contacts with Americans, his reading of William Faulkner, and a bus trip "in homage to Faulkner" (García Márquez' words, my translation) in 1961, the critic examines the influence of the American South in various works, *One Hundred Years of Solitude* being chief among them. Oberhelman's analysis focuses primarily on the presence and significance of the American banana company in the novel, the inclusion of which fits in well with the elements of "decay, decline, and exploitation" usually

associated with the American South when the region appears, in one form or
another, in García Márquez' works. Titles and quotations in Spanish.

Ollivier, Louis L. "*One Hundred Years of Solitude*: Existence Is the Word." *Latin
American Literary Review* 4 (Fall/Winter, 1975): 9-14.
A study of language, and particularly the written word, as the basis of existence and reality in García Márquez' novel. "The word," Ollivier contends, "is
the ultimate reality of Macondo." The significance of the word is analyzed here
on various levels, particularly concerning Melquíades' parchments, as the
critic contends that "a linguistic approach must be considered fundamental to
the understanding" of this novel. An interesting approach. Titles and quotations in English.

Penuel, Arnold M. "Death and the Maiden: Demythologization of Virginity in
García Márquez's *Cien años de soledad*." *Hispania* 66 (December, 1983):
552-560.
Penuel meticulously traces Amaranta's narcissistic behavior and her obsession
with death in *One Hundred Years of Solitude*, showing that "narcissism, pride,
and fear of life condition all that she does." The critic then discusses the
character's insistence on being declared a virgin on her death, before concluding, in part, that "with the juxtaposition of Amaranta's dramatic demand for
certification of her virginity at the end of her life and the manifest sterility and
deconstructiveness of that life the novelist demythologizes . . . the myth of
virginity. This demythologization," Penuel continues, "consists of illuminating
a dark side to the cult of virginity," symbolized in Amaranta by the incapacity
on her part to give of herself. An interesting perspective on the character and
the novel. Detailed and very readable. Titles and quotations in Spanish.

Rodríguez Monegal, Emir. "*One Hundred Years of Solitude*: The Last Three
Pages." *Books Abroad* 47 (Summer, 1973): 485-489.
Rodríguez Monegal discusses these critical pages of the novel and in the
process of his discussion touches on the function of time within Melquíades'
book (particularly as it is similar to Borges' concept of the Aleph), Aureliano
and his relationship to the reader of the novel, and García Márquez' relationship to Melquíades. Not so much an analysis as it is a collection of observations inspired by the last three pages of the novel. Titles and quotations in
English.

Sims, Robert L. "Narrating Violence and the Permutable Violence of Narration:
The Evolution of Focalization in the Works of Gabriel García Márquez from
1947 to 1981." *Hispanic Journal* 10 (Fall, 1988): 53-65.
In the process of tracing the evolution of García Márquez' "narration of
violence and focalization" (employing theories and terminology from Gérard

Genette's *Narrative Discourse: An Essay in Method* and from paleontology), Sims examines *One Hundred Years of Solitude*, specifically the massacre of the banana workers and Fernanda's outburst, to find that the first episode examined fits into the third phase of a four-phase evolution, (this third phase characterized here by interpolated narrative and the blending of zero and internal focalization), while the second episode, with its "variable internal focalization," fits into the third phase as well as presages a type of focalization found in *The Autumn of the Patriarch*. Must be read within the context of the entire article. Titles and quotations in English.

Stevens, L. Robert, and G. Roland Vela. "Jungle Gothic: Science, Myth, and Reality in *One Hundred Years of Solitude*." *Modern Fiction Studies* 26 (Summer, 1980): 262-266.
Stevens and Vela emphasize Western man's efforts to separate illusion from reality, myth from fact. They show that such is not the case, however, with García Márquez in this novel. Citing numerous examples (such as the yellow butterflies that flock to Meme when she falls in love with Mauricio Babilonia and the general presentation of time in the work), the two critics show how the Colombian author demonstrates "a view of reality richer and more exciting than any cross-section of any of its parts could ever reveal." Titles and quotations in English.

Vázquez Amaral, José. "Gabriel García Márquez' *One Hundred Years of Solitude*." In his *The Contemporary Latin American Narrative*. New York: Las Américas, 1970.
An excellent and wide-ranging overview of the Colombian writer's novel. Vázquez Amaral discusses topics as diverse as Macondo, the novel's focus in part on the subject of revolution, the characters of Aureliano Buendia (and his connection to Don Quijote) and Ursula, the treatment of time in the work, the theme of the "solitude of the warrior" after he has attained power, the possible influence on García Márquez of Mexican writers Elena Garro and Juan Rulfo, and the Colombian author's reference in his novel to works by Fuentes and Cortázar, along with several other topics. A very good introduction to the work in question. Titles and quotations in English.

Walter, Richard J. "Literature and History in Contemporary Latin America." *Latin American Literary Review* 15 (January-June, 1987): 173-182.
Walter calls *One Hundred Years of Solitude*, Fuentes' *The Death of Artemio Cruz*, and Vargas Llosa's *The War of the End of the World* "essential reading for any historian of Latin America." The critic contends as well that any reader, historian or not, would better appreciate these works if they knew and understood "the historical context in which they are set." Walter provides this context for each novel (in the case of García Márquez' work, the extended

conflict between Conservatives and Liberals in Colombia), before assessing the value of each work for the historian and concluding that all three writers deal with "the consequences of modernization for traditional societies," the problem of revolution (and its accompanying violence and "ideological confusion"), the role of charismatic leaders, and eventual frustration with the revolution. Particularly useful for the reader unfamiliar with the history of Latin America. Titles (except one in Portuguese with an English translation) and quotations in English.

Watson, Richard A. "A Pig's Tail." *Latin American Literary Review* 15 (January-June, 1987): 89-93.
Playing on the words "tail" and "tale," Watson calls García Márquez' novel "a pig's tail [tale]," a work, the critic contends, whose basic form is a circle. This Watson shows by referring to numerous elements of both the novel's form and its content which reinforce that image. Watson contends that the circular pattern (exemplified most by various forms of repetition) underscores the novel's message concerning, as he puts it, the "sameness of life and death." Titles and quotations in English.

Williams, Raymond L. "*One Hundred Years of Solitude*." In his *Gabriel García Márquez*. Boston: Twayne, 1984.
An excellent twenty-three page overview and analysis of the Colombian author's masterpiece. Divided into sections entitled "Introduction and Plot," "A Critical Overview," "Social and Political Implications," and "Narrative Technique and Universality," this chapter approaches García Márquez' famous novel from various angles and in the process presents the reader with a fine introduction to, analysis of, and reading guide for this novel, which as Williams points out at the beginning of the chapter, "is an utter joy to read yet, paradoxically, an elusive book to write about." A very readable study that should help the reader both better understand and better appreciate the novel in question. Titles in English. Quotations in Spanish with English translations.

JOSÉ LEZAMA LIMA
Cuba

Commentary

Schwartz, Ronald. "Lezama Lima: Cuban Sexual Propensities." In his *Nomads, Exiles, and Émigrés: The Rebirth of the Latin American Narrative, 1960-80*. Metuchen, N.J.: Scarecrow Press, 1980.

This chapter has two purposes: (1) to provide a brief biographical sketch of Lezama Lima and (2) to discuss and evaluate his most famous work, *Paradiso*. The biographical sketch occupies only two pages in this ten-page chapter, but it still, in spite of its brevity, manages to provide considerable information concerning the Cuban writer's life and career. Of particular interest is Lezama Lima's inclination toward poetry over prose (as evidenced by the number of poetic works he produced versus the number of prose works) and his status under the Castro regime following the publication of *Paradiso*. A good starting point for the reader unfamiliar with the writer. Most titles in English. Some in Spanish. Quotations in English.

Siemens, William. "José Lezama Lima." In *Latin American Literature in the Twentieth Century: A Guide*, edited by Leonard S. Klein. New York: Frederick Ungar, 1986.

A brief (roughly two-page) introduction to Lezama Lima's life and works. Discussion of the Cuban writer's poetry and his thoughts on the role and importance of poetic language, as well as two paragraphs on *Paradiso*. Brief consideration of Lezama Lima's place in Cuban and Spanish American literatures. A good starting point for the uninitiated reader. Includes a list of Lezama Lima's other works (in Spanish) not mentioned in the text. Short critical bibliography in Spanish and English.

Paradiso

Cortazar, Mercedes. "Entering Paradise." *Review 74* (Fall, 1974): 17-19.

Cortazar's short article is essentially an introduction to Lezama Lima's complex novel. She contends that "the reader must approach *Paradiso* obliquely, enter its creative space by approximation, assimilate it by osmosis." She goes on to say that "not unlike existence itself, *Paradiso*, is impenetrable." In addition to these and other comments on the nature of the narrative, particularly concerning the "transparent" nature of the narrator and the "yin and yang" aspects of the work, the critic provides a plot summary of the novel, punctuated by interpretative observations. Titles and quotations in English.

Fazzolari, Margarita. "Reader's Guide to *Paradiso*." Translated by Paula Speck. *Review 29* (May-August, 1981): 47-54.

In sections entitled "The Beginnings" (focusing on Lezama Lima's poetry),

"The Paschal Lamb," "American Expression," "Family History," "The Birth of the Image," "The Fall," "Toward Poetry," "The Destruction of Time and Space," and "Attaining Poetry," Fazzolari uses both textual (with emphasis on the novel's poetic nature, particularly concerning the significance of its symbols) and extratextual (references to the Cuban author's life) sources to present an analysis which deciphers some of the complexity of Lezama Lima's novel. Most titles in Spanish with English translations. Quotations in English.

Lezama Lima, José. "Confluences." Translated by Andrée Conrad. *Review 74* (Fall, 1974): 6-16.

As the editor's note so succinctly puts it, "In this essay, Lezama Lima suggests the poetic code of *Paradiso*. He takes his novel and some of its characters back to the point of their origin in his mind, from which they sprang to form his personal universe. At the same time his poetic, symbolic, and philosophical correspondences allow the reader to perceive the labyrinthine working of his creative imagination." Titles in Spanish. Quotations in English.

Müller-Bergh, Klaus. "José Lezama Lima and *Paradiso*." *Books Abroad* 44 (Winter, 1970): 36-40.

This short article provides an introduction to Lezama Lima's novel. The critic begins by briefly examining the Cuban writer's place in Latin American letters and then moves on to a rather detailed, concise overview of Lezama Lima's career. The remainder of the article is devoted to a general discussion of various elements of the novel in question (such as biographical similarities between the author and his protagonist, and numerous elements concerned with Latin American, and particularly Cuban, culture). Titles in Spanish. Quotations in Spanish, French, and English.

Review 74 (Fall, 1974): 5-51. "Focus" section on José Lezama Lima.

This section features nine diverse essays on Lezama Lima's complex novel, the titles and authors of which follow: (1) "Confluences" by José Lezama Lima, (2) "Entering Paradise" by Mercedes Cortazar, (3) "An Approach to Lezama Lima" by Julio Cortázar, (4) "Attempting the Impossible" by Mario Vargas Llosa, (5) "The Text in its Context" by Emir Rodríguez Monegal, (6) "Language as Hero" by Julio Ortega, (7) "A Cuban Proust" by Severo Sarduy, (8) "A Sentimental Realism" by J. M. Alonso, and (9) "An Expanding Imagination" by Andrée Conrad. Almost all titles and quotations in English. A few titles in Spanish and French. A few quotations in French.

Schwartz, Ronald. "Lezama Lima: Cuban Sexual Perpensities." In his *Nomads, Exiles, and Émigrés: The Rebirth of the Latin American Narrative, 1960-80*. Metuchen, N.J.: Scarecrow Press, 1980.

This chapter has two purposes: (1) to provide a brief biographical sketch of

Lezama Lima and (2) to discuss and evaluate *Paradiso*. Discussion of the novel occupies roughly seven-and-a-half pages of this ten-page chapter. Some introductory comments concerning the nature of the Cuban writer's complex novel, followed by an intentionally incomplete plot summary and a brief review of various critical opinions on the work, including some which are quite negative. Schwartz's conclusion is that *Paradiso* is "a linguistic *tour de force* of brilliant descriptions and poetic evocations, an outstanding example of the neo-Baroque element of Latin American literature and, most assuredly, a masterpiece of fiction." A good introduction to the novel. Most titles in English. Some in Spanish. Quotations in English.

Souza, Raymond D. "The Sensorial World of Lezama Lima." In his *Major Cuban Novelists*. Columbia: University of Missouri Press, 1976.
In this lengthy (twenty-seven-page) chapter devoted to *Paradiso*, Souza presents a superb overview and analysis of the work he calls "the most intricate novel in Spanish America," a work in which "the author's imaginative genius both attracts and baffles the readers." The critic uses approximately twenty-three pages of the chapter to present a detailed, step-by-step description of the novel's plot, supplemented throughout by an analysis of the characters, their interrelationships, the technical elements of the narrative, and the thematic implications encountered along the way. This is followed by some concluding observations and limited comparison of Lezama Lima's novel with Carpentier's *Explosion in a Cathedral* (discussed along with other works by Carpentier in the chapter which precedes this one). An excellent introduction and guide to Lezama Lima's complex novel. Titles and quotations in Spanish.

OSMAN LINS
Brazil

Commentary

Andrade, Ana Luiza. "Osman Lins." In *Dictionary of Brazilian Literature*, edited by Irwin Stern. Westport, Conn.: Greenwood Press, 1988.

A brief (roughly two-page) introduction to Lins's life and works. Discusses the main themes of the Brazilian writer's fiction and the three phases of his career, characterized respectively by *Guerra sem testemunhas* (war without witnesses), *Nove, novena* (nine, novena), and *Avalovara*. Brief discussion of the first two works, with more space devoted to *Avalovara*. A good starting point for the reader unfamiliar with Lins. List of additional selected works by Lins (all in Portuguese). Short critical bibliography in Portuguese and English.

Avalovara

Dean, James Seay. "Osman Lins: Plowman 'histórico e mítico.'" *Chasqui* 17 (November, 1988): 3-11.

In this well-documented article, Dean describes the nature of the narrative of *Avalovara* and then turns his attention, in part, to the ten early chapters interspersed in the novel in which Lins himself "explains how the book's structure, its synchronic scheme, and its fragmented characterizations and actions fulfill its theme," as the critic "examines Lins' inset critical comments in the context of his letters, interviews, and others' views of Lins," in the process coming to an evaluation of the novel and its place in twentieth century experimental fiction. Titles and quotations (numerous and lengthy) in Portuguese.

CLARICE LISPECTOR
Brazil

Biography

Fitz, Earl E. "Biography and Background." In his *Clarice Lispector*. Boston:
Twayne, 1986.
An excellent nineteen-page overview of Lispector's life and career. In sections
entitled "The Formative Years," "Influences," "The Making of a Writer," and
"The Works," Fitz meticulously traces the Brazilian writer's life from her birth
in the Ukraine to her death in Rio de Janeiro, all the while highlighting the
author's connection to literature, either through reading or writing, which
played such a major role in her life. In the process, the critic provides an
overview of Lispector's works, which both introduces the individual volumes
to the reader and shows the evolution of Lispector's writing. A superb introduction to the writer and her works. A chronology precedes the chapter. Titles
in Portuguese with English translations when first cited, subsequently in Portuguese. Quotations in English.

Jozef, Bella. "Chronology: Clarice Lispector." *Review 24* (1980): 24-26.
A chronology of Lispector's life and career from her birth in 1925 to her death
in 1977. Entries on her life not only include events but what the writer was
doing in general during the year of the entry (such as the writers' works she
was reading at age twelve). Once her career begins most attention is paid to
her works, with brief descriptive commentary on each one cited. Not an
exhaustive account of the Brazilian writer's life and career by any means, but a
good outline sketch for the reader not concerned with detail. Supplemented by
a brief introduction to Lispector's worldview, the nature of her characters, and
her thoughts on writing. Titles in Portuguese with English translations.

Commentary

Birn, Randi. "Clarice Lispector." In *Critical Survey of Long Fiction*, edited by
Frank N. Magill, Supplement. Pasadena, Calif.: Salem Press, 1987.
A roughly eight-page overview of Lispector's work in long fiction. Contains a
list of her principal novels (some only in Portuguese), a summary of her work
in other literary forms, and an assessment of her achievements. This is followed by a biographical sketch and a six-page overview and analysis of six of
her novels, including *The Apple in the Dark*, *The Passion According to G. H.*,
and *The Hour of the Star*. A good introduction for the reader unfamiliar with
Lispector's work in general and her novels in particular. Includes a list of her
other major works (most in Portuguese) and a short critical bibliography
(almost all in Portuguese). Titles of translated works and quotations in English.

Brower, Keith H. "Clarice Lispector." In *Critical Survey of Short Fiction*, edited by
Frank N. Magill, Supplement. Pasadena, Calif.: Salem Press, 1987.
A roughly six-page overview of Lispector's work in short fiction. Contains a
list of her principal collections of short stories (some only in Portuguese), a
summary of her work in other literary forms, and an assessment of her place in
Brazilian literature. This is followed by a brief biographical sketch and an
analysis (comprising approximately four pages of the article) on the nature and
characteristics of her short stories, with a review of her various collections and
the particular nature of each. Some limited attention to representative stories
from each collection. A ·fine overview of the Brazilian writer's work in the
short story. Provides a list of her other major works (some in Portuguese) and
a short critical bibliography in English. Titles in Portuguese with English
translations.

Fitz, Earl E. "Clarice Lispector." In *Dictionary of Brazilian Literature*, edited by
Irwin Stern. Westport, Conn.: Greenwood Press, 1988.
A brief (roughly three-page) introduction to Lispector's life and career. Includes an assessment of Lispector's place in Brazilian letters, followed by a
brief discussion of her work both as a short story writer (with emphasis on
Family Ties) and as a novelist (focusing primarily on *The Apple in the Dark*).
Quick mention of her later fiction and her nonfiction (including children's
literature). A good starting point for the reader unfamiliar with Lispector. List
of additional selected works in Portuguese and English. Short critical bibliography in English.

——————— . "Clarice Lispector." In *Latin American Literature in the Twentieth
Century: A Guide*, edited by Leonard S. Klein. New York: Frederick Ungar,
1986.
A brief (roughly three-page) introduction to Lispector's life and works. Discussion of the Brazilian writer's *Family Ties* as a prime example of her short
fiction, as well as commentary on her novel *The Apple in the Dark*. Brief
mention of other novels which treat the same themes as *The Apple in the Dark*.
Consideration of Lispector's place in Brazil's post-World War II fiction. A
good starting point for the uninitiated reader. List of Lispector's other works
(in Portuguese) not mentioned in the text. Short critical bibliography in English.

——————— . "Freedom and Self-Realization: Feminist Characterization in the
Fiction of Clarice Lispector." *Modern Language Studies* 10 (Fall, 1980): 51-61.
In this excellent article, Fitz explains and defends Lispector's method of
characterization (the aspect of her narrative which has received the most criticism) and provides, as well, the Brazilian writer's "unique interpretation of
feminism." Some of Fitz's many cogent observations are that Lispector's

characters are presented not according to the tenets of literary realism but those of the "lyrical novel," that her characters "are developed more through what they cogitate about than what they say aloud or actually do," and that the power of Lispector's own nonpolitical, individualized brand of feminism "to break the bond of stagnant quiescence that imprisons her characters actually pushes them forward, occasionally with deleterious results, toward freedom and self-realization." A must read for the reader seeking a better understanding of Lispector's characterization methods, her feminism, and, by extension, her characters. Titles and quotations in English.

Lowe, Elizabeth. "The Passion According to C. L." *Review 24* (1980): 34-37.
Lowe provides an introduction to the nature of Lispector's fictional world as well as a very brief sketch of the Brazilian writer's life and career, before introducing the interview she conducted in Lispector's apartment. In the interview itself, Lispector responds to questions concerning inspiration in literary creation, art as an antidote for madness, her work habits, her dog, the significance she attaches to animals in her stories, Jean-Paul Sartre, when she started to write, city life, what she was like as a girl, and other topics. Personal and insightful, though not particularly in-depth. Titles in English.

Moisés, Massaud. "Clarice Lispector: Fiction and Cosmic Vision." Translated by Sara M. McCabe. *Studies in Short Fiction* 8 (Winter, 1971): 268-281.
Moisés provides a thorough analysis of the nature of Lispector's short fiction, concentrating on the thematics of her works and how various elements of her stories both reflect and support the writer's "cosmic vision." One aspect of Lispector's stories mentioned by the critic is "the privileged moment," in which "the 'I' and the universe meet as if for the first time, framed in a halo of original 'purity,' causing the mutual discovery to become suspended in time, a vision of the most intimate part of reality, without deformation of thought or prejudice." From this, the critic contends, "the person comprehends his own secret and that of the universe, but must return immediately to his previous (un)consciousness, which allows him to live without major anxiety." An excellent article. Titles in Portuguese. Quotations from Lispector's works in English, from other sources in Spanish and French with English translations.

The Apple in the Dark (A maçã no oscuro)
Fitz, Earl E. "The Leitmotif of Darkness in Seven Novels by Clarice Lispector." *Chasqui* 7 (February, 1978): 18-27.
In his conclusion to this excellent article, Fitz states that "the leitmotif of darkness is called upon in its existential, psychological, and linguistic modes, to express and convey the attitudes of angst, nausea, confusion, and desperation that so permeate the lives of the author's characters." *The Apple in the Dark*, in which darkness, Fitz contends, is the central metaphor for the work

from the title onward, is one of the seven works the critic examines on his way
to this conclusion. A superb study of the topic at hand. Titles and quotations in
Portuguese.

——————— . "Novels and Stories." In his *Clarice Lispector*. Boston: Twayne,
1986.

Fitz devotes three pages of this chapter to an overview and analysis of *The
Apple in the Dark*, which the critic contends "anticipates the even more
philosophical and lyrical novels that would follow." Fitz presents a plot summary and focuses his critical attention on the work's themes, characters, and
technical features (chiefly style and structure). An excellent introduction to the
work in question. Titles in Portuguese. Quotations in English.

Family Ties (Laços de família)

Cook, Bruce. "Women in the Web." *Review 73* (Spring, 1973): 65-66.

Essentially a short review article on *Family Ties*, in which Cook warns the
reader looking for picturesque details and local color of Brazil in Lispector's
stories and praises the writer's immense talent for conveying interior reality.
Some comparison of Lispector to Virginia Woolf. Brief reference to a few
stories, with an example of Lispector's convincing description of madness in
"The Imitation of the Rose" cited most prominently. Some comments on the
quality of the translation. Not so much analytical as descriptive. Titles and
quotations in English.

Fitz, Earl E. "Novels and Stories." In his *Clarice Lispector*. Boston: Twayne, 1986.

Fitz devotes roughly eleven pages of this chapter to a discussion of *Family Ties*.
In sections entitled *"Alguns contos"* (some stories)—the title under which six
of the stories of *Family Ties* were first published—and *"Laços de família"*
(the Portuguese title of *Family Ties*), the critic presents an excellent overview
of the nature of the stories that make up the collection, which Fitz calls "one
of the most original and powerful books of its time in Latin America." The
critic concentrates his discussion on the internal nature of Lispector's stories
and the skill with which she renders it. The story "Love," which Fitz calls
"one of her most famous and respected stories" and "one of her most finely
crafted pieces as well," receives almost seven pages of meticulous analysis as a
prime example of the stories that make up *Family Ties*. A superb introduction
to and overview of the collection. Titles and most quotations in Portuguese
with English translations. Some quotations in English only.

Herman, Rita. "Existence in *Laços de família*." *Luso-Brazilian Review* 4 (June,
1967): 69-74.

Herman discusses what she views as the "essential paradox" in Lispector's
Family Ties: "In spite of the fact that existence is viewed as totally negative,

conditioned by interior disunity, according to the author, this very situation must be maintained in order for one to be a human being." This, the critic implies, is why Lispector's protagonists in this collection achieve a new state of awareness only to return to their everyday existences, as, in these stories, the characters, "fully aware of their own useless efforts, know they must stop themselves from making any sort of metaphysical leap. On the contrary, all their psychic energy is utilized towards perpetuating absurdity," which, Lispector implies, is what makes them human. To support her contentions, the critic briefly discusses or refers to several stories from the collection, such as "The Imitation of the Rose," and, most notably, "Love." A solid study. Titles and quotations in Portuguese.

Lastinger, Valérie C. "Humor in a New Reading of Clarice Lispector." *Hispania* 72 (March, 1989): 130-137.
Lastinger contends that while much attention has been paid to Lispector's existentialist leanings and her use of the epiphany in her short stories, the presence and function of humor in her work has been overlooked. The critic first discusses some theories of humor in general and then divides modes of humor present in the stories of *Family Ties* into three types: (1) comedy of situation, (2) comedy of ideas, and (3) comedy of manipulation of narrative techniques. She then examines several stories in the collection before concluding, in part, that humor in Lispector's works is "a very effective way for her to mark her idiosyncrasy and independence from the authors to whom she owes so much, allowing her to introduce the feminine presence in philosophical discourse." An interesting piece on a generally ignored element of Lispector's works. Titles and quotations in English.

Nunes, Maria Luisa. "Narrative Modes in Clarice Lispector's *Laços de família*: The Rendering of Consciousness." *Luso-Brazilian Review* 14 (Winter, 1977): 174-184.
Using the examples provided by several stories in *Family Ties* (including "The Imitation of the Rose," "Love," "The Daydreams of a Drunken Woman," and "The Crime of the Mathematics Professor"), Nunes examines how Lispector renders the consciousness of her protagonists, contending from the outset that the Brazilian writer employs "certain traditional techniques," these being "*style indirect libre* or narrated monologue, interior monologue, internal analysis including sensory impressions, direct discourse in the form of 'asides,' and the mixture of many of the above techniques." The critic explains each technique and shows how they are deftly used by Lispector to convey the inner workings of her characters. An excellent, very readable article. Titles and quotations from Lispector's works in Portuguese.

Peixoto, Marta. "*Family Ties*: Female Development in Clarice Lispector." In *The Voyage In: Fictions of Female Development*, edited by Elizabeth Abel, Marianne Hirsch, and Elizabeth Langland. Hanover, N.H.: University Press of New England, 1983.

In this article on female development in Lispector's fiction, Peixoto concentrates on the female protagonists of the stories in *Family Ties*, stories which the critic believes "can be read as versions of a single developmental tale that provides patterns of female possibilities, vulnerability, and power in Lispector's world." Peixoto meticulously examines several stories and shows how their female protagonists, through an epiphany, usually break out of their "metaphoric prisons formed by their eager compliance with conforming social roles." Their escape is only momentary, however, as they return to the role which imprisons them, as their "potential development . . . again and again falters and stops short" of permanent change. Peixoto does view "The Smallest Woman in the World" as an ironic exception to this pattern, of this "predominantly bleak view of female possibilities." A solid, complete article. Titles and quotations in English.

The Hour of the Star (A hora da estrela)

Fitz, Earl E. "Novels and Stories." In his *Clarice Lispector*. Boston: Twayne, 1986.

Fitz devotes three pages of this chapter to a discussion of *The Hour of the Star* about which the critic writes, "Lispector wrote in *A hora da estrela* [*The Hour of the Star*] a novel that attempts to merge the lyricism and hermeticism so characteristic of her best work with a theme of overt 'social relevancy.'" Fitz's discussion of the novel features a plot summary and critical consideration of the work's themes, its characters, and its technical elements (chiefly with respect to style and structure). A fine introduction to this novel. Titles in Portuguese. Quotations in Portuguese with English translations.

The Passion According to G. H. (A paixão segundo G. H.)

Dixon, Paul B. "*A paixão segundo G. H.*: Kafka's Passion according to Clarice Lispector." *Romance Notes* 21 (Spring, 1981): 298-304.

Dixon uses his article "to show that Clarice Lispector's *A paixão segundo G. H.* [*The Passion According to G. H.*] is a retelling of [Franz Kafka's] 'The Metamorphosis,' that the essential structure of the two tales is the same, and that the thematic richness óf Clarice's work is heightened when it is read as a corroboration of Kafka's story." A concise and detailed study of the topic. Titles and quotations from Lispector's work in Portuguese, from Kafka's work in English (though some German terms are used occasionally by the critic, though always with English translations).

Fitz, Earl E. "The Leitmotif of Darkness in Seven Novels by Clarice Lispector." *Chasqui* 7 (February, 1978): 18-27.

Fitz concludes his excellent article by stating that "the leitmotif of darkness is called upon in its existential, psychological, and linguistic modes . . . to express and convey the attitudes of angst, nausea, confusion, and desperation that so permeate the lives of the author's characters." *The Passion According to G. H.*, in which the protagonist's "psychic odyssey" begins in the darkness of night (reflecting her confused mind) and ends in the light of dawn (reflecting her "newly acquired sense of space, time, and being."), is one of the seven novels Fitz examines on his way to his conclusion. A superb and very readable study of the topic. Titles and quotations in Portuguese.

_____ . "Novels and Stories." In his *Clarice Lispector*. Boston: Twayne, 1986.
Three pages of this chapter are given over to a discussion of *The Passion According to G. H.*, which Fitz calls "one of the most singular Latin American novels of the 1960s." The critic's treatment of the novel features a summary of its plot and analytical observations concerning its themes, characters, and technical aspects (principally with regard to style and structure). An excellent introduction to the work. Titles in Portuguese. Quotations in Portuguese with English translations.

García, Rubén. "The Unexpected Correspondences: *A Paixão segundo G. H.* and *Dom Casmurro*." *Hispanófila* 29 (January, 1986): 55-61.
García contends that in spite of her connection to numerous Brazilian psychological novelists, such as Cornélio Penna and Lúcio Cardoso, Lispector belongs to a broader tradition of Brazilian literature, specifically that represented by Machado de Assis. To support his contention, he compares numerous aspects of Machado's *Dom Casmurro* and Lispector's *The Passion According to G. H.*, using numerous examples from the two texts to establish their similarities regarding the concern for identity, the "absolute obsession with time," similar first-person narrators, the emphasis on interior as opposed to exterior time, the lack of a "rigorous distinction between the inner world of the imagination and the outer world of the concrete," and sight, photography, mask, and ritual as symbols. Titles and quotations in Portuguese.

"The Buffalo" ("O búfalo")
Peixoto, Marta. "*Family Ties*: Female Development in Clarice Lispector." In *The Voyage In: Fictions of Female Development*, edited by Elizabeth Abel, Marianne Hirsch, and Elizabeth Langland. Hanover, N.H.: University Press of New England, 1983.
In an article focusing on female development in Lispector's fiction in general and *Family Ties* in particular, Peixoto considers "The Buffalo," in which the protagonist "focuses on the buffalo in her effort to force herself from her own compulsion to be the loving and pardoning female." The critic interprets the end of the story as both negative and positive from the standpoint of female development. Part of an excellent article and best read within the context of the entire piece. Titles and quotations in English.

"The Chicken" ("A galinha")

Lastinger, Valérie C. "Humor in a New Reading of Clarice Lispector." *Hispania* 72 (March, 1989): 130-137.

"The Chicken" receives the majority of Lastinger's attention in this article focusing exclusively on humor in the stories of *Family Ties*. The story is examined from several angles, first as a "comedy of situation," then for the humor expressed through the reference to the chicken's "female characteristics," and finally for the manner in which the narrator plays with the reader ("as he would with a yo-yo," Lastinger contends). Part of an article on a largely overlooked aspect of Lispector's fiction and best read within the context of the entire piece. Titles and quotations in English.

Peixoto, Marta. "*Family Ties*: Female Development in Clarice Lispector." In *The Voyage In: Fictions of Female Development*, edited by Elizabeth Abel, Marianne Hirsch, and Elizabeth Langland. Hanover, N.H.: University Press of New England, 1983.

In this article which focuses primarily on the theme of female development as expressed in *Family Ties*, Peixoto discusses "The Chicken" as a story in which "the limitations of the female role take on the sharpness of caricature," a story which "repeats the plot of failed escape from the confining roles of nurturing and submission" found throughout the collection. Part of an excellent article and best read within the context of the entire piece. Titles and quotations in English.

"The Daydreams of a Drunk Woman" ("Devaneio e embriaguez duma rapariga")

Lastinger, Valérie C. "Humor in a New Reading of Clarice Lispector." *Hispania* 72 (March, 1989): 130-137.

In this article focusing on humor in *Family Ties*, Lastinger very briefly examines humor in "The Daydreams of a Drunk Woman." She finds that the juxtaposition of two events "creates a comical situation: as the husband's friend tries to seduce the woman, and is therefore probably taking inventory of her sexual features, a fly lands on the woman's breast!" The critic goes on to state that "the reader imagines either the seducer noticing the fly on the bosom he admires, or the woman discreetly trying to chase it away." Part of an interesting article on this overlooked aspect of Lispector's fiction and best read in the context of the entire piece. Titles and quotations in English.

"The Dinner" ("O jantar")

Lastinger, Valérie C. "Humor in a New Reading of Clarice Lispector." *Hispania* 72 (March, 1989): 130-137.

While analyzing the presence, expression, and significance of humor in Lispector's fiction in general and in *Family Ties* in particular, Lastinger discusses

"The Dinner," the humor of which she classifies as "humor of narration." She focuses on the story's point of view and its resulting tone. Part of an interesting article on this overlooked aspect of Lispector's fiction and best read within the context of the entire piece. Titles and quotations in English.

"Family Ties" ("Laços de família")

Peixoto, Marta. "*Family Ties*: Female Development in Clarice Lispector." In *The Voyage In: Fictions of Female Development*, edited by Elizabeth Abel, Marianne Hirsch, and Elizabeth Langland. Hanover, N.H.: University Press of New England, 1983.

In the process of examining female development in Lispector's fiction, and particularly *Family Ties*, Peixoto analyzes the female protagonist of the title story. As the critic points out at one point, the stories of this collection "present the dark side of family ties, where bonds of affection become cages and prison bars," and such, Peixoto finds, is the case in this story, in which "the power the woman yields within the family has a negative, constricting side: deprived of the chance to develop herself beyond the scope of the family, she attempts to control those close to her." Part of an excellent article and best read in context of the entire piece. Titles and quotations in English.

"Happy Birthday" ("Feliz aniversário")

Lastinger, Valérie C. "Humor in a New Reading of Clarice Lispector." *Hispania* 72 (March, 1989): 130-137.

In the process of studying humor in Lispector's works in general and in *Family Ties* in particular, Lastinger discusses the comic elements found in "Happy Birthday." The critic categorizes this story in the comic mode of "comedy of situation" and, after some references to the text, concludes that the "comical effect here lies on the one hand on the discrepancy between the hypocritical atmosphere of harmony and the candor of the mother's gesture," while "on the other hand, it is also humorous because the mother is not clearly conscious of having spat." Part of an interesting article on a largely overlooked element of Lispector's fiction and best read in the context of the entire piece. Titles and quotations in English.

Peixoto, Marta. "*Family Ties*: Female Development in Clarice Lispector." In *The Voyage In: Fictions of Female Development*, edited by Elizabeth Abel, Marianne Hirsch, and Elizabeth Langland. Hanover, N.H.: University Press of New England, 1983.

In this article which focuses primarily on the theme of female development in *Family Ties*, Peixoto devotes considerable attention to the theme as expressed through the protagonist of "Happy Birthday." She focuses on the symbolism of many of the actions and images associated with the protagonist, claiming that "Lispector suggests that the role of matriarch affords a false power that entraps women as well as their families." The critic concludes, however, that the old woman, as is the case with so many of Lispector's female protagonists, returns at the end to her initial situation, "an action typical of this collection which expresses, as Peixoto calls it, a "predominantly bleak of female possibilities." Part of an excellent article and best read within the context of the entire piece. Titles and quotations in English.

"The Imitation of the Rose" ("A imitaçao da rosa")

Peixoto, Marta. "*Family Ties*: Female Development in Clarice Lispector." In *The Voyage In: Fictions of Female Development*, edited by Elizabeth Abel, Marianne Hirsch, and Elizabeth Langland. Hanover, N.H.: University Press of New England, 1983.

In the process of examining the theme of female development in Lispector's fiction, specifically as expressed in *Family Ties*, Peixoto discusses the female protagonist of "The Imitation of the Rose." The critic finds, as is the case in many stories from this collection, "a familiar domestic world threatened and undercut by the laws of another realm." Peixoto examines the protagonist's conflict between sanity and madness and places this struggle within the context of the theme of female development. Part of an excellent article and best re⸀ ⸀ within the context of the entire piece. Titles and quotations in English.

"Love" ("Amor")

Fitz, Earl E. "Novels and Stories." In his *Clarice Lispector*. Boston: Twayne, 1986.

Of the eleven pages of this chapter given over to a discussion of *Family Ties*, almost seven are devoted to a meticulous analysis of the story "Love." Fitz states that "all of the elements characteristic of Lispector's work can be found in this story, which is perhaps her best known and most anthologized piece of writing." The critic's analysis proceeds step-by-step through the story's plot, as Fitz stops to point out significant aspects of the narrative as they present themselves. Emphasis is on theme, style, structure, narrative perspective, and ambiguity, as the critic presents an excellent analysis of the story in question. Title and some quotations in Portuguese with English translations. Other quotations in English.

Herman, Rita. "Existence in *Laços de família*." *Luso-Brazilian Review* 4 (June, 1967): 69-74.

Herman establishes what she considers the "essential paradox" in the stories of Lispector's *Family Ties*: "In spite of the fact that existence is viewed as totally negative, conditioned by interior disunity, according to the author, this very situation must be maintained in order for one to be a human being." For this reason, the critic contends, in *Family Ties*, the characters, "fully aware of their own useless efforts, know they must stop themselves from making any sort of metaphysical leap. On the contrary, all their psychic energy is utilized towards perpetuating absurdity." A protagonist who does this, and who receives the bulk of Herman's attention, is Ana of "Love." The critic shows how Ana, like other protagonists in *Family Ties*, achieves a state of new awareness, only to return to her everyday existence. She, the critic states, "has returned to contradiction, to duplicity, to failure—a failure that for Clarice Lispector signifies success." A solid study. Titles and quotations in Portuguese.

Lastinger, Valérie C. "Humor in a New Reading of Clarice Lispector." *Hispania* 72 (March, 1989): 130-137.
"Love" is one of several stories from *Family Ties* discussed in this article on humor in Lispector's fiction in general and in this collection in particular. Lastinger finds comical the fact that Lispector's pregnant protagonist suffers from nausea brought on by morning sickness, not comical itself, but comical given the fact that Lispector is playing a semantic game with the work "nausea," also associated with existentialism. Part of an article on this overlooked element of the Brazilian writer's fiction and best read within the context of the entire piece. Titles and quotations in English.

Lindstrom, Naomi. "Clarice Lispector: Articulating Woman's Experience." *Chasqui* 8 (November, 1978): 43-52.
Lindstrom examines the narrative voice employed in "Love" and its relationship to the emerging (and then fading) self-awareness of the protagonist, Ana. Lindstrom states that the "handling of narrative voice in this story draws attention to a phenomenon frequently explored in the social essays of feminists [that of voicelessness before self-awareness and growth]." To quote the critic again, "the narrator's varying degrees of intervention give an index of Ana's progress and regression," as the narrator first dominates the story (in comparison to Ana's relative inarticulateness), then allows the more expressive Ana to speak, only to take over the narrative in the end as the protagonist "finds no supportive response." An interesting reading of the story. Titles and quotations from Lispector's work in Portuguese.

Peixoto, Marta. "*Family Ties*: Female Development in Clarice Lispector." In *The Voyage In: Fictions of Female Development*, edited by Elizabeth Abel, Marianne Hirsch, and Elizabeth Langland. Hanover, N.H.: University Press of New England, 1983.
In this article focusing on female development in Lispector's fiction in general and in *Family Ties* in particular, Peixoto analyzes the female protagonist of "Love." The critic examines Anna's symbolic connection to the blind man and to the plants and the epiphany she experiences. Peixoto concludes, however, that as "Anna puts out the light of her confused enlightenment, a flame that would threaten her domestic life if it were allowed to burn," her potential development, like that of most of the female protagonists in this collection,

"falters and stops short." Part of an excellent article and best read in the context of the entire piece. Titles and quotations in English.

"Mystery in São Cristóvão" ("Mistério em São Cristóvão")

Peixoto, Marta. "*Family Ties*: Female Development in Clarice Lispector." In *The Voyage In: Fictions of Female Development*, edited by Elizabeth Abel, Marianne Hirsch, and Elizabeth Langland. Hanover, N.H.: University Press of New England, 1983.

Examining female development in Lispector's fiction, and particularly in *Family Ties*, Peixoto briefly touches on the female protagonist of "Mystery in São Cristóvão," comparing the girl to the broken hyacinth. This story falls into the category of adolescent initiation, and the message of both this story and "Preciousness," when compared to "The Beginnings of a Fortune" (with a male protagonist), is that development, "for the young girls, clearly will not proceed according to the male model." Part of an excellent article and best read within the context of the entire piece. Titles and quotations in English.

"Preciousness" ("Preciosidade")

Peixoto, Marta. "*Family Ties*: Female Development in Clarice Lispector." In *The Voyage In: Fictions of Female Development*, edited by Elizabeth Abel, Marianne Hirsch, and Elizabeth Langland. Hanover, N.H.: University Press of New England, 1983.

In this article focusing primarily on the theme of female development as expressed in the stories of *Family Ties*, Peixoto analyzes "Preciousness" as a story in which the protagonist "accepts and turns to advantage" her negative experience. On the one hand, she realizes that she is "precious." On the other, however, she "retreats into a profound passivity" as a result of the experience. Peixoto finds that the protagonist fits a pattern common to all but one in this collection, a pattern in which the character has a moment of progress, or development, only to return to the confines of that which imprisoned her. Part of an excellent article. Titles and quotations in English.

"The Smallest Woman in the World" ("A menor mulher do mundo")

Lastinger, Valérie C. "Humor in a New Reading of Clarice Lispector." *Hispania* 72 (March, 1989): 130-137.

In this article on humor in Lispector's work in general and *Family Ties* in particular, Lastinger briefly (two lengthy paragraphs) discusses humor in "The Smallest Woman in the World." The critic points out similarities between Lispector's story and Voltaire's *Micromégas*, and later lists several comic elements in the story: "the false feeling of superiority of the readers of the Sunday paper; the short focuses on each family's reaction which catches each one of them red-handed as they quickly claim ownership of the woman; the irony of the defense they put up in front of the savage human nature they feel has been exposed in them." Lastinger contends that the main comic event comes when the explorer finds the woman also "is primarily preoccupied by material possession." Best read within the context of entire article. Titles and quotations in English.

Peixoto, Marta. "*Family Ties*: Female Development in Clarice Lispector." In *The Voyage In: Fictions of Female Development*, edited by Elizabeth Abel, Marianne Hirsch, and Elizabeth Langland. Hanover, N.H.: University Press of New England, 1983.

In this article focusing primarily on the theme of female development as expressed in *Family Ties*, Peixoto finds the protagonist of "The Smallest Woman in the World" to be an ironic exception to the "predominantly bleak view of female possibilities" largely expressed by the female protagonists of the other stories in the collection. She does not experience an epiphany but does cause "moments of insight in other characters" and "manages to retain the tranquil independence sought eagerly by city-bred women in then civilized world of enclosed spaces, prescribed behavior and family ties." Part of an excellent article and best read within the context of the entire piece. Titles and quotations in English.

LYA LUFT
Brazil

Commentary

Stern, Irwin. "Lya Luft." In his *Dictionary of Brazilian Literature*. Westport,
Conn.: Greenwood Press, 1988.

Stern presents a brief introduction to Luft's career and works. A short statement concerning the nature of her novels is followed by a paragraph containing
succinct comments about two of her works, including *The Island of the Dead*.
In a final paragraph, Stern compares aspects of Luft's works to those of
Virginia Woolf and Clarice Lispector, as well as Adélia Prado. A good starting
point for the reader unfamiliar with Luft. A list of additional works by the
writer in Portuguese and a short critical bibliography in Portuguese and English.

The Island of the Dead (O quarto fechado)

McClendon, Carmen Chaves. "Theoretical Dialogue in *O Quarto Fechado*." *Chasqui* 17 (November, 1988): 23-26.

McClendon cites Luft's background as a professor of literature, a teacher of
literary theory, and poses the question, "How does a professor of literature,
who is a talented writer, think through a particularly confusing theoretical
point?" Her answer: "She writes a novel." The critic states that "rather than
framing her writing theory, Luft seems to enter into a dialogue with literary
theory." McClendon supports this contention by analyzing "the reflection of
[Michel] Foucault's 'Language to Infinity' mirrored in Luft's *O Quarto
Fechado [The Island of the Dead]*." The results of her detailed analysis are
intriguing and present a unique view of Luft's novel. Prior knowledge of
Foucault's theories is not absolutely necessary, but helpful. Titles and quotations in Portuguese.

MANUEL PUIG
Argentina

Biography

Schwartz, Ronald. "Puig: Argentine 'Camp.'" In his *Nomads, Exiles, and Émigrés: The Rebirth of the Latin American Narrative, 1960-80*. Metuchen, N.J.: Scarecrow Press, 1980.

A chapter with two apparent purposes: (1) to provide a brief biographical sketch of Puig; and (2) to discuss in some detail *Kiss of the Spider Woman*. The biographical sketch occupies roughly six pages of this twelve-page chapter. It is filled with details of Puig's life, with considerable emphasis on the role of movies in his life. The sketch also provides information on his novels, including a fair amount of commentary on each one, producing, in effect, both a biography and an overview of the writer's works. A good starting point for the reader unfamiliar with Puig. Titles in English.

Commentary

Bacarisse, Pamela. "The Projection of Peronism in the Novels of Manuel Puig." In *The Historical Novel in Latin America*, edited by Daniel Balderston. Gaithersburg, Md.: Ediciones Hispamérica, 1986.

Bacarisse contends that "politics—that is to say, Peronism—are in evidence in all" of Puig's novels, "even if only in the background, constituting a vaguely-discernible substructure to a society that is being remembered and even, one might claim, analyzed, by the author." She studies how Peronism specifically manifests itself in Puig's writing and what thematic role it plays in general. Article is laced with considerable background on the Peronist Argentina of which the critic speaks. Titles and quotations in Spanish.

Bouman, Katherine A. "Manuel Puig at the University of Missouri-Columbia." *The American Hispanist* 2, no. 17 (1977): 11-12.

An account of a question-and-answer session conducted by Puig at the University of Missouri at Columbia on April 4, 1977. The account is a mix of summaries of the Argentine writer's comments, direct quotations, and background description of the event itself. The text presents an overview of Puig's career through *Kiss of the Spider Woman*, supplemented by Puig's personal comments on the role of films in his life and his writing, women in Argentine society, Argentine politics, and critics. A very general account. Titles in English.

Christ, Ronald. "An Interview with Manuel Puig." *Partisan Review* 44 (1977): 52-61.

In an interview with the critic, Puig provides insightful and somewhat lengthy responses to questions concerning what he writes about and how he does it, the presence of social criticism in his works, how he finds a form for his novels, his work as art, the influence of films in his works and those of other Latin American writers, translations of his novels, the thematic focus of his works, the women's movement, and other topics. Interesting and informative. Titles and quotations in English.

Lindstrom, Naomi. "Manuel Puig." In *Critical Survey of Long Fiction* (Foreign Language Series), edited by Frank N. Magill, vol. 3. Pasadena, Calif.: Salem Press, 1984.

A twelve-page introduction to Puig and his work in long fiction. Contains a list of his principal novels (almost all with English translations), a summary of his work in other literary forms, and an assessment of his achievements. This is followed by a biographical sketch and an eight-page overview and analysis of his major novels. A good introduction for the reader unfamiliar with Puig's work in general and his novels in particular. Includes a list of the Argentine writer's other works (most in Spanish only) and a short critical bibliography almost exclusively in English. Titles of translated works in English.

——————————. "The Problem of Pop Culture in the Novels of Manuel Puig." *The American Hispanist* 4 nos. 30-31 (November/December, 1978): 28-31.

Lindstrom sets out in her article to address two questions: "First, how does 'pop' culture manifest itself in Puig's novels? Secondly, what is Puig's novelistic attitude toward this culture?" She gathers numerous clear examples and draws conclusions from four of Puig's novels before stating in the final paragraph that "Puig shows how massive and multifaceted a role pop culture and the media play in the lives of contemporary Western society." A very readable piece on a prominent aspect of Puig's works. Titles and quotations in Spanish.

Mitchell, Phyllis. "The Reel Against the Real: Cinema in the Novels of Guillermo Cabrera Infante and Manuel Puig." *Latin American Literary Review* 11 (Fall/Winter, 1977): 22-29.

In this article on the influence of the movies in the works of Puig and Cabrera Infante, Mitchell makes reference to Puig's *Betrayed by Rita Hayworth*, *Heartbreak Tango*, and *The Buenos Aires Affair*. In the course of her analysis, the critic makes several cogent observations concerning the role of movies in the Argentine writer's works, finding, for example, that Puig's characters are essentially poor, small-town, nonliterary people who "long to escape to the glamour of the big city," characters for whom "films provide a shared experience about which the characters can talk or against which they measure themselves and each other." She concludes, that "because they mistake entertainment for reality, the film becomes a trap which gives the characters no incentive to come to grips with their situation and no way to ever feel satisfied with themselves." Titles and quotations in English.

Puig, Manuel. "Growing Up at the Movies: A Chronology." *Review 72* (Winter/ Spring, 1971-1972): 49-51.

A brief, personal, almost year-by-year account of Puig's life and career through 1969 by the author himself, with considerable reference, as the title suggests, to the influence and place of movies in his life and work. Not in-depth but informative. Titles of Puig's works in Spanish.

Southard, David R. "Betrayed by Manuel Puig: Reader Deception and Anti-Climax in His Novels." *Latin American Literary Review* 9 (1976): 22-28.

Southard examines Puig's "use of deception as a technical device which, by misleading the reader, contributes to the sense of anti-climax." Following a detailed analysis of reader deception and anticlimax in *Betrayed by Rita Hayworth*, *Heartbreak Tango*, and *The Buenos Aires Affair*, Southard concludes, in part, that the evolution of this aspect of Puig's novels reflects the writer's increasing interest in reader involvement and in plot in his works. The anticlimax, Southard contends, also plays an important part in Puig's manipulation of time and is "possibly the most significant element of Puig's works. Interesting perspective. Titles and quotations in Spanish.

Williams, Raymond L. "Manuel Puig." In *Latin American Literature in the Twentieth Century: A Guide*, edited by Leonard S. Klein. New York: Frederick Ungar, 1986.

A brief (roughly two-page) introduction to Puig's life and works and a quick overview of his major works, followed by a description of his dominant thematic concerns. Provides a two-paragraph discussion of *Betrayed by Rita Hayworth*, with emphasis on the novel's thematic and technical characteristics. A good starting point for the reader unfamiliar with Puig. "Further Work" section provides one title (in Spanish) not mentioned in the text. Short critical bibliography in English.

Betrayed by Rita Hayworth (La traición de Rita Hayworth)

Review 72 (Winter/Spring, 1971-1972): 48-64. A "Focus" section devoted to Puig and *Betrayed by Rita Hayworth*.

The first piece of this section, "Growing Up at the Movies: A Chronology," by Puig himself, provides a brief but personal account of the Argentine author's life and career through 1969, with emphasis on the influence of movies in his life and work. In "The New Art of Narrating Films," Marta Morello Frosch discusses the influence of movies on the characters of the novel in question, and Emir Rodríguez Monegal, in his "A Literary Myth Exploded," discusses Puig's novel as one which, in part at least, "explodes some of the cultural principles of experimental and avant-garde novels." Informative, providing valuable perspectives on the novel. Titles (except in Puig's chronology) and quotations in English.

Southard, David R. "Betrayed by Manuel Puig: Reader Deception and Anti-Climax in His Novels." *Latin American Literary Review* 9 (1976): 22-28.

In this article, Southard examines "the use of deception as a technical device which, by misleading the reader, contributes to the sense of anti-climax." The first work he analyzes with respect to this aspect of Puig's writing is *Betrayed by Rita Hayworth*. Southard identifies the misplaced letter, revealed in the last chapter, as the "main element of the novelist's deception by withholding information." The letter, appearing out of sequence, "eliminates any climactic ending which could neatly resolve the story lines in the novel." Comparison of the reader-deception and anticlimax factor in this novel with that of *Heartbreak Tango* and *The Buenos Aires Affair*. Conclusions concerning this aspect of Puig's novels. Titles and quotations in Spanish.

The Buenos Aires Affair

Kelly, John R. "*The Buenos Aires Affair*." In *Magill's Literary Annual*, 1977, edited by Frank N. Magill, vol. 1. Pasadena, Calif.: Salem Press, 1977.

Kelly begins his four-page overview of *The Buenos Aires Affair* with a discussion of the "Boom" in Latin American fiction and the place of Puig's works within the "Boom." This is followed by a discussion of various elements of the novel in question, including the interaction of the principal characters, the novel as detective fiction (with reference to Jorge Luis Borges' "Emma Zunz") and as a parody of that genre, and the Argentine author's incorporation of film and cinematic techniques into his work. An excellent introduction to the novel. "Sources for Further Study" section lists review articles of the work (in English). Titles and quotations in English.

Southard, David R. "Betrayed by Manuel Puig: Reader Deception and Anti-Climax in His Novels." *Latin American Literary Review* 9 (1976): 22-28.

Southard sets out to examine "the use of deception as a technical device which, by misleading the reader, contributes to the sense of anti-climax" in Puig's novels. One of the works Southard examines in this respect is *The Buenos Aires Affair*, in which much of the reader deception and anticlimax come from the "out-of-context action" of the "murder" scene and Leo's self-deception. *Betrayed by Rita Hayworth* and *Heartbreak Tango* are also discussed. Offers conclusions on the significance of this aspect of Puig's fiction. Titles and quotations in Spanish.

Eternal Curse on the Reader of These Pages (Maldición eterna a quien lea estas páginas)

De Feo, Ronald. "Manuel Puig's *Eternal Curse on the Reader of These Pages*." *Review 31* (January-April, 1982): 16-18.

A review article in which De Feo describes Puig's first novel written in English as "an extended psychodrama for two devious players, two alienated souls who in their verbal exchanges sometimes connect and even merge on occasion, but who still, paradoxically, remain at a distance." The critic discusses the novel's relationship to Puig's other works, its style, the presence (or relative lack thereof) of elements of pop culture in the novel, the difficulty of discerning reality from illusion, the work's characters and their interrelationships, as well as Puig's use of dialogue and his success (mostly concerning cultural authenticity) at producing a novel in English. A good introduction to the novel. Titles and quotations in English.

Liberti di Barrio, Olga. *"Eternal Curse on the Reader of These Pages."* In *Magill's Literary Annual*, 1983, edited by Frank N. Magill, vol. 1. Pasadena, Calif.: Salem Press, 1983.

Liberti di Barrio begins her roughly four-page article on *Eternal Curse on the Reader of These Pages* with background information on this novel which "was written in English, then translated to Spanish," with the published English text being "based upon the original, unpublished English version and the Spanish text." This is followed by background on Puig's career and a discussion of various elements of the novel in question, including how it fits into the author's oeuvre, its plot, its principal characters, their actions and interactions (and the thematic significance of these), and the reader's role in the text. An excellent introduction to the novel. "Sources for Further Study" section lists review articles on the work (in English). Titles in Spanish with English translations. Quotations in English.

Heartbreak Tango (Boquitas pintadas)

Southard, David R. "Betrayed by Manuel Puig: Reader Deception and Anti-Climax in His Novels." *Latin American Literary Review* 9 (1976): 22-28.

In the process of examining "the use of deception as a technical device which, by misleading the reader, contributes to the sense of anti-climax" in Puig's novels, Southard analyzes this aspect of *Heartbreak Tango*, finding that reader (and character) deception occurs through the identity of the writer of the letters to Nélida, long thought by the reader (and Nélida herself) to be Juan Carlos' mother when it was actually his sister, Celina. The anticlimax element is also found in the merging of the radio soap operas into the characters lives. *Betrayed by Rita Hayworth* and *The Buenos Aires Affair* are also discussed. Conclusions drawn concerning the significance of this aspect of Puig's novels. Titles and quotations in Spanish.

Weiss, Judith. "Dynamic Correlations in *Heartbreak Tango*." *Latin American Literary Review* 3 (Fall/Winter, 1974): 137-141.

A study of the nature and role of female characters in this novel (characters which Weiss views as "all too often ignored as complex central characters in Latin American fiction"), the presence and significance of the tango (and tango lyrics in particular) in the work, and the serial nature of the narrative. Weiss concludes that the "question remains in the case of both the choice of females as pivotal characters and of these forms as mediums for his novel, whether Puig himself had in mind a nihilistic laugh or a valiant attempt— reminiscent in a way of Cervantes—at turning the weakest links in fiction into instruments of force." Titles and quotations in English.

Kiss of the Spider Woman (El beso de la mujer araña)

Crispin, Ruth Katz. "The Orphic Substructure of Manuel Puig's *El beso de la mujer araña.*" In *Selected Proceedings of the Mid-America Conference on Hispanic Literature*, edited by Luis T. González-del-Valle and Catherine Nickel. Lincoln, Nebr.: Society of Spanish and Spanish-American Studies, 1986.

In her study of Puig's novel, Crispin attempts "to show how the plotline parallels an archetype of imitation, and how and why the ritual, in *El beso*, finds its metaphoric expression specifically in the tradition of Orpheus and Orphism." To this end, she examines the characters and the evolution of their personalities and their relationships, in addition to the characters' proper names and the numbers "which most frequently and significantly appear in the novel." An interesting reading of the novel, with considerable background reference to the Orpheus myth. Titles and quotations (with one exception) in Spanish.

Masiello, Francine R. "Jail House Flicks: Projections by Manuel Puig." *Symposium* 32 (Spring, 1978): 15-24.

Masiello contends that "basic to the unity of [*Kiss of the Spider Woman*] is a contrapuntal interplay of episodes in which various tales and narrative modes duplicate or correct one another and call to question the text as a fictional contrivance." The purpose of her study is analyze the "contrapuntal interplay" to which she refers, which she does in a detailed and clear manner before concluding, in part, that through the "play of mirror images and polar oppositions which interweaves prison bleakness and garish celluloid fantasy, Puig assembles a highly original and coherent novel in which language emerges as the central protagonist." Titles and quotations in Spanish.

Merrim, Stephanie. "Through the Film Darkly: Grade 'B' Movies and Dreamwork in *Tres tristes tigres* and *El beso de la mujer araña.*" *Modern Language Studies* 15 (Fall, 1985): 300-312.

In this discussion of the presence and function of B movies in *Kiss of the Spider Woman* and Cabrera Infante's *Three Trapped Tigers*, Merrim states that in Puig's novel the "movie-stories quickly begin to play the same role as dreams in psychoanalysis," adding later that "it is no accident . . . that the movie-stories touch off discussion of concerns to the characters, for the emotions and circumstances from their present . . . provide the scaffolding of the films." Citing various aspects of Sigmund Freud's theories on dreams and numerous examples from the text, the critic meticulously examines the specific purpose and function of the B films used in Puig's novel. Titles and quotations in Spanish.

Rice-Sayre, Laura. "Domination and Desire: A Feminist-Materialist Reading of Manuel Puig's *Kiss of the Spider Woman*." In *Textual Analysis: Some Readers Reading*, edited by Mary Ann Caws. New York: Modern Language Association of America, 1986.

Rice-Sayre begins by defining feminist-materialist textual analysis and then applies such an analysis to *Kiss of the Spider Woman*, contending that the majority of readers and critics who have separated "the political from the sexual and the individual from the institutional" have misread the work. She examines the Molina-Valentín relationship to show, among other things, their growth and awareness concerning "the imbrication of political and sexual repression by the exercise of domination." Titles and quotations in English.

Schwartz, Ronald. "Puig: Argentine 'Camp.'" In his *Nomads, Exiles, and Émigrés: The Rebirth of the Latin American Narrative, 1960-80*. Metuchen, N.J.: Scarecrow Press, 1980.

A chapter with two apparent purposes: (1) to provide a brief biographical sketch of Puig and (2) to discuss in some detail *Kiss of the Spider Woman*. Discussion of the novel occupies roughly six pages of this twelve-page chapter. Provides a good plot summary, in addition to commentary (from Schwartz and various other critics, as well as Puig himself) on the technical elements of the novel, the presence of camp in the work, Puig's audience, and the work's potential political message. A good introduction to the novel. Titles and quotations in English.

Weyers (Weber), Frances. "Manuel Puig at the Movies." *Hispanic Review* 49 (Spring, 1981): 163-181.

A rather lengthy article focusing on the movies and their relationship, on various levels (concerning plot, theme, technique, and effect on the reader), to Puig's *Kiss of the Spider Woman*. After a detailed analysis, the critic concludes that "Molina and Valentín put the ideologies and images of Hollywood to their own use and we are invited to do the same," in this novel which "stimulating our movie memories, leads us back and forth between two media so that our perception becomes certainly richer and more private, but more communal as well, because we sense the continuity of movie viewers from Chicago to General Villegas." An exhaustive study of a fascinating aspect of Puig's novel. Titles and quotations in Spanish.

AUGUSTO ROA BASTOS
Paraguay

Biography

Foster, David William. "The Watcher of the Night: Roa Bastos's Life and Times." In his *Augusto Roa Bastos*. Boston: Twayne, 1978.

This chapter provides a thirteen-page introduction to Roa Bastos' life and the cultural, historical, and political background from which he, and, by extension, his writings, come. The chapter is divided into sections entitled "The Archetypic Exile," "Paraguayan Roots," "Argentine Exile," and "A Historico-Cultural Excursus." Short on details on Roa Bastos' life and no real discussion (such as an overview) of his works. The purpose of this chapter seems to be to place the Paraguayan writer into literary and (more so, it seems) extraliterary contexts, and it achieves its purpose admirably. A chronology of Roa Bastos' life and career precedes the chapter. Titles in Spanish with English translations. Quotations in English.

Commentary

Foster, David William. *Augusto Roa Bastos*. Boston: Twayne, 1978.

Foster presents an overview of Roa Bastos' life and career, and a detailed structuralism-based analysis of several of the Paraguayan writer's short stories and his two novels. Chapters include "The Watcher of the Night: Roa Bastos's Life and Times," "*Hijo del hombre*: The Christ-Symbol Accommodated," and "*Yo el Supremo*: The Curse of Writing," in addition to two chapters on the writer's short fiction, and a conclusion. A good introduction to the writer and his works. A chronology of Roa Bastos' life and career. Provides a good index, a primary bibliography in Spanish, and an annotated critical bibliography in Spanish and English. Titles in Spanish with English translations. Quotations in English.

McMurray, George R. "New Directions." In his *Spanish American Writing Since 1941: A Critical Survey*. New York: Frederick Ungar, 1987.

McMurray devotes approximately five pages of this section of his book to an overview of Roa Bastos' fiction. Following an introductory paragraph, the critic offers concise commentary on the Paraguayan writer's major fiction. A good starting point for the reader unfamiliar with Roa Bastos. Titles in Spanish with English translations.

Scott, Robert H. "Augusto Roa Bastos." In *Latin American Literature in the Twentieth Century: A Guide*, edited by Leonard S. Klein. New York: Frederick Ungar, 1986.

A brief (roughly three-page) introduction to Roa Bastos' life and works. Discussion of the Paraguayan writer's short fiction, focusing of themes and technique, and his two novels, *Son of Man* and *I the Supreme*. A good starting point for the uninitiated reader. Includes a list of Roa Bastos' other work (in Spanish) not mentioned in the text and a short critical bibliography in Spanish and English.

I the Supreme (Yo el Supremo)

Berg, Mary G. "*I the Supreme*." In *Magill's Literary Annual*, 1987, edited by Frank N. Magill, vol. 1. Pasadena, Calif.: Salem Press, 1987.

Berg begins her roughly five-page overview of *I the Supreme* with a brief introduction to the novel in question, which she states has been viewed "as the culmination of a distinguished series of novels by major Latin American writers . . . which consider the phenomenon of dictatorship and the nature of power." This is followed by background information on José Gaspar Rodríguez de Francia, who was the dictator of Paraguay from 1814 to 1840 and who serves as "the central subject and primary narrative voice of *I the Supreme*." The rest of Berg's article is devoted to not only what the novel communicates, with respect to both plot and theme, but also how it communicates it. An excellent introduction to the novel. "Sources for Further Study" section lists review articles on the work (in English). Titles in English with Spanish translations. Quotations in English.

Foster, David William. "Augusto Roa Bastos' *I, the Supreme*: The Image of a Dictator." *Latin American Literary Review* 4 (Fall/Winter, 1975): 32-35.

This short article is essentially an introduction to the nature of the narrative of Roa Bastos' novel and to the portrait the Paraguayan author paints of his protagonist, real-life dictator, Dr. José Gaspar Rodríguez de Francia. Foster discusses how this portrait is painted and to what degree Roa Bastos attempts to condemn or defend Francia. A piece, particularly suited, it seems, for the reader who has not yet read the work. Titles and quotations in English.

——————— . "*Yo el Supremo*: The Curse of Writing." In his *Augusto Roa Bastos*. Boston: Twayne, 1978.

In sections entitled "Introduction," "Image of a Dictator," "History Versus Novel," "Myth and 'Writing Degree Zero,'" and "Conclusion," Foster presents a fine overview and structuralist analysis of *I the Supreme*, focusing on, among other things, the nature of the novel's narrative, the characterization of the protagonist, the use of documents in the work, and the levels of writing found in the text. Titles in Spanish with English translations. Quotations in English.

Martin, Gerald. "*Yo el Supremo*: The Dictator and His Script." In *Contemporary Latin American Fiction*, edited by Salvador Bacarisse. Edinburgh: Scottish Academic Press, 1980.

Martin presents a fine overview of _I the Supreme_, as he "seeks to sketch out an approach to the novel which will establish the outlines of the literary and historical conjuncture within which the work is situated, and to suggest what its place might turn out to be in the development of Latin American literature." In the process, the critic compares the novel to Domingo Faustino Sarmiento's _Facundo: Civilization and Barbarism_, as well as to Carpentier's _Reasons of State_ and García Márquez' _The Autumn of the Patriarch_. Martin also considers Roa Bastos' treatment of Francia and Francia's role in Paraguayan history, before concluding that the novel has found "a means of fusing 'literary revloution' with 'revolutionary literature' in a way that has allowed the novel to be hailed both by the radicals and the aesthetes among Latin American critics. . . ." Titles and quotations in English.

Ugalde, Sharon Keefe. "Binarisms in _Yo el Supremo_." _Hispanic Journal_ 2 (Fall, 1980): 69-77.

Ugalde first studies the aspects of myth present in the work (focusing on the concept of time and the protagonist's godlike attributes) and then turns her attention to the binary oppositions to be found in the work, identifying and examining several, "Yo-El," "Absolute Power-No Power," "Genuine Utopia-Reign of Terror," and "Reality-Illusion" being chief among them. The critic then treats what she calls "The Ironic Dimension: The Destruction of Language and the Unresolved Polarizations." Here she states, in part, that the novel "offers the reader no satisfying resolutions of the oppositions presented, as do myths, but rather a twentieth-century ironic vision," adding later, "the deep lying contradiction of Latin American society[,] . . absolute power of the dictator opposed to no power of the people is never resolved," concluding finally that in this work the "structure is after all the message. Life's enigmas: irresolvable oppositions." Some reference to Claude Lévi-Strauss' concept of myth and structuralist theory. Titles and quotations in Spanish.

Son of Man (Hijo del hombre)

Foster, David William. "_Hijo del hombre_: The Christ-Symbol Accommodated." In his _Augusto Roa Bastos_. Boston: Twayne, 1978.

Using a structuralist approach to Roa Bastos' _Son of Man_, Foster presents a detailed and lengthy (twenty-seven-page) analysis of the work. Following an introduction, he discusses various elements of the novel in sections entitled "Narrative Structure," "An Organizing Symbol: The Christ of Itapé," "Cristóbal Jara: The Fulfillment of the Figure," and "Narrative Point of View in _Son of Man_," followed by a conclusion. A good overview and analysis of the novel in question. Titles and quotations in English.

——————— . "_Hijo del hombre_: The Crucifixion and Universal Suffering of Mankind." In his _The Myth of Paraguay in the Fiction of Augusto Roa Bastos_.

Chapel Hill: University of North Carolina Press, 1969.

Approximately half of Foster's book is devoted to a study of *Son of Man*. After a brief introduction to the work, Foster turns his attention to an analysis of the work in sections entitled "The *Cristo de Itapé* as a Symbol," "Alexis Dubrovsky—The Misconception of a Symbol," "Cristóbal Jara—The Realization of a Symbol," and "'Ex combatientes'—The Legacy of a Symbol," followed by a short conclusion. Titles and quotations in Spanish.

JOÃO GUIMARÃES ROSA
Brazil

Commentary

Clark, Fred M. "João Guimarães Rosa." In *Latin American Literature in the Twentieth Century: A Guide*, edited by Leonard S. Klein. New York, Frederick Ungar, 1986.
A brief, (roughly three-page) introduction to Guimarães Rosa's life and works. An overview of the Brazilian writer's major works with limited discussion of each, with most attention paid to *The Devil to Pay in the Backlands*. Much of the discussion of each work focuses on Guimarães Rosa's unusual ideas about and use of language. A good starting point for the uninitiated reader. Supplies a list of the Brazilian author's other works (in Portuguese) not mentioned in the text. Short critical bibliography in English.

Daniel, Mary L. "João Guimarães Rosa." In *Dictionary of Brazilian Literature*, edited by Irwin Stern. Westport, Conn.: Greenwood Press, 1988.
A brief (roughly five-page) introduction to Guimarães Rosa's life and career. Considerable (given space limitations) information on the Brazilian writer's life followed by a one-paragraph summary of his career, and a consideration of the effect of his arrival on the Brazilian literary scene. Limited discussion (one paragraph each, with the exception of the two paragraphs devoted to *The Devil to Pay in the Backlands*) of each of his works. A summary of the characteristics of his narrative and an assessment of his place in Brazilian literature. A good starting point for the reader unfamiliar with Guimarães Rosa. Includes a short critical bibliography in Portuguese and English.

Harss, Luis, and Barbara Dohmann. "João Guimarães Rosa, or the Third Bank of the River." In their *Into the Mainstream: Conversations with Latin American Writers*. New York: Harper & Row, 1967.
An interview-based discussion of Guimarães Rosa and his works. Contains considerable information on the Brazilian writer's life and early career, as well as background information on the Brazilian backlands which play such a role in the writer's fiction. The major part of the chapter, however, is devoted to a discussion of the nature of Guimarães Rosa's fictive world and his works through the mid-1960's. This discussion consists chiefly of the cogent observations of Harss and Dohmann, but is supplemented nicely with comments from Guimarães Rosa himself. A classic piece of criticism and an excellent introduction to the Brazilian writer and his works. Titles in Portuguese with English translations. Quotations in English.

Vincent, Jon S. *João Guimarães Rosa*. Boston: Twayne, 1978.
An excellent book-length overview and analysis of Guimarães Rosa's literary

production. Seven chapters, each one dedicated to a separate work, present background, considerable plot summary, detailed analysis, and assessment of the Brazilian writer's major works, from *Sagarana* to *The Devil to Pay in the Backlands* to *Tutaméia*. An epilogue brings together the conclusions drawn from the chapters on the disparate works. A superb introduction to Guimarães Rosa's prose in general and to the individual works discussed. Easily one of the best books in the Twayne series. Provides a chronology of the writer's life and career, a primary bibliography in Portuguese and English (mostly Portuguese), and a critical bibliography in Portuguese and English. Titles in Portuguese with English translations. Quotations in English.

The Devil to Pay in the Backlands (Grande sertão: veredas)

Davis, William Myron. "Indo-Iranian Mythology in *Grande sertão: veredas*." *Luso-Brazilian Review* 17 (Winter, 1980): 119-131.

Davis discusses Guimarães Rosa's apparent interest in the Far East, even listing works of literature on Far Eastern subjects taken from the Brazilian author's library. The critic goes on to contend that sharp similarities (including those of names, of characters' traits, their actions and interactions) among Zoroastrian and Hindu mythology and *The Devil to Pay in the Backlands* "justify the assertion that Guimarães Rosa actually borrowed from Indo-Iranian mythology and did not merely utilize a conventional fertility myth pattern widespread in the Near East." This is particularly true with respect to Iranian myth, from which, the critic contends, Guimarães Rosa borrows much more than he does from the *Vedas* and *Upanishads*. The critic specifically identifies the similarities mentioned. Titles and quotations in Portuguese.

Frizzi, Adria. "'The Demonic Texture': Deferral and Plurity in *Grande sertão: veredas*." *Chasqui* 17 (May, 1988): 25-29.

"The Demonic Texture" of *The Devil to Pay in the Backlands* for Frizzi concerns the elusive, ever-changing, and plural aspects of the narrative and its story, characteristics similar to those attributed to the devil, both in Christian tradition and in Riobaldo's narration. Relying heavily on deconstructionist principles and terminology, Frizzi examines "the proliferation of names, the joining of antithetical terms," and what she calls "the 'open' [or unresolved] enigma" of the narrative to show how "the text is . . . inscribed in a system which, like the devil, is open to change and endless nomination." Knowledge of deconstructionist theories helpful but not absolutely essential. Titles and quotations in Portuguese.

Martins, Wilson. "Structural Perspectivism in Guimarães Rosa." In *The Brazilian Novel*, edited by Heitor Martins. Bloomington: University of Indiana Department of Spanish and Portuguese, 1976.

Martins states that "Guimarães Rosa is one of those writers born classic," which, in the modern sense of the word, the critic seems to suggest, is a writer who "makes of literature a special kind of language, the author's own dialect, with its peculiar grammar and vocabulary, its autonomous syntax and its exclusive semantics," at the same time attempting "the most supreme originality, the kind which not only refuses to imitate, but also tries to prevent all imitations." With this in mind, Martins examines various aspects of *The Devil to Pay in the Backlands*, with emphasis on "structural perspectivism" ("For structure is structural perspectivism, and it is this which 'crystallizes' the written work into a work of literature"), with considerable reference to *Don Quijote*. Titles and quotations (from Guimarães Rosa's work) in Portuguese with English translations. Other quotations in Spanish, French, and English.

Valente, Luis Fernando. "Affective Response in *Grande sertão: veredas*." *Luso-Brazilian Review* 23 (Summer, 1986): 77-88.
Valente begins by analyzing the first paragraph of *The Devil to Pay in the Backlands*, showing, among other things, how a dialogue is immediately established between the narrator and the reader (as well as between the narrator and his in-text listener). He goes on to discuss the "affective involvement" of the reader in the text, noting not only how such involvement begins but also how it continues and is even intensified as the narrative progresses, due in part to both the nature of the narrative and the nature of the narrator himself. An excellent study of the reader's response to the text and the factors which cause said response. Titles and quotations in Portuguese.

Vincent, Jon S. "*Grande sertão: veredas*: The Critical Imperative." In his *João Guimarães Rosa*. Boston: Twayne, 1978.
An amazing chapter on Guimarães Rosa's masterpiece. Amazing because of the difficult work with which it deals and the ease with which it does it. Describing Guimarães Rosa's novel as a book that "must be approached with caution," Vincent discusses the nature of its narrative, its plot (in a concise, roughly one-page plot summary), its narrator, its "listener," its language (including the difficulties of translating it), its similarities to epic literature, its structure, and its theme. An excellent, detailed, and very readable twenty-six-page study of the novel. Essential for the reader seeking a deeper understanding and appreciation of the work. Title in Portuguese with English translation. Quotations in English.

JUAN RULFO
Mexico

Biography

Leal, Luis. "Son of Affliction: Rulfo's Life and Times." In his *Juan Rulfo*. Boston: Twayne, 1983.

A fifteen-page chapter which, just as the title indicates, provides a sketch of Rulfo's life (both personal and professional) and times (that is, the literary and political context into which Rulfo was born and within which he matured both as a man and as a writer). Very informative. Includes a chronology of Rulfo's life and career (through 1982) which precedes the chapter. Titles of Rulfo's works in Spanish with English translation. Other titles vary. Quotations (most from Rulfo himself) in English.

Commentary

Harss, Luis, and Barbara Dohmann. "Juan Rulfo, or the Souls of the Departed." In their *Into the Mainstream: Conversations with Latin American Writers*. New York: Harper & Row, 1967.

An interview-based discussion of Rulfo and his works. Contains considerable information about the Mexican writer's life and career. The major portion of the chapter, however, is devoted to an overview of Rulfo's works, consisting primarily of the cogent observations of Harss and Dohmann, but supplemented nicely with comments from Rulfo himself. A classic piece of criticism and an excellent introduction to Rulfo and his works. Titles of Rulfo's works in Spanish with English translations. Titles of other writers' works (very few) in Spanish only. Quotations in English.

Leal, Luis. *Juan Rulfo*. Boston: Twayne, 1983.

An excellent study of Rulfo's life and career. Includes a chapter on the Mexican writer's life as well as one on his early writings. Two chapters are devoted to *The Burning Plain* (one on "The Early Stories" and another on "The Later Stories") and two as well to *Pedro Páramo* ("Context and Genesis" and "Structure and Imagery"). A seventh chapter covers Rulfo's other writings, followed by a conclusion. A superb introduction to Rulfo and his works. Includes a chronology of the Mexican author's life and career through 1982, an excellent index, and primary and secondary bibliographies (the latter annotated) in Spanish and English. Titles in Spanish with (eventually) English translations. Quotations in English.

McMurray, George R. "Juan Rulfo." In *Latin American Literature in the Twentieth Century: A Guide*, edited by Leonard S. Klein. New York: Frederick Ungar, 1986.

A brief (two-page) introduction to Rulfo's life and works. Short summary of the Mexican writer's literary career and some of the characteristics common to all of his narrative. Limited discussion of *The Burning Plain* (with brief mention of several stories therein) and *Pedro Páramo*. A good starting point for the reader unfamiliar with Rulfo. Provides a short critical bibliography in English.

_____ . "New Directions." In his *Spanish American Writing Since 1941: A Critical Survey*. New York: Frederick Ungar, 1987.

McMurray devotes roughly four pages of this section of his book to a brief overview of Rulfo's fiction. Following two paragraphs of introduction, the critic offers concise commentary, first, on *The Burning Plain* and a number of stories from the collection, and, then, on *Pedro Páramo*, before a final paragraph in which McMurray cites the contribution to Spanish American fiction of Rulfo and two other natives of Jalisco (Mexico): Yáñez and Arreola. A good introduction for the reader unfamiliar with Rulfo. Titles in Spanish with English translations.

Ramírez, Arthur. "Juan Rulfo: Dialectics and the Despairing Optimist." *Hispania* 65 (December, 1982): 580-585.

In a unique reading of Rulfo, Ramírez emphasizes the Mexican writer's tendency toward dualities, such as life and death, and illusion and disillusion, and contends that in spite of general critical opinion that Rulfo's literary world is negative and pessimistic, the Mexican author actually "stresses the negative (death, hate, violence, etc.) to bring out all the more vividly their opposites—life, love, compassion, and hope." Much of Pedro Páramo's negative behavior, for example, is motivated by his love for Susana San Juan. Ramírez examines even the most negative elements (and points out some essentially ignored positive elements, such as the hospitality offered Juan Preciado by numerous characters) in Rulfo's narratives to show their positive side and how the writer "transcends his despairing vision of humanity and makes manifest an embodiment of the universally acknowledged highest values of mankind. Titles and quotations in Spanish.

The Burning Plain (El llano en llamas)

Borgeson, Paul W., Jr. "The Turbulent Flow: Stream of Consciousness Techniques in the Short Stories of Juan Rulfo." *Revista de Estudios Hispánicos* 13 (May, 1979): 227-252.

After briefly discussing what he calls the "unsettling effect" of Rulfo's stories, Borgeson presents an analysis of some of the specific techniques used by the author to achieve this effect, all of which have to do with the stream-of-consciousness approach. The critic defines this approach and then examines techniques associated with it which appear in Rulfo's stories (including association, sensory impression, suspended coherence, and recurrent devices), concluding, in part, that Rulfo not only uses "virtually all of the devices identified with stream of consciousness fiction," but "in several instances he extends their application significantly," in the process creating, as the critic states later, "a magnificently gloomy picture of his characters'—and mankind's—situation." Titles and quotations in Spanish.

Brotherston, Gordon. "Province of Dead Souls: Juan Rulfo." In his *The Emergence of the Latin American Novel*. London: Cambridge University Press, 1977.
This chapter serves essentially as an introduction to Rulfo's fictional work. The critic discusses both *Pedro Páramo* and *The Burning Plain*, though considerably less attention is paid to the latter. The collection of stories is treated primarily as part of the Mexican author's oeuvre. Some individual stories are cited, though none receives any sort of in-depth analysis (such not being the critic's intent here). Some consideration as well of both *Pedro Páramo* and *The Burning Plain* within the context of literature of the Mexican Revolution. A good introduction to Rulfo's works and to his fictional world. Titles in Spanish with English translations (or vice versa). Quotations in English or in Spanish with English translations.

Gyurko, Lanin A. "Rulfo's Aesthetic Nihilism: Narrative Antecedents of *Pedro Páramo*," *Hispanic Review* 40 (Autumn, 1972): 451-466.
Gyurko shows how Rulfo's stories, and in particular "Macario," "The Man," and "Luvina," prefigure the "somber vision" of *Pedro Páramo*. Citing numerous examples from both the stories and the novel, the critic shows, for example, how the protagonist of "Macario" "creates within his conscience a psychic purgatory that adumbrates the world of lost souls" in *Pedro Páramo*, how narrative devices employed in "The Man" (particularly those concerned with the nonchronological presentation of time and shifts of point of view) presage similar techniques used in the novel, and how the town in "Luvina," "with its muted, stagnant life anticipates the ghost town of Comala." An interesting and very readable piece. Titles and quotations in Spanish.

Leal, Luis. "*The Burning Plain*: The Early Stories" and "*The Burning Plain*: The Later Stories." In his *Juan Rulfo*. Boston: Twayne, 1983.
Leal divides the stories of *The Burning Plain* according to the date they were written and places them in the two separate chapters cited above. Each chapter begins with a short introduction to the stories to be discussed, followed by individual two- and three-page overviews and analyses of each story. The two chapters together provide an excellent guide to Rulfo's collection of stories. Titles in Spanish with English translations provided in end notes. Quotations in English.

Mancing, Howard. "The Art of Literary Allusion in Juan Rulfo." *Modern Fiction Studies* 23 (Summer, 1977): 242-244.

Mancing examines the possible connection of literary allusion between Rulfo's story "¡Diles que no me matan!" ("Tell them not to kill me!") and *Lazarillo de Tormes* and (if only by extension through *Lazarillo de Tormes*) Penelope's web. The allusion centers on the repeated fence mending and breaking in Rulfo's story, seen by the critic as a possible allusion to the repeated mending and breaking into of the bread chest in the Spanish novel and to Penelope's repeated weaving and unweaving. The critic does not seek to prove deliberate allusion, but instead seems to wish to show, through Rulfo's story, that though one can read past works ignorant of current authors, reading current authors' works ignorant of past works "is to run the risk of limiting—perhaps severely—our appreciation of their works." Titles and quotations in Spanish.

Pedro Páramo

Adams, Ian M. "Landscape and Loss in Juan Rulfo's *Pedro Páramo*." *Chasqui* 9 (November, 1979): 24-29.

Adams studies the styles of the novel, the connection of these styles to the situations of the characters, the various types of loss presented in the work, and the relation of all these elements to the landscape of Comala, before concluding that "if Comala is a Mexican hell, Rulfo is specific about its nature: it is the hell of the loss of origins, the impossibility of finding them, and the loss of the ties that define life. Living becomes the exercise of hate created by loss. The landscape, deprived of any vitality, reflects the human situation." An interesting piece. Titles and quotations in Spanish.

Álvarez, Nicolás Emilio. "Structuralism and *Pedro Páramo*: A Case in Point." *Kentucky Romance Quarterly* 24 (1977): 419-431.

Essentially an article which approaches Rulfo's novel using structuralist ideas both in order to examine aspects of the work in question and to measure the effectiveness of some of the structuralist methods. The critic finds, for example, that "structuralist literary criticism with its biased synchronic method unjustifiably neglect[s] to consider the ideological and socio-historical codes of a narrative text," namely Rulfo's. Structuralist methods, however, do work well "in dealing with the symbolic code," again as applied here to *Pedro Páramo*. More space is dedicated to the structuralist ideas of Roland Barthes and Claude Lévi-Strauss (which helps the reader unfamiliar with these ideas) than to Rulfo's novel, which seems at times more of a test case for structuralism than the focus of the study. Still a solid article and an interesting approach to Rulfo's work. Titles and quotations in Spanish and French (particularly concerning structuralism).

Brotherston, Gordon. "Province of Dead Souls: Juan Rulfo." In his *The Emergence of the Latin American Novel*. London: Cambridge University Press, 1977.

In essence, this chapter serves as an introduction to Rulfo's fictional world.

The critic discusses both *Pedro Páramo* and *The Burning Plain*, but places more emphasis on the former (a lengthy passage from which opens the chapter). Brotherston presents an overview of the work with emphasis on the novel's plot, the nature of its narrative, its themes, and its atmosphere. Some consideration as well of the place of *Pedro Páramo* (and *The Burning Plain*) within the context of literature concerned with the Mexican Revolution. A good introduction to the novel in question and to Rulfo's fictional world. Titles in Spanish with English translations (or vice versa). Quotations in English or in Spanish with English translations.

D'Lugo, Carol Clark. "*Pedro Páramo*: The Reader's Journey Through the Text." *Hispania* 70 (September, 1987): 468-474.

D'Lugo contends that in this novel Rulfo frees his readers "from the assumed narrative conventions by means of a complicated discourse which, without blatant, exterior guidelines, maneuvers the reader through stages of (1) traditional assumptions; (2) attempts at coherence; (3) shock of dislodgement; and (4) adjustment to a liberated status through reassessment, rereading, and a free-flowing enjoyment." She shows this by going step by step through the first half of the novel to examine what Rulfo does with his narrative voice and the effects it all has (and is intended to have) on the reader. Consideration as well of the question of narrative unity in the work (particularly in consideration of Rulfo's deliberate use of fragmentation on many levels). A solid study. Titles and quotations in English.

Gyurko, Lanin A. "Rulfo's Aesthetic Nihilism: Narrative Antecedents of *Pedro Páramo*," *Hispanic Review* 40 (Autumn, 1972): 451-466.

Gyurko contends that the "somber vision" of *Pedro Páramo* finds its antecedents in Rulfo's short stories, and in three of them in particular: "Macario," "The Man," and "Luvina." He examines the three stories and their connections to *Pedro Páramo* in order to illustrate how the protagonist of the first story "creates within his conscience a psychic purgatory that adumbrates the world of lost souls" in the novel, the narrative devices employed in the second story (particularly concerning the nonchronological presentation of time and shifts of point of view) "prefigure the intricate structural techniques of the novel," and the town in the third story, "with its muted, stagnant life anticipates the ghost town of Comala." A valuable and very readable piece. Titles and quotations in Spanish.

Leal, Luis. "*Pedro Páramo*: Context and Genesis." In his *Juan Rulfo*. Boston: Twayne, 1983.

In twelve pages, Leal discusses Rulfo's novel within the context of the novel of the Mexican Revolution (featuring a rather detailed discussion of this subgenre) and then traces the novel's genesis to the Mexican author's short stories, some ten years before the novel was published. A final section treats the presence of, and the potential reasons for, violence and death in Rulfo's works in general and in *Pedro Páramo* in particular. An interesting chapter. Most titles in English. Quotations in English.

——————— . "*Pedro Páramo*: Structure and Imagery." In his *Juan Rulfo*. Boston: Twayne, 1983.

In a section entitled "Souls in Purgatory," Leal studies the characters of *Pedro Páramo* and their individual roles within the text. A second section consists of a study of the novel's structure, with emphasis on critics' initial reactions to it, a deciphering of its complexities, and a review of the multiple narrative threads and the techniques used to present them. In a final section, Leal examines the various images (such as water, red light, the wind, the horse) which play a significant role in the work and which integrate, the critic contends, the three narrative threads. A concise, detailed study. Titles and quotations in English.

Levine, Suzanne J. "*One Hundred Years of Solitude* and *Pedro Páramo*: A Parallel." *Books Abroad* 47 (Summer, 1973): 490-495.

Levine examines the many similarities and some of the differences that exist between Rulfo's novel and García Márquez' *One Hundred Years of Solitude*. The critic finds that both works deal with "social and political problems common to most Latin American countries"; are stories of intricate rural societies, with the focus on one family in a small town; make use of Biblical and Greek myth; question machismo and feudalism; and superimpose different moments of time. The novels differ, however, in the personalities and behavior of their female characters, the fact that Rulfo's novel is more Faulknerian, and, most important, in that *Pedro Páramo* leaves the reader with a final affirmation of death, while *One Hundred Years of Solitude* leaves the reader with a final affirmation of life. An interesting piece on two works rarely compared to each other. Titles and quotations in English.

Peavler, Terry J. "Textual Problems in *Pedro Páramo*." *Revista de Estudios Hispánicos* 19 (January, 1985): 91-99.

Peavler cites the precise analysis required of the contemporary novel in general, but implies that *Pedro Páramo* makes a shambles of even the most precise reading, stating that the novel "has probably on one occasion or another made fools of us all . . . for it creates the beautiful illusion of lyric precision, yet when we place it under our critical microscopes, it proves to be in a state of continual flux." This "continual flux" derives from the numerous and distinct Spanish editions of the work. The critic cites variations of structure (number of sections), language (vocabulary), and punctuation (chiefly the use of italics, quotation marks, and dashes) in the four Spanish editions of the work, making, he implies, definitive analysis impossible because of the lack of a definitive text. A fascinating article. Titles and quotations in Spanish.

Ramírez, Arthur. "Spatial Form and Cinema Techniques in Rulfo's *Pedro Páramo*." *Revista de Estudios Hispánicos* 15 (May, 1981): 233-249.

Ramírez analyzes "spatial" form in literature according to the theories of Joseph Frank (essentially, as applied in *Pedro Páramo*, the practice of beginning a story or reference in one place and returning to it in various separated places, "and finishing it, if at all, in still another," thus forcing the reader to put the pieces together) and then examines its use in Rulfo's novel. The second half of the article is devoted to an analysis of cinematic techniques (particularly montage—and principally time-montage—and, within montage, flashback and "flash-forward," as well as cinema-based transition techniques) used by the author, before concluding that the novel's structure, though "seemingly chaotic, is actually internally consistent, ordered." Title and quotations from Rulfo's work in Spanish.

Sommers, Joseph. "Through the Window of the Grave: Juan Rulfo." In his *After the Storm: Landmarks of the Modern Mexican Novel*. Albuquerque: University of New Mexico Press, 1968.

In this classic work on Rulfo's *Pedro Páramo*, Sommers prefaces his commentary with a brief sketch of Rulfo's literary career, followed by a general overview of the nature of the novel in question. The critic then dedicates individual sections of the chapter to detailed analysis of the work's narrative perspective, its structure, the presentation of characters in the work, and the novel's, as the critic calls it, "mythic underpinnings." In a final section entitled "World View," Sommers focuses principally on the novel's theme, with some comparison between Rulfo's view of the world and that of Agustín Yáñez. A widely read piece of criticism. Titles and quotations in English.

ERNESTO SÁBATO
Argentina

Biography

Oberhelman, Harley Dean. "Sábato and His Universe." In his *Ernesto Sábato*. New York: Twayne, 1970.

An eleven-page sketch of Sábato's life and career, divided into three sections. The first section, entitled "The Boy from the Pampa," discusses the writer's childhood and the Argentine setting in which it occurred. The second section, "A Disquieting Career in Science," covers Sábato's university years, both as a student and as a professor of physics, with reference to his gradual move toward literature. The final section, "A Journey through Tunnels and Tombs," traces his literary career, beginning in 1943 with his resignation of his professorship and his move to Córdoba to write. A good and surprisingly detailed introduction to the Argentine writer's life and career. Titles in Spanish with English translations. Quotations in English.

Commentary

Gertel, Zunilda. "Ernesto Sábato." In *Latin American Literature in the Twentieth Century: A Guide*, edited by Leonard S. Klein. New York: Frederick Ungar, 1986.

A Brief (two-and-a-half-page) introduction to Sábato's life and works. Some commentary on his essays, but the discussion of Sábato's literary production largely focuses on *The Outsider*, *On Heroes and Tombs*, and a third novel, *Abbadón el exterminador* (Abbadon the exterminator), with an emphasis on thematic concerns. A good starting point for the uninitiated reader. Provides a list of Sábato's other works (in Spanish) not mentioned in the text and a short critical bibliography in Spanish and English.

McMurray, George R. "New Directions." In his *Spanish American Writing Since 1941: A Critical Survey*. New York: Frederick Ungar, 1987.

McMurray devotes roughly four pages of this section of his book to a brief overview of Sábato's fiction. Following one paragraph dealing with the Argentine writer's background and another with his essays, the critic offers concise commentary on Sábato's three novels. A good starting point for the reader unfamiliar with Sábato. Titles in Spanish with English translations.

Nelson, F. William. "Ernesto Sábato." In *Critical Survey of Long Fiction* (Foreign Language Series), edited by Frank N. Magill, vol. 3. Pasadena, Calif.: Salem Press, 1984.

A roughly eight-page introduction to Sábato and his work in long fiction. Contains a list of his novels (most with English translations), a summary of his work in other literary forms, and an assessment of his achievements. This is followed by a biographical sketch and an overview and analysis of his novels. A good introduction to Sábato for the reader unfamiliar with his work in general and his novels in particular. Includes a list of his major works (in Spanish) and a short critical bibliography in English and Spanish. Titles of translated works in English.

Oberhelman, Harley Dean. *Ernesto Sábato*. New York: Twayne, 1970.

A book-length overview and analysis of Sábato's life and works. Contains an introductory chapter on the Argentine writer's life and career, followed by a chapter on his work as an essayist. One chapter is dedicated to an analysis of *The Outsider* and three to *On Heroes and Tombs*. A chapter entitled "In Search of Ernesto Sábato" concludes Oberhelman's study. An excellent introduction to the writer and his works. Provides a chronology of his life and career through 1963 and a chronology of Argentine history, a good index, and both primary and secondary bibliographies in various languages. Most titles in Spanish only. Quotations in English.

On Heroes and Tombs (Sobre héroes y tumbas)

Foster, David William. "Ernesto Sábato and the Anatomy of National Unconscious." In his *Currents in the Contemporary Argentine Novel: Arlt, Mallea, Sábato, and Cortázar*. Columbia: University of Missouri Press, 1975.

Foster prefaces this chapter with a concise one-page introduction to Sábato and his career. This is followed by an opening quotation taken from *On Heroes and Tombs*, a brief introductory section, and sections entitled "The Anatomy," "A Memorandum of Truth," and "Novelistic Unity," as the bulk of the chapter is devoted to an overview and analysis of *On Heroes and Tombs*. Foster's analysis is detailed and punctuated with cogent interpretative observations which should help the reader better understand Sábato's complex work. Very readable. Titles first cited in Spanish with English translations, subsequently cited in English. Quotations in English.

Holzapfel, Tamara. "Metaphysical Revolt in Ernesto Sábato's *Sobre héroes y tumbas*." *Hispania* 52 (December, 1969): 857-863.

Holzapfel discusses the concept of metaphysical rebellion as defined by Albert Camus (in part a definition which implies that "the individual must constantly strive for freedom, justice and self-improvement") and contends that unlike *The Outsider*, Sábato's *On Heroes and Tombs* "echoes in its basic outline Camus' philosophy of creative humanism." The rest of her article offers an analysis of Fernando, Alejandra, Martín, and Bruno as characters who "have the essential traits of the metaphysical rebel." Titles and quotations in Spanish.

Kennedy, William. "Sábato's Tombs and Heroes." *Review 29* (May-August, 1981): 6-9.

A concise and thoughtful (as well as thought-provoking) introduction to *On Heroes and Tombs*. Kennedy begins with some brief comments concerning Sábato's career and the time and thought (on Sábato's part) leading up to the novel in question. This is followed by a rather detailed plot description. The remainder of the article (divided into two sections) suggests possible interpretations of the novel's themes, with emphasis on the work's political and psychological overtones, and the fact that, as the critic contends, *On Heroes and Tombs* "is a book of hope." Titles and quotations in English.

Oberhelman, Harley Dean. "Martín and Alejandra," "An Idiot's Tale," and "The Unknown God." In his *Ernesto Sábato*. New York: Twayne, 1970.
Oberhelman divides his sixty-seven-page overview and analysis of *On Heroes and Tombs* into three chapters, each one dealing with a separate plot division within the novel. The first plot division and the first chapter deal with the "tragic, frustrating love affair" between Martín and Alejandra, the second with the section of the novel concerning Fernando, and the third with the final part of the novel dealing with Bruno. The critic's discussion of the work is long on plot summary, character analysis, and thematic interpretation. An excellent and very readable study of the work in question. Most titles in Spanish. Quotations in English.

Smith, Gilbert. "*On Heroes and Tombs*." In *Magill's Literary Annual*, 1982, edited by Frank N. Magill, vol. 2. Pasadena, Calif.: Salem Press, 1982.
Smith begins his roughly five-page overview of *On Heroes and Tombs* with a brief introduction to this complex novel, which, the critic contends, "may seem too esoteric and disparate for the average serious reader of fiction." This is followed by a discussion of various aspects of the novel, including the nature of its narrative, the significance of the appearance of Jorge Luis Borges in it, the work's principal characters and their actions and interactions, followed by a brief assessment of the work as a whole. An excellent introduction to the novel. "Sources for Further Study" section lists review articles on the work (in English). Titles and quotations in English.

Souza, Raymond D. "Fernando as Hero in Sábato's *Sobre héroes y tumbas*." *Hispania* 55 (March, 1972): 241-246.
Souza discusses Fernando as the "synthesizing axis" of *On Heroes and Tombs*, a novel in which, the critic contends, "the hero motif is one of the major elements." Souza identifies Fernando as the hero of the work as his story "parallels that of the hero-archetype," as he, similar to the mythic hero, "withdraws from his surroundings, narrates his encounter with the primordial force of existence, and returns and leaves his testimony." Fernando's heroic encounter, as with most contemporary heroes, is internal, his testimony passed on to Martín, on whom it effects profound changes. Titles and quotations in Spanish.

The Outsider (El túnel)

Baker, Armand F. "Psychic Integration and the Search for Meaning in Sábato's *El túnel.*" *Hispanic Journal* 5 (Spring, 1984): 113-125.

Baker cites critical opinion which contends that Sábato's view and message as expressed in *The Outsider* are negative. The critic then examines some of Sábato's essays and the novel in question, and "the psychic disposition of the three main characters . . . from a Jungian perspective, with the assumption that a person's psychic balance, or lack of it, has a direct bearing on the success of his or her relations with others, as well as his or her metaphysical outlook on life." Baker's conclusion is that "this negative interpretation of the above-mentioned critics is unjustified and that, despite the tragic conclusion of his first novel, Sábato has had some very positive things to say about the problem of communion and the meaning of life." A solid study. Titles and quotations in Spanish.

Francis, Nathan T., and William F. Adams. "The Limits of Rationalism in Sábato's *El túnel.*" *Revista de Estudios Hispánicos* 13 (January, 1979): 21-27.

Francis and Adams agree with other critics that *The Outsider* treats the subject of the alienated individual, but they contend that it treats another subject as well, that of "modes of cognition." The critics suggest that the author "presents two approaches to reality: a rational approach exemplified by Juan Pablo Castel, and the intuitive approach of María Iribarne Hunter." Francis and Adams analyze the aspects of these two characters and their relationship which reveal their disparate approaches to reality, concluding, in part, that the protagonist's efforts to "impose a rational structure on an inexplicable universe" are responsible for his personal downfall. Titles and quotations in Spanish.

Gibbs, Beverly J. "*El túnel*: Portrayal of Isolation." *Hispania* 48 (September, 1965): 429-436.

Gibbs calls *The Outsider* "one of the most tightly structured portrayals of a character's existential isolation to be published in recent decades" and then proceeds with a meticulous analysis of Juan Pablo Castel's character, his actions, his relationship with María, and other elements of the narrative (such as various images) which focus on and portray what becomes for him, as Gibbs states, "complete isolation." Detailed and very readable. Titles and quotations in Spanish.

Heck, Francis S. "Sábato, Robbe-Grillet, and the New Novel." *Revista de Estudios Hispánicos* 12 (January, 1978): 41-54.

Heck compares *The Outsider* to Alain Robbe-Grillet's *Les Gommes*, finding that, despite their apparent differences, they have much in common (chiefly the use of the Oedipus myth and the detective-story motif) and are not, in spite of their authors' disparate views on the novel, "polarized at two extremes of the modern novel." The critic also examines Sábato's views on the novel (as expressed in an essay intended as a condemnation of the New Novel and of Robbe-Grillet's theories) and those of the Frenchman to find that the two novelists, like their novels, are much more closely related than they appear to be. Titles and quotations in Spanish and French.

Holzapfel, Tamara. "Dostoevsky's *Notes from the Underground* and Sábato's *El túnel.*" *Hispania* 51 (September, 1968): 440-446.
Holzapfel examines Dostoevsky's "underground hero" and Sábato's "tunnel man," as well as their lovers, to show that while the two works discussed are similar in many respects (their "metaphors derived from terms denoting subterranean separation from life" being the most obvious), the most important parallel between the two works lies in their "philosophical affinity." Both works feature protagonists who are "anguished individuals living in bitter conflict with reality," though the Russian author, Holzapfel contends, suggests a Christian solution, while Sábato "offers no solution whatsoever to man's estrangement from his fellows." An interesting comparison. Title and quotations from Sábato's work in Spanish.

Nelson, William. "Sábato's *El túnel* and the Existential Novel." *Modern Fiction Studies* 32 (Autumn, 1986): 459-467.
Nelson's purpose in this article is "to establish the terms of the 'existential' novel and to present evidence that identifies *El túnel* [*The Outsider*] as an example of that form." The critic begins by establishing, largely through evidence in Sábato's essays, that the Argentine writer was indeed familiar with existentialist philosophy at the time of the novel's composition. This established, the critic examines various characteristics of the existentialist novel (such as the first-person narrator, particularly one who "ostensibly witnesses and reveals but is unable to understand what he experiences") and compares them to the characteristics of Sábato's work, before declaring that "in both content and form, Sábato's novel meets the criteria for existentialist fiction." A detailed and solid discussion. Titles (except for *El túnel*) and quotations from all sources in English.

Oberhelman, Harley Dean. "The Defeat of Reason." In his *Ernesto Sábato*. New York: Twayne, 1970.
A very clear and readable sixteen-page overview and analysis of *The Outsider*. Contains an excellent, detailed plot summary, followed by consideration of the novel's similarities (most thematic, but others of style as well) and connections to existentialism (and existentialist works by Jean-Paul Sartre and Albert Camus), Magical Realism, Franz Kafka's *The Metamorphosis*, the works of Fyodor Dostoevsky (particularly *Notes from Underground*), and Spanish picaresque (*Lazarillo de Tormes*) and *Tremendista* works (Camilo José Cela's *The*

Family of Pascual Duarte). Some consideration as well of the author's use of time and space as a parallel to the protagonist's subjectivity and fluctuating behavior. Titles in Spanish. Quotations in English.

Petersen, Fred. "Sábato's *El túnel*: More Freud Than Sartre." *Hispania* 50 (May, 1967): 271-276.
Petersen contends that *The Outsider* is not just a novel on the subject of human isolation, "but rather on something far more obvious, the universally valid fact of human psychology: The Oedipus Complex." Stating that "Juan Pablo Castel lives out a well-nigh classic example of oedipal involvement and conflict," and that the work "could almost be called a 'Freudian primer,'" the critic enters into a detailed and convincing analysis of this work in which, he contends, almost all significant elements, from scenes to symbols, have to do with womanhood or motherhood. Special emphasis is placed on the protagonist's dreams and nightmares, and his painting *Maternidad* (motherhood) and its connection to the action of the novel. Offers an interesting perspective on Sábato's novel. Titles and quotations in Spanish.

Richards, Henry J. "The Characterization of the Ontologically Insecure in *El túnel*." *Kentucky Romance Quarterly* 24 (1977): 151-162.
An interesting study of *The Outsider*'s Juan Pablo Castel and María Iribarne Hunter "based on a concurrent reading of that novel and R. D. Laing's study of schizoid and schizophrenic individuals, *The Divided Self*." The critic contends that the "behavior patterns exhibited by the two characters in question suggest that they are victims of 'ontological insecurity,' a mental disorder which, according to Laing, causes great anxiety in the victims who, in their relationships with others, experience themselves in a number of unusual ways." A detailed and very readable study with interesting observations and conclusions. Titles and quotations in Spanish.

Scott, Robert H. "*El túnel*: The Novel as Psychic Drama." *The American Hispanist* 2, no. 14 (1977): 13-15.
Scott studies *The Outsider* as the presentation of "the conflict of a divided self on a quest for psychic integration." The critic contends that examining the internal conflict of the protagonist, "as he attempts to come to terms with his unconscious," can lead one to a comparison with the myths of Dionysus and Orpheus. Scott analyzes "the symbolic use of names, characters, dreams, and the painting 'Maternidad,'" as well as the interaction of the characters, to show that the novel "is as much an inner psychic drama as an external one," as the protagonist "is as much isolated and alienated from himself as he is from others." Titles and quotations in Spanish.

MARIO VARGAS LLOSA
Peru

Biography

Gerdes, Dick. "Biographical Introduction." In his *Mario Vargas Llosa*. Boston: Twayne, 1985.

A superb seventeen-page introduction to Vargas Llosa's life and career through 1984. Covers in concise fashion the writer's background, his personal life (family and children), his development as a writer, the evolution of his career, both as a writer and a scholar, and his thoughts on literature and politics. Contained within the information concerning his career is a general overview of his work in the novel, short story, and drama, as well as treatment of his work in literary criticism and the political essay. A chronology precedes the chapter. Titles and quotations in English.

Commentary

Brody, Robert. "Mario Vargas Llosa and the Totalization Impulse." In *Mario Vargas Llosa: A Collection of Critical Essays*, edited by Charles Rossman and Alan Warren Friedman. Austin: University of Texas Press, 1978.

Brody states that attempts to define the nature of Latin American narrative since the 1940's "have resulted in the delineation of at least two fundamental forms, which are not necessarily mutually exclusive." One of these, "magical realism," concerns texts which portray fantasy. The other, "totalization impulse," encompasses texts which attempt to create a "total reality." The critic briefly examines the nature of the latter type of narrative, its evolution and prominence in contemporary Latin American fiction, and its presence and sources in Vargas Llosa's work. Brody concludes that this "impulse" is certainly present in the Peruvian writer's works, most notably *The Green House*. Titles in Spanish. Quotations in English.

Davis, Mary E. "The Haunted Voice: Echoes of William Faulkner in García Márquez, Fuentes, and Vargas Llosa." *World Literature Today* 59 (Autumn, 1985): 531-535.

Davis devotes considerable space in her study to the nature and development of Faulkner's unique voice and to how and why that voice plays so well in Latin America. When she turns her attention to the presence of Faulkner in Vargas Llosa's works, she, among other things, compares *The Green House* to *Absalom, Absalom!*, *Conversation in the Cathedral* to *Sanctuary*, and *Aunt Julia and the Scriptwriter* to "Spotted Horses." Titles and quotations in English.

_____ . "Mario Vargas Llosa." In *Critical Survey of Long Fiction* (Foreign Language Series), edited by Frank N. Magill, vol. 4. Pasadena, Calif.: Salem Press, 1984.

A roughly eleven-page introduction to Vargas Llosa and his work in long fiction. Contains a list of his novels (all with English translations), a summary of his work in other literary forms, and an assessment of his achievements. This is followed by a biographical sketch and an overview and analysis of his principal novels. A good introduction for the reader unfamiliar with Vargas Llosa's work in general and his novels in particular. Supplies a list of his other major works (most in Spanish only) and a short critical bibliography in Spanish and English. Titles of translated works in English.

_____ . "Mario Vargas Llosa: The Necessary Scapegoat." In *Mario Vargas Llosa: A Collection of Critical Essays*, edited by Charles Rossman and Alan Warren Friedman. Austin: University of Texas Press, 1978. Also appears in *Texas Studies in Literature and Language* 19 (Winter, 1977): 530-544.
Davis identifies the scapegoat and its ritual sacrifice as common elements in Vargas Llosa's works. She first traces the historical development of the scapegoat and then examines the presence and significance of the figure in the Peruvian writer's novels, contending prior to said examination that he "frustrates the basic purpose of sacrifice; that is, the death of the *pharmakos* [scapegoat] does not achieve the purification of society," but serves instead "to emphasize the lack of morality with modern society." A detailed study with revealing conclusions. Titles in Spanish. Quotations in English.

_____ . "William Faulkner and Mario Vargas Llosa: The Election of Failure." *Comparative Literature Studies* 16 (1979): 332-343.
Davis meticulously traces the influence (and the evolution of said influence) of Faulkner on Vargas Llosa. She discusses various ways in which the influence of Faulkner is seen in Vargas Llosa's works, through similarities with respect to narrators, style, mood, and the Peruvian writer's "most significant parallel with Faulkner—the creation of a ground of being essentially tragic." Davis concludes by stating that "perhaps the most significant progress in Vargas Llosa's prose has been in his use of failure," as *Captain Pantoja and the Special Service* and *Aunt Julia and the Scriptwriter* "posit failure as a vital step toward a viable identity," an aspect of Vargas Llosa's fiction that positions him even closer to Faulkner than he was earlier in his career, as he has "added to his dominion those aspects of style which capture man's generosity and nobility in a universe which demands defeat and failure." Titles and quotations from Vargas Llosa's works in Spanish. Other titles and quotations in French and English.

Feustle, Joseph A., Jr. "Mario Vargas Llosa: A Labyrinth of Solitude." In *Mario Vargas Llosa: A Collection of Critical Essays*, edited by Charles Rossman and Alan Warren Friedman. Austin: University of Texas Press, 1978. Also appears in *Texas Studies in Literature and Language* 19 (Winter, 1977): 522-529.

Feustle cites solitude as a common theme in Latin American literature and contends that this theme has appeared as well in Vargas Llosa's works. After discussing various aspects of the concept of solitude (within a Latin American context) as expressed by Argentine essayist Ezequiel Martínez Estrada and Mexican poet-essayist Octavio Paz, the critic focuses on Latin American racism and class prejudice, and, more important, the Latin American code of *hombría*, or manhood (particularly as it concerns the concepts of love, sex, and domination) as the primary expressions of the solitude theme in Vargas Llosa's works. Particular attention is paid to the presence of these topics in *The Time of the Hero*. A detailed and enlightening study. Most titles in Spanish only. Quotations in English. Most Spanish terms presented with English translations.

Gallagher, D. P. "Mario Vargas Llosa (Peru, 1936-   )." In his *Modern Latin American Literature*. New York: Oxford University Press, 1973.
Gallagher's twenty-two-page chapter on Vargas Llosa serves as an excellent introduction to the writer and his novels through 1970. The critic discusses the thematic focus and technical nature of the Peruvian author's narrative as manifested in *The Time of the Hero*, *The Green House*, and *Conversation in the Cathedral*. Gallagher also addresses Vargas Llosa's purpose in presenting his novel's stories in such a complex manner. There is ample discussion of each work in the process. Very readable. Titles in Spanish. Quotations (except for one in French and a few Spanish words) in English.

Gerdes, Dick. *Mario Vargas Llosa*. Boston: Twayne, 1985.
An excellent book-length introduction to the work of Vargas Llosa. Includes a "Biographical Introduction," as well as a chapter devoted to the Peruvian writer's short stories, with a separate chapter focusing on *The Cubs*. Each of Vargas Llosa's novels is treated at length in individual chapters (such as "*The Time of the Hero*: Lost Innocence"), with emphasis on plot synopsis and an analysis of the work's technical elements. Also contains a chapter dedicated to his plays. Well organized and very readable. Provides a chronology of Vargas Llosa's life and career (through 1984), a good index, a bibliography of Vargas Llosa's works in Spanish and English, and a critical bibliography in Spanish and English. Titles and quotations in English.

Harss, Luis, and Barbara Dohmann. "Mario Vargas Llosa, or the Revolving Door." In their *Into the Mainstream: Conversations with Latin American Writers*. New York: Harper & Row, 1967.
An interview-based discussion of Vargas Llosa and his works. Contains a considerable amount of information on the Peruvian writer's life and his early career, as well as brief consideration of the legacy of Peruvian literature inherited by the writer. The major portion of the chapter, however, is devoted

to an overview of his works through the mid-1960's (including *The Green House*), consisting chiefly of the cogent observations of Harss and Dohmann, but supplemented nicely with comments from Vargas Llosa himself. A classic piece of criticism and an excellent introduction to the writer and his early works (just after they were published). Titles of Vargas Llosa's works in Spanish with English translations. Titles of other writers' works (very few) in Spanish only. Quotations in English.

Kerr, Roy A. "Recurrent Modes of Characterization in Mario Vargas Llosa's Fiction." *Hispanófila* 91 (September, 1987): 55-64.
Kerr identifies four recurring modes of characterization in Vargas Llosa's works: (1) the Outsider; (2) the Conformer; (3) the Victim; and (4) the Manipulator. The first three categories are associated with protagonists, the final one with secondary characters. The critic places various characters from the Peruvian writer's novels into what he believes is their appropriate category, before concluding, in part, that Vargas Llosa's plots feature "man against man," where "individuals of protagonistic importance are either Outsiders fighting against society, Conformers whose quarrel is with a particular group, or random Victims of society's rage or indifference. In any case, a main character has an extremely limited possibility of success against such unscrupulous secondary figures as the Manipulator." An excellent, very readable study. Titles and quotations in Spanish.

McMurray, George R. "Major Figures of the Boom." In his *Spanish American Writing Since 1941: A Critical Survey*. New York: Frederick Ungar, 1987.
McMurray devotes approximately six pages of this section of his book to a brief overview of Vargas Llosa's fiction. Following two introductory paragraphs, the critic offers concise commentary on each of the Peruvian writer's major fictional works, before providing a concluding paragraph in which he focuses on Vargas Llosa's favorite authors. A good starting point for the reader unfamiliar with Vargas Llosa. Titles in Spanish with English translations.

_____ . "Mario Vargas Llosa." In *Latin American Literature in the Twentieth Century: A Guide*, edited by Leonard S. Klein. New York: Frederick Ungar, 1986.
A brief (roughly three-page) introduction to Vargas Llosa's life and works. McMurray gives a quick summary of the Peruvian writer's views on the creative process and limited discussion (one paragraph each) of his major works, in addition to two of his works of literary criticism. There is some consideration of the general nature of his works. A good starting point for the reader unfamiliar with Vargas Llosa. Includes a list of the writer's other works (most only in Spanish) not mentioned in the text. Short critical bibliography in English and Spanish.

_____ . "The Novels of Mario Vargas Llosa." *Modern Language Quarterly*
29 (September, 1968): 329-340.
McMurray discusses *The Time of the Hero* and *The Green House* (the only two
novels by Vargas Llosa published at the time the critic wrote the article), but
in the process (and outside that process as well) he also discusses the Peruvian
writer's "new novelist" approach to various elements of the narrative, such as
the presentation of time, characterization, and narrative voice. The critic also
discusses the writer's penchant for shifting dialogue and intentional ambiguity
meant to encourage reader participation. Consideration as well of Vargas
Llosa's concern for plot and social justice (unlike the French "new novelists"),
and his expression of the philosophies of social determinism and existentialism. An excellent introduction to the nature of Vargas Llosa's narrative, despite
the article's publication date, as virtually all of what the critic says about the
writer rings true in the more mature Vargas Llosa as well. Titles and quotations
in Spanish.

Rossman, Charles, and Alan Warren Friedman, eds. *Mario Vargas Llosa: A Collection of Critical Essays*. Austin: University of Texas Press, 1978. This collection,
with only minor changes, also appears in *Texas Studies in Literature and
Language* 19 (Winter, 1977).
A wide-ranging collection of critical essays (and one interview) on Vargas
Llosa's work. The first half of the book contains essays dedicated to individual
works (such as Michael Moody's "A Small Whirlpool: Narrative Structure in
The Green House"), while the second half of the book is devoted to essays
which present, as the editors put it, "more general discussions" and concerns
(such as Robert Brody's "Mario Vargas Llosa and the Totalization Impulse").
An excellent and important collection. Includes a chronology of Vargas Llosa's
life and career through 1977. Most titles in Spanish, some in English. Quotations in English.

Schwartz, Ronald. "Vargas Llosa: The Peruvian Experience." In his *Nomads, Exiles, and Émigrés: The Rebirth of Latin American Narrative, 1960-80*.
Metuchen, N.J.: Scarecrow Press, 1980.
This chapter has two purposes: (1) to provide a brief biographical sketch of
Vargas Llosa and (2) to discuss at some length the novel *Captain Pantoja and
the Special Service*. The biographical sketch occupies five pages of this fifteen-
page chapter, but despite its brevity it provides considerable information concerning the Peruvian writer's life and career, tracing the two almost year by
year from 1952 (after presenting a lengthy paragraph on his life until that date).
The sketch includes, in the process, a quick chronological overview of Vargas
Llosa's works, not only in prose fiction but in literary criticism, theater, and
screenwriting as well. Concise and informative. Titles in English.

Solares, Ignacio. "An Interview with Mario Vargas Llosa." Translated by Alfred J. Mac Adam. *Partisan Review* 51, no. 3 (1984): 347-355.

In an interview first published in Mexico in 1982, Vargas Llosa discusses his first attempts at writing; his reading of Leo Tolstoy's *War and Peace* at fifteen (an event "decisive in his development"); his belief that "physical health is essential for aesthetic creation"; writers he reads (such as Spanish writer Azorín) to stay in touch with the music of the Spanish language; the absence of religion in his works (and later, the presence of religion in his life); his character Antonio Conselheiro (from *The War at the End of the World*); the presence of violence in his works; the problems of fanaticism, political confusion, and misunderstanding in the modern world; Albert Camus; the question of neurosis and artistic creativity; and other topics. A personal and insightful piece. Titles in Spanish with English translations.

Williams, Raymond Leslie. "The Boom Twenty Years Later: An Interview with Mario Vargas Llosa." *Latin American Literary Review* 15 (January-June, 1987): 201-206.

In a rather brief interview conducted at Washington University in April, 1986, Vargas Llosa comments on the tendency in recent Latin American fiction to "hide the structure and technique in the story," to move away from the "formal revolution" of the 1960's. The Peruvian writer also discusses how he writes, focusing on "material that comes in an irrational way," this "in spite of all the rational planning." Finally, Vargas Llosa offers his observations on the presence of violence in novels, the recent trend in Latin American fiction of dealing with historical and political themes, and the role of intellectuals in Latin America (with emphasis on the blame they deserve concerning many historical and political tragedies). Titles in English.

World Literature Today 52 (Winter, 1978). Mario Vargas Llosa issue.

Pages 5-75 of this issue are devoted to articles on the works of Vargas Llosa following his visit to the University of Oklahoma (the home base of the journal) and participation in a conference in his honor in 1977. Articles in the issue include "Social Commitment and the Latin American Writer" by Vargas Llosa himself, "The Transfiguration of the Chivalric Novel" by Alexander Coleman, "Green House Mirrors" by Luis Harss, and "Secrecy: A Structural Concept of *The Time of the Hero*" by J. J. Armas Marcelo. A rather detailed chronology of Vargas Llosa's life and career through 1978. Includes a primary and secondary bibliography in various languages and numerous photographs. Most titles and quotations in English.

Aunt Julia and the Scriptwriter (La tía Julia y el escribidor)

Gerdes, Dick. "*Aunt Julia and the Scriptwriter*: Fiction as Artifact." In his *Mario Vargas Llosa*. Boston: Twayne, 1985.

Gerdes begins his twenty-four-page overview and analysis of Vargas Llosa's novel by placing it, particularly given its humor and parody, in the Peruvian writer's career. He then moves on to a rather lengthy plot synopsis and analysis of the two sides, or tracks, of the narrative: that of autobiography and that of soap operas, or the "reality" versus the fiction. The critic addresses the novel's theme and the presentation of theme in a section entitled "Metafiction: The Novel as a Process of its Own Making." A detailed and readable selection. Titles and quotations in English.

Kerr, Roy A. "Recurrent Modes of Characterization in Mario Vargas Llosa's Fiction." *Hispanófila* 91 (September, 1987): 55-64.

Kerr establishes the Outsider, the Conformer, the Victim, and the Manipulator as the four recurrent modes of characterization present in Vargas Llosa's fiction, and identifies Pedro Camacho of *Aunt Julia and the Scriptwriter* as an Outsider and Mario Vargas of the same novel as a Conformer. The critic shows how each character fits into the particular category to which Kerr assigns him. The critic later discusses how such character types interrelate in Vargas Llosa's novels in general and what that indicates about the Peruvian writer's mode of fiction. An excellent and very readable study. Titles and quotations in Spanish.

Liberti di Barrio, Olga. "*Aunt Julia and the Scriptwriter.*" In *Magill's Literary Annual*, 1983, edited by Frank N. Magill, vol. 1. Pasadena, Calif.: Salem Press, 1983.

Liberti di Barrio begins her roughly five-page overview of *Aunt Julia and the Scriptwriter* with a brief comment on the novel genre and what Latin American writers such as Vargas Llosa have done with it. The critic then describes the general nature of the novel in question followed by observations on Vargas Llosa's thoughts on the nature of fiction and fictional reality. This is followed by a discussion of various elements of *Aunt Julia and the Scriptwriter*, including the two planes of narration and their interrelationship, and the characters, with emphasis on the thematic significance of their situations and actions. An excellent introduction to the novel. "Sources for Further Study" section lists review articles on the work (in English). Titles in Spanish with English translations. Quotations in English.

Machen, Stephen. " 'Pornoviolence' and Point of View in Mario Vargas Llosa's *La tía Julia y el escribidor.*" *Latin American Literary Review* 9 (Fall/Winter, 1980): 9-16.

Machen contends that the use of "porno-violence" in *Aunt Julia and the Scriptwriter* "first, . . . allows Vargas Llosa to exorcise one of his own 'inner demons,' which is the problem of presenting this type of material in a serious work of fiction; and second, it gives him free rein to criticize the mass media by parodying a mode of presentation within it that embodies the essence of the form." The critic concentrates on Tom Wolfe's definition of "porno-violence" (which demands that "the reader's point of view . . . always be the aggressor") and examines Camacho's soap opera in which the man rapes a thirteen-year-old girl as an example of this type of narrative. The critic concludes that Vargas Llosa "utilizes 'porno-violence' to make a legitimate comment about the state of contemporary culture." Titles in Spanish with English translations. Quotations in English.

Oviedo, José Miguel. "A Conversation with Mario Vargas Llosa about *La tía Julia y el escribidor*." In *Mario Vargas Llosa: A Collection of Critical Essays*, edited by Charles Rossman and Alan Warren Friedman. Austin: University of Texas Press, 1978. Also appears in *Texas Studies in Literature and Language* 19 (Winter, 1977): 546-559.
In an interview conducted at the University of Oklahoma in 1977, the Peruvian writer responds to questions concerning this novel, the manuscript of which he was revising at the time the interview was conducted. Oviedo poses questions concerning, for example, how the novel took shape, how the author handles the imaginary world and the more real world within the narrative structure, and what the title of the novel would be (an interesting question since Vargas Llosa provides a title he was to change before the novel's actual publication). Not intended as an analytical piece, but intriguing because of the timing of the interview. Published bilingually in Spanish and English. Titles in Spanish.

——————————. "*La tía Julia y el escribidor*, or the Coded Self-Portrait." In *Mario Vargas Llosa: A Collection of Critical Essays*, edited by Charles Rossman and Alan Warren Friedman. Austin: University of Texas Press, 1978.
Oviedo discusses the autobiographical background of several elements of the Mario Vargas chapters of *Aunt Julia and the Scriptwriter*, and examines both halves of the novel (the Varguitas half and the Pedro Camacho half) and their protagonists, and the relationship of each half to the question of "the writer in the process of writing," before concluding, in part, that "the apparent simplicity of the book is deceiving: it appears to be an autobiography; but it is the negation of autobiography, it appears to have two distinct levels of the story, but it has many more, of great complexity; it appears to be a double melodrama, but it is quite a different thing—a persistent working out of Vargas Llosa's theory of the 'demons' and a glance into the incandescent center in which the experience of a writer becomes imagination." Titles in Spanish. Quotations in English and French.

Captain Pantoja and the Special Service (Pantaleón y las visitadoras)
Boland, R. C. "*Pantaleón y las visitadoras*: A Novelistic Theory Put Into Practice." *Revista de Estudios Hispánicos* 16 (January, 1982): 15-33.
Boland cites the opinions of several critics who view the novel as inferior to

Vargas Llosa's other works. Boland contends, however, that the work is actually "a meticulously constructed novel in which Vargas Llosa puts into practice a theory which he has been steadily developing ever since he began writing novels in the late 1950's." Elements of this theory (all of which Boland finds in the novel's text) include the concept of the novel as a borrower from other genres (in this case letters, reports, sermons, radio broadcasts, even film), minimal intrusion of author, narrative unity, social criticism, and, new to the Vargas Llosa's theory with this novel, humor. Titles and quotations in Spanish.

Jones, Julie. "The Search for Paradise in *Captain Pantoja and the Special Service*." *Latin American Literary Review* 9 (Fall/Winter, 1981): 41-46.
Jones examines the theme of the quest for paradise in this novel, a theme suggested, she states, "by both the lush tropical setting and the nature of Panta's mission (the providing of love)." She identifies those seeking paradise as Captain Pantoja, the prostitutes, and the Brothers of the Arc. The Captain's quest receives the most attention. Jones concludes that all the quests fail, as Pantoja, in particular, "returns gratefully to his family and to routine duty: his own refuge from the 'maddening crowd' and the closest approach to paradise which he can hope to reach in the world of Vargas Llosa." Titles and quotations in English.

Kerr, Roy A. "Recurrent Modes of Characterization in Mario Vargas Llosa's Fiction." *Hispanófila* 91 (September, 1987): 55-64.
In an article in which he establishes the Outsider, the Conformer, the Victim, and the Manipulator as the four recurrent modes of characterization present in Vargas Llosa's fiction, Kerr identifies Pantoja as a Conformer and General Collazos, General Victoria, Colonel López López, and Germán Laúdano Rosales as Manipulators in *Captain Pantoja and the Special Service*. The critic shows how the characters fit into the categories into which he has placed them and then later discusses how such character types interrelate in Vargas Llosa's works in general and what that indicates concerning the Peruvian writer's mode of fiction. An excellent and very readable study. Titles and quotations in Spanish.

Morello-Frosch, Marta. "Of Heroes and Martyrs: The Grotesque in *Pantaleón y las visitadoras* [*Captain Pantoja and the Special Service*]." *Latin American Literary Review* 14 (Spring/Summer, 1979): 40-44.
Citing Wolfgang Kayser's definition of the grotesque as "the expression that renders a formerly familiar world into an alien one," Morello-Frosch studies the humor in *Captain Pantoja and the Special Service* as expressed through the unconventional (or alien—and in this way grotesque) situations of Captain Pantoja (who is ordered by the army to organize a prostitute service for the soldiers) and the Brother (the religious leader who is crucified). The critic

examines the grotesque nature of their situations and precisely how these situations contribute to the "delightful parody of misapplied righteousness and zeal." Titles in Spanish with English translation.

Schwartz, Ronald. "Vargas Llosa: The Peruvian Experience." In his *Nomads, Exiles, and Émigrés: The Rebirth of the Latin American Narrative, 1960-80.* Metuchen, N.J.: Scarecrow Press, 1980.
The chapter appears to have two purposes: (1) to provide a biographical sketch of Vargas Llosa and (2) to examine to some degree the novel *Captain Pantoja and the Special Service*. The second purpose occupies roughly the final ten pages of the fourteen-page chapter, as the critic examines the novel's plot, the nature of its narrative, its humor, and its themes. A very good overall introduction to the work in question. Titles and quotations in English.

Siemens, William L. "Apollo's Metamorphosis in *Pantaleón y las visitadoras*." In *Mario Vargas Llosa: A Collection of Critical Essays*, edited by Charles Rossman and Alan Warren Friedman. Austin: University of Texas Press, 1978. Also appears in *Texas Studies in Literature and Language* 19 (Winter, 1977): 481-493.
Siemens contends that Vargas Llosa "has grasped the essence of classical concerns and played the ludicrous Peruvian situation off against them in *Captain Pantoja and the Special Service*." These concerns deal with "the preservation of order against the encroachments of ever threatening chaos." The critic states that in cultural systems which view periods of chaos as inevitable, such periods have frequently been institutionalized so as to control it better. Siemens states that "this tradition took the form of the replacement of Apollo by Dionysus in the Temple of Delphi for a period of three months out of the year." He goes on to contend that "underneath all the zany occurrences and transformations of Vargas Llosa's novel what is really going on is a process analogous to that replacement of Apollo by Dionysus at Delphi." He finds much to support his contention, producing interesting conclusions, the first of which is that Pantoja plays the parts of both Apollo and Dionysus, though with considerable modification. Titles and quotations in Spanish.

Smith, Gilbert. "*Captain Pantoja and the Special Service*." In *Magill's Literary Annual*, 1979, edited by Frank N. Magill, vol. 1. Pasadena, Calif.: Salem Press, 1987.
Smith begins his roughly five-page overview with an introduction to some of the narrative techniques used by Vargas Llosa in the novel, with reference to how such techniques fit into the context of contemporary Latin American fiction. This is followed by a discussion of various elements of the novel, with emphasis on the work's themes. An excellent introduction. "Sources for Fur-

ther Study" section lists review articles on the work (in English). Titles and quotations in English.

Williams, Raymond L. "The Narrative Art of Mario Vargas Llosa: Two Organizing Principles in *Pantaleón y las visitadoras.*" In *Mario Vargas Llosa: A Collection of Critical Essays*, edited by Charles Rossman and Alan Warren Friedman. Austin: University of Texas Press, 1978. Also appears in *Texas Studies in Literature and Language* 19 (Winter, 1977): 469-480.

Williams discusses the criticism *Captain Pantoja and the Secret Service* has received for its so-called "facile" humor and presents a detailed study of the two organizing principles which he believes, in spite of general criticism, reflect the rigid control of the narration typical of Vargas Llosa's other works and "are fundamental to an appreciation of Vargas Llosa's narrative art both as a humorous entertainment and as a work subversively critical of the society it describes." The two principles concern "Pantoja's organization (the novel's content as described by use of a nuclear verb)" and "Vargas Llosa's organization (the novel's structure)," together creating a "parody of military organization in both form and content." Titles and quotations in Spanish.

Conversation in the Cathedral (Conversación en la Catedral)

Cheuse, Alan. "Mario Vargas Llosa and *Conversation in the Cathedral*: The Question of Naturalism." In *Mario Vargas Llosa: A Collection of Critical Essays*, edited by Charles Rossman and Alan Warren Friedman. Austin: University of Texas Press, 1978. Also appears in *Texas Studies in Literature and Language* 19 (Winter, 1977): 445-451.

Cheuse opens his article with the question, "Where have all the critics gone wrong?" He goes on to contend that Vargas Llosa's works contain "a hardy strain of Naturalism." The Peruvian writer's brand of Naturalism, however, though linked to the Naturalism of Honoré de Balzac, Gustave Flaubert, and Émile Zola in theme, differs from them in presentation. The critic uses *Conversation in the Cathedral* to prove his point, focusing on "the manipulation of the 'environment' of time" in the novel, a manipulation which Cheuse believes produces the same thematic effect as the nineteenth century masters though through a radically different method. Titles and quotations in English.

Franco, Jean. "Conversations and Confessions: Self and Character in *The Fall* and *Conversation in the Cathedral.*" In *Mario Vargas Llosa: A Collection of Critical Essays*, edited by Charles Rossman and Alan Warren Friedman. Austin: University of Texas Press, 1978. Also appears in *Texas Studies in Literature and Language* 19 (Winter, 1977): 452-468.

Franco presents a detailed analysis of the concept of character in *Conversation in the Cathedral* compared to the same concepts in Albert Camus' *The Fall* and, to a lesser degree, Jean-Paul Sartre's *The Reprieve*, finding that because the three writers "view the individual in terms of consciousness, they create literary projections of that individual that verge on impersonality." Specifically, Franco contends, "in *The Fall*, an individual who might be Everyman postures before the silence of nature," while in *The Reprieve*, "characters sink deeply into the undifferentiated crowd of history," and in Vargas Llosa's novel, "they attempt to assert themselves as individuals only to be revealed as agents in the reader's act of self-awareness." Titles and quotations in English.

Gallagher, D. P. "Mario Vargas Llosa (Peru, 1936-   )." In his *Modern Latin American Literature*. New York: Oxford University Press, 1973.
The chief purpose of this excellent twenty-two-page introduction to Vargas Llosa and his novels through 1970 is to introduce the reader to the thematic focus and technical nature of the Peruvian writer's narrative. In the process of achieving this, *Conversation in the Cathedral* receives considerable attention as Gallagher illustrates exactly how Vargas Llosa's thematic concerns (particularly relating to Peruvian society) and technical practices (such as "interlocking parallel stories") are reflected in the work. Titles in Spanish. Quotations (except for one in French and a few Spanish words) in English.

Gerdes, Dick. "*Conversation in the Cathedral*: Life as a Shipwreck." In his *Mario Vargas Llosa*. Boston: Twayne, 1985.
Gerdes presents a detailed and very readable overview and analysis of the sociopolitical background from which this massive novel sprang, as well as the work's plot, technique, and theme, in sections entitled "Introduction: Historical Biography," "Plot: Conversation as (In)Action," "Structure as Whirlwind," and "Moral Implications: A Sadder and a Wiser Man." Supplemented by numerous references to the text. An excellent guide for the reader seeking a better understanding of Vargas Llosa's complex and difficult novel.

Johnson, Phillip. "Vargas Llosa's *Conversacion en la Catedral*: A Study of Frustration and Failure in Peru." *Symposium* 30 (Fall, 1976): 203-212.
Johnson begins by discussing the theme of frustration and failure in Vargas Llosa's early novels and the Peruvian writer's thoughts concerning Peru before turning his attention to an in-depth study of the character of Santiago Zavala, the protagonist of *Conversation in the Cathedral*, who Johnson contends "is Vargas Llosa's most complete expression of defeat and represents the total pessimism the author feels for Peru." Titles and quotations in Spanish.

Kerr, R. A. "The Janus Mask: Hidden Identities and the Reader's Role in Mario Vargas Llosa's Early Fiction." *Chasqui* 13 (November, 1983): 18-31.
Kerr examines the use and significance of Janus mask, or multi-name, multi-identity characters in *The Time of the Hero*, *The Green House*, and *Conversation in the Cathedral*. His analysis of *Conversation in the Cathedral* centers on

Santiago, Hortensia, and Fermin, all of whom have other identities. Kerr shows how the use of the Janus mask is most significant in this novel as "character duality and its consequences are . . . responsible for the generation of an incident [La Musa's murder] that stands at the center of the narration." Kerr goes on to state that "the murder clarifies narrative references prior to it and prepares the reader for the explanations that follow." An interesting, detailed, and highly readable study. Titles and quotations in Spanish.

——————————. "Recurrent Modes of Characterization in Mario Vargas Llosa's Fiction." *Hispanófila* 91 (September, 1987): 55-64.
Kerr establishes the Outsider, the Conformer, the Victim, and the Manipulator as the four recurrent modes of characterization in Vargas Llosa's fiction, and identifies Cayo Bermúdez of *Conversation in the Cathedral* as an Outsider and Amalia and Hortensia of the same novel as Victims. Kerr shows how the characters fit into the categories to which he has assigned them and then later discusses how such character types interrelate in Vargas Llosa's novels in general and what that indicates concerning the Peruvian writer's mode of fiction. An excellent and very readable study. Titles and quotations in Spanish.

Lipski, John M. "Narrative Textures in *Conversación en la Catedral*." *Revista de Estudios Hispánicos* 13 (January, 1979): 65-79.
Lipski's article examines "the ways in which the author allows the narrative to traverse a number of parallel sub-paths, while remaining tied to and dominated by a major plot-line." The critic hopes that such an analysis will highlight the interaction between language and textual structures in this highly complex novel." One of the critic's conclusions is that the "verbal maze into which the reader is drawn accurately mirrors the lives and actions of the characters of the novel, and a simpler linguistic structure would not have adequately portrayed the meaningless and absurd situation which is the human condition." Titles and quotations in Spanish.

Review 75 (Spring, 1975): 5-36. "Focus" section on Vargas Llosa and *Conversation in the Cathedral*.
This section features a preface by José Miguel Oviedo and a chronology of Vargas Llosa's life and career through 1975 (also by Oviedo), followed by five diverse essays devoted to *Conversation in the Cathedral*: (1) "Masochism, Anyone?" by Wolfgang A. Luchting, (2) "A Conversation with the Translator" [Gregory Rabassa], (3) "The Serpent of Remorse" by Jorge Edwards, (4) "A Complex Space" by Fernando Moreno Turner, and (5) "Novel Form, Novel Space" by Ronald Christ. Titles and quotations in English or in Spanish with English translations.

The Green House (La casa verde)
Brody, Robert. "Mario Vargas Llosa and the Totalization Impulse." In *Mario*

Vargas Llosa: A Collection of Critical Essays, edited by Charles Rossman and Alan Warren Friedman. Austin: University of Texas Press, 1978. Also appears in *Texas Studies in Literature and Language* 19 (Winter, 1977): 514-521.

Brody first defines "totalization impulse" (essentially the attempt to present a "total reality" in a novel) and then examines its presence and its sources in Vargas Llosa's works. Most of the critic's analysis and conclusions concern *The Green House*, the work in which Brody finds that this impulse is strongest. The critic's analysis centers on the author's use of a "purposeful ambiguity" in general and the application of this ambiguity to what Brody terms the "hidden identity characteristic" in particular. Titles in Spanish. Quotations in English.

Díez, Luys A. "The Sources of *The Green House*: The Mythical Background of a Fabulous Novel." In *Mario Vargas Llosa: A Collection of Critical Essays*, edited by Charles Rossman and Alan Warren Friedman. Austin: University of Texas Press, 1978. Also appears in *Texas Studies in Literature and Language* 19 (Winter, 1977): 429-444.

Díez states early in this article that he intends to deal with fiction in *The Green House* by comparing the text of the novel "with information provided in interviews with Vargas Llosa, the writer's log book, and my own personal impressions after visiting the locales of the action." What follows is just that, as the critic discusses Piura and Peru's Amazon jungle, and Vargas Llosa's connection to them, as well as local characters which correspond to characters in the novel (such as Tushía—a source for Fushía). Díez contends that the writer combines his experiences and interest in Piura and the Amazon jungle to create "a dual composition." Includes several comments by Vargas Llosa and provides interesting information on the novel's sources. Titles and quotations in English.

Gallagher, D. P. "Mario Vargas Llosa (Peru, 1936-   )." In his *Modern Latin American Literature*. New York: Oxford University Press, 1973.

Gallagher uses this excellent twenty-two-page introduction to Vargas Llosa and his novels through 1970, in part, to introduce the reader to the thematic focus and technical nature of the Peruvian writer's narrative. In the process of doing this, *The Green House* receives considerable attention as the critic illustrates exactly how Vargas Llosa's thematic concerns and technical practices (particularly the latter) are reflected in the work. Some comparison as well of *The Green House* with the "jungle novels" produced in Latin America in the 1920's and 1930's. A very readable piece. Titles in Spanish. Quotations (except one in French and a few Spanish words) in English.

Gerdes, Dick. "*The Green House*: Formal Invention, Greater Realism." In his *Mario Vargas Llosa*. Boston: Twayne, 1985.

Gerdes begins this twenty-two-page treatment of Vargas Llosa's novel with a

202 Contemporary Latin American Fiction

two-and-a-half page introduction focusing on the Peruvian writer's interest in "the key phenomena of multiplicity, intensity, ambiguity, and totality" in fiction and how these all play a significant role in *The Green House*. The critic also discusses the novel's immediate success on publication, as well as the background (much of it personal to Vargas Llosa) from which the novel's story sprang, before presenting a synopsis of the plot (in a section entitled "Plot: Five Stones, One Paralyzed Society") and an analysis of Vargas Llosa's narrative technique (with emphasis on time and structure) and its thematic implications. Should prove very helpful to the reader attempting to decipher this complex novel. Titles and quotations in English.

Hazera, Lydia D. "Strategies for Reader Participation in the Works of Cortázar, Cabrera Infante and Vargas Llosa." *Latin American Literary Review* 13 (July-December, 1985): 19-34.

In an excellent article on ways in which these three authors "trigger the reader's active participation," Hazera examines Vargas Llosa's *The Green House* to show that the Peruvian writer encourages the reader to participate through his work's complex narrative structure, the lack of moral judgement (leaving the reader to be "the sole agent in the formation of any moral evaluation"), the "paradoxical behavior and lack of identity" of the characters, and various areas of ambiguity in the text. Interesting comparison of the issue of reader participation in the three writers' works. Titles and quotations in English.

Jones, Julie. "Vargas Llosa's Mangachería: The Pleasures of Community." *Revista de Estudios Hispánicos* 20 (January, 1986): 77-89.

Jones opens her article citing Vargas Llosa's interest in Alexandre Dumas and Victor Hugo, and the lack of critical attention directed at the Mangache episodes in *The Green House*. The critic studies "the relation of Dumas' musketeer novels and Hugo's *Notre Dame de Paris*" to these episodes, "showing how Vargas Llosa adapts motifs from the earlier novels to a very different sort of narration." The critic then focuses "on the role that La Mangachería plays in the novel as a whole, arguing that it "provides a positive counterpoint to the sales of failed lives that have attracted so much critical attention." Titles and quotations in Spanish.

Kerr, R. A. "The Janus Mask: Hidden Identities and the Reader's Role in Mario Vargas Llosa's Early Fiction." *Chasqui* 13 (November, 1983): 18-31.

Kerr examines the use and significance of Janus mask figures, or multi-name, multi-identity characters in *The Time of the Hero*, *The Green House*, and *Conversation in the Cathedral*. His analysis of this aspect of *The Green House* focuses on Don Anselmo, Bonifacia, and Lituma, all of whom have second identities. Kerr analyzes precisely how Vargas Llosa "first fragments and then rewrites the two sides of each of these Janus mask personalities," showing that "as one protagonist's Janus mask personality is revealed, that character in turn is in the act of revealing the merging sides of the other two characters." An interesting, detailed, and very readable study. Titles and quotations in Spanish.

_____ . "Recurrent Modes of Characterization in Mario Vargas Llosa's Fiction." *Hispanófila* 91 (September, 1987): 55-64.

In an article in which Kerr identifies the Outsider, the Conformer, the Victim, and the Manipulator as the four recurrent modes of characterization found in Vargas Llosa's fiction, the critic identifies Fushía and Don Anselmo of *The Green House* as Outsiders and Bonifacia of the same novel as a Victim. Kerr shows how the characters fit into the categories to which he assigns them and then later discusses how such character types interrelate in Vargas Llosa's novels in general and what that indicates concerning the Peruvian writer's mode of fiction. An excellent and very readable study. Titles and quotations in Spanish.

Moody, Michael. "A Small Whirlpool: Narrative Structure in *The Green House*. In *Mario Vargas Llosa: A Collection of Critical Essays*, edited by Charles Rossman and Alan Warren Friedman. Austin: University of Texas Press, 1978. Also appears in *Texas Studies in Literature and Language* 19 (Winter, 1977): 408-428.

An excellent article on the novel's structure and its relationship to the manipulation of time in the narrative, the work's plot, and its theme. Moody contends that "the quality of formlessness in *The Green House* is, to a considerable degree, an artfully contrived illusion created for its particular power of expression rendering the novel's thematic issues." The critic meticulously sorts out the work's plot, the interrelationships of its characters, and its various time frames. One of the critic's many cogent conclusions is that "the breakup of order in structural arrangement corresponds to a human condition in which man loses his identity as an organic being and exists only contingently, as one element of a larger pattern of relationships." An insightful piece and very helpful for anyone trying to decipher the many complexities of the novel associated with Vargas Llosa's manipulation of structure and time. Titles and quotations in English.

Vázquez Amaral, José. "*The Green House*: Mario Vargas Llosa and the Contemporary Indian." In his *The Contemporary Latin American Narrative*. New York: Las Américas, 1970.

A thirteen-page chapter devoted chiefly to (as implied in the title) Vargas Llosa's portrayal of the Indian in his novel and, to a lesser degree, the jungle itself as a significant element in the work. Considerable background on Peru's Indian problem and a discussion of how it is illustrated in the novel. Provides discussion as well of *The Green House* as it compares in many respects to Rómulo Gallego's *Doña Bárbara* and José Eustacio Rivera's *The Vortex*. Limited discussion also of *The Time of the Hero* as an example of a novel by Vargas Llosa not related to the jungle. Enlightening article in large part because of its extrinsic background information. Titles and quotations in English.

The Real Life of Alejandro Mayta (Historia de Mayta)

Brower, Keith H. "*The Real Life of Alejandro Mayta*." In *Magill's Literary Annual*, 1987, edited by Frank N. Magill, vol. 2. Pasadena, Calif.: Salem Press, 1987.
A five-page overview of the novel in question. The work is first placed within the context of Vargas Llosa's career. This is followed by a concise plot summary. The majority of the article, however, is devoted to an analysis of the novel's main (and, to some degree, its secondary) characters, the technical elements of the work (particularly concerning the manipulation of time and narrative focus), and its themes. An excellent introduction to the novel. "Sources for Further Study" lists other reviews of the work (in English). Titles and quotations in English.

Newman, Kathleen. "Historical Knowledge in the Post-Boom Novel." In *The Historical Novel in Latin America*, edited by Daniel Balderston. Gaithersburg, Md.: Ediciones Hispamérica, 1986.
Newman discusses the concept of metahistory and the interest of some Latin American novelists of the 1980's in recent historical events. The critic examines *The Real Life of Alejandro Mayta* as a novel which reflects this interest. Citing various examples, she finds Vargas Llosa's novel to be, in part, "a critique of the twenty-five years of history of the Latin American left," and the Peruvian author's critique, is, to use Newman's terms, "antagonistic." Newman also examines Ricardo Piglia's *Respiración artificial* (artificial respiration) in this light and compares it to Vargas Llosa's novel. Titles and quotations in Spanish.

The Time of the Hero (La ciudad y los perros)

Baker, Rilda L. " 'Of how to be and what to see while you are being': The Reader's Performance in *The Time of the Hero*." In *Mario Vargas Llosa: A Collection of Critical Essays*, edited by Charles Rossman and Alan Warren Friedman. Austin: University of Texas Press, 1978. Also appears in *Texas Studies in Literature and Language* 19 (Winter, 1977): 396-407.
Baker studies the reader's "engrossment or involvement" in this Vargas Llosa novel, analyzing what she calls "the essential markers within the work that determine the reader's performance." She shows in part that the novel consists of "multilevel alteration: third-person narration vs. first-person narration, fictive past vs. fictive present, past-tense verbs vs. present-tense verbs, the city vs. the academy." One result of this, Baker claims, is that reading the novel is

"a retrogressive procedure in which the reader is required to retreat three steps and retrieve lost pieces of the chain of events in order to advance four steps in pursuit of the accelerating action." Titles and quotations in English.

Feustle, Joseph A., Jr. "Mario Vargas Llosa: A Labyrinth of Solitude." In *Mario Vargas Llosa: A Collection of Critical Essays*, edited by Charles Rossman and Alan Warren Friedman. Austin: University of Texas Press, 1978. Also appears in *Texas Studies in Literature and Language* 19 (Winter, 1977): 522-529.
In this article on the theme of solitude in Vargas Llosa's works, Feustle pays most attention to the theme as expressed in *The Time of the Hero*, a novel replete with examples of what the critic views as the chief expression of the solitude theme in the Peruvian writer's works: racial and class prejudice and, more important, the Latin American code of *hombría*, or manhood (particularly as it concerns the concepts of love, sex, and domination). A detailed and enlightening study. Most titles in Spanish only. Most Spanish terms presented with English translations. Quotations in English.

Gallagher, D. P. "Mario Vargas Llosa (Peru, 1936-   )." In his *Modern Latin American Literature*. New York: Oxford University Press, 1973.
The main purpose of this excellent twenty-two-page introduction to Vargas Llosa and his novels through 1970 is to introduce the reader to the thematic focus and technical nature of the Peruvian writer's narrative. *The Time of the Hero* receives considerable attention as Gallagher illustrates through numerous references to the work exactly how Vargas Llosa's thematic concerns (particularly concerning Peruvian society and class discrimination) and technical practices (the use of the flashback) are reflected in this novel. Very readable. Titles in Spanish. Quotations (except for one in French and a few Spanish terms) in English.

Gerdes, Dick. "*The Time of the Hero*: Lost Innocence." In his *Mario Vargas Llosa*. Boston: Twayne, 1985.
An excellent twenty-page overview and analysis of Vargas Llosa's prizewinning first novel. In a brief introductory section, followed by sections entitled "Plot: Banal Events, Moral Struggles"; "Structure and Point of View"; and "Conclusion: The Moral Implications of Ambiguity" Gerdes discusses the novel's place in the Spanish American "Boom" and its theme—all in a detailed yet concise manner, with numerous references to the text. An excellent, well-organized, and very readable introduction to the work in question. Titles and quotations in English.

Hancock, Joel. "Animalization and Chiaroscuro Techniques: Descriptive Language in *La ciudad y los perros* (The City and the Dogs)." *Latin American Literary Review* 4 (Fall/Winter, 1976): 37-47.

In an effort to show how descriptive language in *The Time of the Hero* parallels and contributes to the novel's themes, Hancock focuses on the use of animalization (in the characters' names, their physical descriptions, and their actions) and the chiaroscuro technique (employing "an interplay of light and darkness to create moods, highlight certain features for special attention, sketch grotesque characters, and represent a concept in symbolic terms"), providing numerous examples of both. A solid and very readable article. Titles and quotations in Spanish with English translations.

Johnson, Phillip. "The Shadow of the City: Society and Disorder in *La ciudad y los perros.*" *The American Hispanist* 1, no. 6 (1976): 12-15.
Johnson contends that in *The Time of the Hero* "the school is represented as a microcosm of the larger Peruvian society, where the same order of corruption, injustice, hypocrisy, and violence prevails as in the city of Lima." This connection between the school and the city (and the society of the city) is supported, the critic contends, by the novel's structure, with flashbacks to the characters' lives outside the confines of the school, "organized in such a way that the two district settings intertwine and contaminate one another." The critic devotes considerable attention to the flashbacks concerning the cadets' pasts and contends that the flashbacks show that the behavior of the cadets in the school is simply a product of what they learned in society, concluding finally that "the city feeds the school and the school replenishes society. The vicious circle is perpetuated." Titles and quotations in Spanish.

Kerr, R. A. "The Janus Mask: Hidden Identities and the Reader's Role in Mario Vargas Llosa's Early Fiction." *Chasqui* 13 (November, 1983): 18-31.
Kerr examines the use and significance of Janus mask figures, or multi-name, multi-identity characters in *The Time of the Hero*, *The Green House*, and *Conversation in the Cathedral*. From the first novel, the critic discusses the dual identities of three of the work's characters (most notably Jaguar), showing how the reader comes to divine that they in fact possess dual identities and what effect these identities and the manner in which they are slowly revealed have on the reader. Consideration as well of how "the Janus mask figure as a method of character presentation and as a way of structuring our perception of such presentation . . . mirrors thematic occupations in the novel." An interesting, detailed, and very readable study. Titles and quotations in Spanish.

——————————— . "Recurrent Modes of Characterization in Mario Vargas Llosa's Fiction." *Hispanófila* 91 (September, 1987): 55-64.
Kerr establishes the Outsider, the Conformer, the Victim, and the Manipulator as the four recurrent modes of characterization in Vargas Llosa's fiction, and identifies Alberto Fernández and Lieutenant Gamboa of *The Time of the Hero* as Conformers, Richi Arana of the same novel as a Victim, and all the "senior

officers of the Leoncio Prado Academy as prototypical Manipulators." Kerr shows how the characters fit into the categories to which he assigns them and then later discusses how such character types interrelate in Vargas Llosa's novels in general and what that indicates concerning the Peruvian writer's mode of fiction. An excellent and very readable study. Titles and quotations in Spanish.

_____ . "The Secret Self: Boa in Vargas Llosa's *La ciudad y los perros*." *Romance Notes* 24 (Winter, 1983): 111-115.
Kerr examines the monologues of Boa Valdevieso in *The Time of the Hero* to show that they reveal a side of the character not evident in other areas of the narrative. The critic shows that Boa's own comments, directed at himself or to his dog, reveal, for example, a character of "childlike superstitions and fears," who "can act responsibly and demonstrate affection," all this in stark contrast to the portrait painted of him elsewhere. Interesting piece. Titles and quotations in Spanish.

McMurray, George R. "Form and Content Relationships in Vargas Llosa's *La ciudad y los perros*." *Hispania* 56 (September, 1973): 579-586.
An interesting article in which McMurray cites Vargas Llosa's own comments on the creative process and Carlos Fuentes' observations on the nature of the modern Spanish American novel to explain what the critic calls the "variety of styles and techniques puzzling to the casual reader" of *The Time of the Hero*. Using numerous lengthy examples (supplemented with diagrams), McMurray shows how the novelist uses "form—essentially an esthetic aspect of literature—as a subtle device to reflect the tensions in the strife-torn society he portrays and, in this way, to imply his disenchantment with present-day conditions." Focuses on various stages in Alberto's development in the novel and the style and technique (form) used to reflect these stages and the thematic significance therein. Titles and quotations in Spanish.

Magnarelli, Sharon. "*The Time of the Hero*: Liberty Enslaved." *Latin American Literary Review* 4 (Spring/Summer, 1976): 35-45.
Magnarelli refutes the wealth of criticism concentrating on this novel's sociological elements and, particularly, its so-called realist nature, contending that because of the unusual nature of its first-person narration, "if realism is present in the novel, it is only as a mask or a question mark." The critic presents a detailed analysis of the first-person narration, citing Vargas Llosa's novel and numerous literary theorists, before concluding, in part, that the first-person narration "is essential to the novel's themes," that "its use and the disorientation it causes underline the falseness of our perceptions. . . ." She goes on to conclude that the "text ultimately presents a rather complex and multifaceted theory of literature and language and clearly recognizes that all

literature is both free and enslaved." Titles and quotations in Spanish and French with English translations.

The War of the End of the World (La guerra del fin del mundo)

Conlon, John J. *"The War of the End of the World."* In *Magill's Literary Annual*, 1985, edited by Frank N. Magill, vol. 2. Pasadena, Calif.: Salem Press, 1985.

Conlon begins his roughly five-page overview of the novel in question with an introduction to the historical and literary background (the latter represented by Brazilian Euclides da Cunha's *Rebellion in the Backlands*) from which Vargas Llosa's novel sprang, with emphasis on changes and alterations made by the Peruvian author. This is followed by a discussion of various elements of the novel, including the nature of its story, its characters, and Vargas Llosa's handling of history. An excellent introduction to the novel. "Sources for Further Study" section lists review articles on the work (in English). Titles (except for two in Portuguese, one of which is translated to English) in English.

Gerdes, Dick. *"The War of the End of the World*: A Modern Romance." In his *Mario Vargas Llosa*. Boston: Twayne, 1985.

In this twenty-two-page analysis of Vargas Llosa's sixth novel, Gerdes begins by discussing in some detail the actual historical events (the Canudos rebellion and massacre in Brazil in 1896-1897) on which (along with Euclides da Cunha's *Rebellion in the Backlands*) the novel is based. The critic then discusses and analyzes the story, plot, and structure, with emphasis on the various characters and the context, nature, and significance of the work's numerous parts, chapters, and segments. A final section is devoted to the novel's "Form and Meaning." An excellent overview and analysis of the work. Titles in Spanish (and one in Portuguese) with English translations or in English. Quotations in English.

Kerr, Roy A. "Recurrent Modes of Characterization in Mario Vargas Llosa's Fiction." *Hispanófila* 91 (September, 1987): 55-64.

Kerr establishes the Outsider, the Conformer, the Victim, and the Manipulator as the four recurrent modes of characterization found in Vargas Llosa's fiction, and identifies Antonio of *The War of the End of the World* as an Outsider, Jurema of the same novel as a Victim, and Epamonidas Gonçalves as a Manipulator. Kerr shows how the characters fit into the categories to which he assigns them and then later discusses how such character types interrelate in Vargas Llosa's novels in general and what that indicates concerning the Peruvian writer's mode of fiction. An excellent and very readable study. Titles and quotations in Spanish.

Oviedo, José Miguel. "Vargas Llosa in Canudos." Translated by David Draper Clark. *World Literature Today* 60 (Winter, 1986): 51-54.

This short article serves as an introduction to and review of *The War of the End of the World*. Oviedo discusses both the literary and historical models for Vargas Llosa's work (respectively, Euclides da Cunha's *Rebellion in the Backlands* and the Canudos episode on which da Cunha's work is based) and then treats some of the diverse characters which populate the novel. The rest of Oviedo's article is devoted to the nature of the work's narrative, with emphasis on how *The War of the End of the World* compares to the Peruvian author's other works. The critic concludes by recommending the novel in question, contending that the "internal, ethical, and esthetic fidelity to the author's creative intuition makes his modern version of a classic story a classic itself." Titles in Spanish with English translations. Quotations in English.

Walter, Richard J. "Literature and History in Contemporary Latin America." *Latin American Literary Review* 15 (January-June, 1987): 173-182.
Walter calls *The War of the End of the World*, Fuentes' *The Death of Artemio Cruz*, and García Márquez' *One Hundred Years of Solitude* "essential reading for any historian of Latin America." The critic contends as well that any reader, historian or not, would better appreciate these works if said reader knew and understood "the historical context in which they are set." Walter provides this context (in the case of Vargas Llosa's novel, the Canudos uprising in 1897) before assessing each work's value for the historian (Vargas Llosa's novel, in part, Walter contends, "brings to life again the events at Canudos and underscores and reflects their impact on Brazilian society as a whole"). He concludes that all three writers deal with "the consequences of modernization for traditional societies," the problem of revolution (and its accompanying violence and "ideological confusion"), the role of charismatic leaders, and eventual frustration with the revolution. Particularly useful for the reader unfamiliar with Latin American history. Titles (except for one in Portuguese with an English translation) and quotations in English.

AGUSTIN YÁÑEZ
Mexico

Commentary

Flasher, John. "Agustín Yáñez." In *Latin American Literature in the Twentieth Century: A Guide*, edited by Leonard S. Klein. New York: Frederick Ungar, 1986.

A brief (two-and-a-half-page) introduction to Yáñez' life and works. A quick summary of the nature of the Mexican writer's narrative and limited discussion of his major works, with *The Edge of the Storm* and *The Lean Lands* receiving most attention. A good starting point for the uninitiated reader. Supplies a list of Yáñez' other works (in Spanish) not mentioned in the text. Short critical bibliography in Spanish and English.

McMurray, George R. "New Directions." In his *Spanish American Writing Since 1941: A Critical Survey*. New York: Frederick Ungar, 1987.

McMurray devotes approximately three pages of this section of his book to a brief overview of Yáñez' fiction. Following an introductory paragraph, the critic offers concise commentary on the Mexican writer's novels. A good starting point for the reader unfamiliar with Yáñez. Titles in Spanish with English translations.

The Edge of the Storm (Al filo del agua)

Brushwood, John S. "The Lyric Style of Agustín Yáñez." *Symposium* 26 (Spring, 1972): 5-14.

Brushwood uses various examples from Yáñez' writings, including the "Overture" of *The Edge of the Storm*, to examine some of the techniques the Mexican author employs in order to produce "verbal melody and rhythm" in his prose. Among the techniques the critic identifies in his detailed study of the texts examined is the use of "series of substantives and series of verbless phrases" (this being a particular feature of the "Overture"). Brushwood also draws conclusions concerning when such prose is used ("in works that depend entirely on the creation of a special ambience, and in special passages of the other works" [such as the "Overture"]). A very readable piece. Titles and quotations in Spanish.

Doudoroff, Michael J. "Tensions and Triangles in *Al filo del agua*." *Hispania* 57 (March, 1974): 1-12.

Doudoroff claims that in *The Edge of the Storm* there are "certain abstract patterns of organization which, in combination with important features of pacing and character development, complicate and enrich the total effect of the novel and qualify its theme." The "pattern of organization" he studies in this article is the interlocking triangle, which he identifies as the main technical device in the novel's "dynamic representation of the process of fundamental change." His chapter-by-chapter analysis of the triangle patterns reveals, in part, that "the position of each figure is defined in terms of two other people, and all such groups lead back to Don Dionisio." He concludes that it is "the patterning of relationships . . . that defines and qualifies the collective psychology, revealing the meaning of the events of 1909-1911, and lifting its significance above the regional limits of its setting." Titles and quotations in Spanish.

Durand, Frank. "The Apocalyptic Vision of *Al filo del agua.*" *Symposium* 25 (Winter, 1971): 333-346.
Durand concerns himself "with the workings of inevitability in religious and social terms, as well as with its unifying artistic role" in *The Edge of the Storm*, a novel in which, the critic contends, "from every aspect, including structure and style, . . . is an apocalyptic exposure of the evils and fears that beset a Mexican town . . . striving for heavenly salvation but overwhelmed by a sense of doom and of punishment in the Day of Judgment." An interesting and thoughtful study, with a solid conclusion. Titles and quotations in Spanish.

Franz, Thomas R. "Three Hispanic Echoes of Tolstoi at the Close of World War II." *Hispanic Journal* 6 (Fall, 1984): 37-51.
In this article on the presence of Leo Tolstoi's *War and Peace* in *The Edge of the Storm*, Asturias' *El Señor Presidente*, and Spanish novelist Camilo José Cela's *La colmena* (*The Hive*), Franz devotes most of his attention (more than four pages) concerning Yáñez' novel to the "prolonged, symbolic use of the comet" in this work and in *War and Peace*, finding numerous similarities between the presence and significance of the comet in the two novels. Franz also cites several other traces of Tolstoi in Yáñez' novel, such as "the common use of a final section or epilogue which does not round out the novel, but rather stands apart from it, therefore implying an exposition of the foregoing segments but, more importantly, pointing to an uncertain future where the 'laws' that govern may be vaguely intuited but are as yet unknown." An interesting piece. Titles and quotations from the Hispanic works in Spanish. All others in English.

Merrill, Floyd. "Structure and Restructuration in *Al filo del agua.*" *Chasqui* 17 (May, 1988): 51-60.
In sections entitled "An Overview," "Intransigent Polarities," "Conflict of Cosmologies," and "Blurred Dichotomies," Merrill studies *The Edge of the Storm* "insofar as it reveals the rupture of an established hierarchal order, and insofar as this rupture parallels certain global transformations found in Western history and thought." A detailed study and an interesting perspective on Yáñez' novel. Titles and quotations in Spanish.

O'Neill, Samuel J. "Interior Monologue in *Al filo del agua.*" *Hispania* 51 (September, 1968): 447-456.

A thorough study of the use of interior monologues in *The Edge of the Storm*. O'Neill provides considerable information on the interior monologue in general and divides such monologues in Yanez' novel into three types, explaining the characteristics of each one. He then examines these types of monologues in the work before concluding that "direct interior monologue is not as technically perfected as indirect interior monologue," and that Yáñez "achieves greater success with a combination of direct and indirect interior monologue and psychological (internal) analysis where his preference for stage direction can integrate these techniques with omniscient narration." A solid study. Titles and quotations in Spanish.

Sommers, Joseph. "Genesis of the Storm: Agustín Yáñez." In his *After the Storm: Landmarks of the Modern Mexican Novel*. Albuquerque: University of New Mexico Press, 1968.

Sommers prefaces his analysis of *The Edge of the Storm* with a brief sketch of Yáñez' career, followed by a general overview of the nature of the novel in question. This is followed by individual sections dedicated to detailed analysis of "Narrative Technique and Reality" in the novel, characterization, and setting. In a final section entitled "World View," Sommers focuses on the thematics of the Mexican writer's important novel. A classic piece of criticism. Titles and quotations in English.

Walker, John L. "Timelessness through Memory in the Novels of Agustin Yáñez." *Hispania* 57 (September, 1974): 445-451.

Walker explains the concept of timelessness in general and of timelessness through memory (the latter being essentially the past experiences of a person which "exist more or less unaffected by stimuli brought into the mind through new events" and which "exert a continuous influence" on the person's character) and then examines the presence, role, and significance of these concepts in seven of Yáñez' works, including *The Edge of the Storm*. His analysis of the novel shows, in part, that the priests attempt to create an artificial timelessness, one that eventually "falls to the changes brought in from the outside world." The critic contends that "true timelessness in the Proustian sense is in the private recollections of the people, only some of whose memories are explored." Titles and quotations in Spanish.

CONTEMPORARY LATIN AMERICAN FICTION

INDEX

INDEX